The Four Doctrines

The Lord
Sacred Scripture
Life
Faith

by Emanuel Swedenborg

English translation by John Faulkner Potts
Edited by Alice Spiers Sechrist

Swedenborg Foundation
New York
Established 1850

Originally published in Latin at Amsterdam, 1763
First English translation published in U.S.A., 1838
51st Printing, 1984

ISBN 0-87785-064-X
Library of Congress Catalog Card Number 67-1465
Cover design by John N. Tierney
Manufactured in the United States of America

Swedenborg Foundation, Inc.
139 East 23rd Street
New York, NY 10010

INTRODUCTION

The justification for reprinting a book written over two hundred years ago is that its contents continue to be significant and relevant in the Twentieth Century.

Over one hundred and seventy-five years have passed since English translations of these four works found their way to London bookstalls. Later the four related dissertations were appropriately and conveniently brought together into a single volume. Numerous editions of THE FOUR DOCTRINES have been published in many languages through the years to meet a constant demand.

One who opens this book for the first time soon discovers the reason for this long-sustained interest in Swedenborg's exposition of the four basic religious doctrines: THE LORD, SACRED SCRIPTURE, LIFE, and FAITH. In simple language and basic logic, buttressed by copious quotations from both the Old and New Testaments, the author reinterprets Christianity in terms which are at once readable, scriptural, practical, and stimulating—to students of *all* religions.

CONTENTS

THE DOCTRINE OF THE LORD

FOR

THE NEW JERUSALEM

————

I.

ALL HOLY SCRIPTURE TREATS OF THE LORD: THE LORD IS THE WORD.

1. We read in John:

In the beginning was the Word, and the Word was with God, and God was the Word. The same was in the beginning with God. All things were made by Him, and without Him was nothing made that was made. In Him was life, and the life was the light of men. And the light shineth in the darkness, and the darkness comprehended it not (1:1-5).

The Word was made flesh, and dwelt among us, and we beheld His glory, the glory as of the Only-begotten of the Father, full of grace and truth (verse 14).

The light is come into the world, but men loved the darkness rather than the light, because their deeds were evil (3:19).

While ye have the light, believe in the light, that ye may be sons of light. I am come a light into the world, that whosoever believeth in Me may not abide in the darkness (12:36, 46).

From these passages it is evident that the Lord is God from eternity, and that this God is the selfsame Lord who was born in the world; for it is said that the Word was with God, and God was the Word, and also that without Him was nothing made that was made; and it is added that the Word was made flesh, and they beheld Him.

It is but little understood in the church why the Lord is called the Word. It is because "the Word" signifies divine

1

truth or divine wisdom, and the Lord is divine truth itself
or divine wisdom itself. And this is why He is called the
Light, of which also it is said that it came into the world.
As the divine wisdom and the divine love make one, and
in the Lord had been one from eternity, it is said, "In Him
was life, and the life was the light of men." "Life" is divine
love; and "light" is divine wisdom. It is this *one* that is
meant by, "In the beginning the Word was with God, and
God was the Word." "With God," is in God; for wisdom is
in love, and love in wisdom. So in another place in John:

> And now, O Father, glorify Thou Me with Thine own Self, with
> the glory which I had with Thee before the world was (17:5).

"With Thine own Self," is in Thyself, and therefore it is
said, "and God was the Word"; and elsewhere, that the
Lord is in the Father, and the Father in Him; and that He
and the Father are one. As therefore the Word is the divine
wisdom of the divine love, it follows that it is Jehovah Himself, thus the Lord by whom all things were made that are
made; for all things have been created from divine love by
means of divine wisdom.

2. That the Word here specifically meant is the same
Word that was manifested through Moses, the prophets,
and the evangelists, is very evident from the fact that the
Word is the divine truth itself from which angels have all
their wisdom, and men all their spiritual intelligence. For
this same Word that is among men in this world is also
among the angels in the heavens, but in this world among
men it is natural, whereas in the heavens it is spiritual. And
as the Word is the divine truth, it is also the Divine proceeding*; and this is not only from the Lord, but is also the Lord

---

* In the expression "Divine proceeding," *Divine* is not to be understood as
an adjective qualifying *proceeding*, but *proceeding* is to be taken as a verb (or
participle) describing the act which the Divine there performs. Thus the expression does not mean a proceeding which is divine, but a Divine that is in the
act of proceeding forth. "Divine proceeding," thus understood, exactly translates
Swedenborg's *Divinum procedens*. [Tr.]

Himself. Being the Lord Himself, it follows that each and all things of the Word have been written about Him alone. From Isaiah to Malachi there is nothing that is not either concerning the Lord, or, in the opposite sense, against Him. Heretofore, no one has ever seen this to be so, and yet every one can see it, provided he is aware of it, and thinks of it while he is reading, especially if he knows that the Word contains not only a natural but also a spiritual sense, and that in this sense the names of persons and places signify something about the Lord, and, consequently, something of heaven and the church from Him, or else something opposite to them. As all the details of the Word both in general and in particular treat of the Lord; and as the Word, being the divine truth, is the Lord, it is evident why it is said, "And the Word was made flesh, and dwelt among us, and we beheld His glory"; and also why it is said, "While ye have the light, believe in the light, that ye may be sons of light: I am come a light into the world, that whosoever believeth in Me should not abide in the darkness." The "light" is the divine truth, thus the Word. This is why, even at this day, every one who, while reading the Word, approaches the Lord alone, and prays to Him, is enlightened in the Word.

3. Briefly stated, the subjects concerning the Lord that are treated of in all the Prophets of the Old Testament; from Isaiah to Malachi, both in general and in particular, are these:

i. The Lord came into the world in the fullness of times, which was when He was no longer known by the Jews, and when, consequently, there was nothing of the church left; and unless He had then come into the world and revealed Himself, mankind would have perished in eternal death. As He Himself says in John: "Except ye believe that I am, ye shall die in your sins" (8:24).

ii. The Lord came into the world to execute a last judgment, and thereby to subdue the existing dominance of the hells; which was effected by means of combats (that is, temptations) admitted into His maternal human, and the attendant continual victories; for unless the hells had been subjugated no man could have been saved.

iii. The Lord came into the world in order to glorify His Human, that is, unite it to the Divine which was in Him from conception.

iv. The Lord came into the world in order to set up a new church which should acknowledge Him as the Redeemer and Saviour, and be redeemed and saved through love to Him and faith in Him.

v. He at the same time reduced heaven into order, so that it made one with the church.

vi. The passion of the cross was the last combat or temptation, by means of which He completely conquered the hells and fully glorified His Human.

In the following small work on *The Sacred Scripture* it will be seen that the Word treats of no other subjects than these.

4. In confirmation of this, I shall in this first chapter merely cite passages from the Word which contain the expressions "that day," "in that day," and "in that time;" in which, by "day," and "time," is meant the Lord's advent.

In Isaiah:

It shall come to pass in days to come that the mountain of the house of Jehovah shall be established in the top of the mountains. Jehovah alone shall be exalted in that day. The day of Jehovah of hosts shall be upon every one that is proud and lofty. In that day a man shall cast away his idols of silver and of gold (2:2, 11, 12, 20).

In that day the Lord Jehovih will take away their ornament (3:18).

In that day shall the branch of Jehovah be beautiful and glorious (4:2).

In that day it shall roar against him, and he shall look unto the land, and behold darkness and distress, and the light shall be darkened in the ruins (5:30).

It shall come to pass in that day that Jehovah shall hiss for the fly that is in the uttermost part of the rivers of Egypt. In that day the Lord shall shave in the crossings of the river. In that day He shall vivify. In that day every place shall be for briers and thorns (7:18, 20, 21, 23).

What will ye do in the day of visitation, which shall come? In that day Israel shall stay upon Jehovah, the Holy One of Israel, in truth (10:3, 20).

It shall come to pass in that day, that the Root of Jesse, which standeth for an ensign of the peoples, shall the nations seek, and His rest shall be glory. Chiefly in that day shall the Lord seek again the remnant of His people (11:10, 11).

In that day thou shalt say, I will confess unto Thee, O Jehovah. In that day shall ye say, Confess ye to Jehovah, call upon His name (12:1, 4).

The day of Jehovah is at hand, as a laying waste from Shaddai shall it come. Behold, the day of Jehovah cometh, cruel, and of indignation, and of wrath, and of anger. I will move the heaven, and the earth shall be shaken out of her place, in the day of the wrath of His anger. His time is near, and it cometh, and the days shall not be prolonged (13:6, 9, 13, 22).

It shall come to pass in that day, that the glory of Jacob shall be made thin. In that day shall a man look unto his Maker, and his eyes to the Holy One of Israel. In that day shall the cities of refuge be as the forsaken places of the forest (17:4, 7, 9).

In that day there shall be five cities in the land of Egypt that speak with the lip of Canaan. In that day there shall be an altar to Jehovah in the midst of Egypt. In that day there shall be a path from Egypt to Assyria, and Israel shall be in the midst of the land (19:18, 19, 23, 24).

The inhabitant of the island shall say in that day, Behold our expectation (20:6).

A day of tumult, and of treading down, and of perplexity, from the Lord Jehovih of hosts (22:5).

In that day shall Jehovah visit upon the army of the height, and upon the kings of the earth. After many days shall they be visited; then shall the moon blush, and the sun be ashamed (24:21, 22, 23).

It shall be said in that day, Lo, this is our God, for whom we have waited, that He may deliver us (25:9).

In that day shall this song be sung in the land of Judah, We have a strong city (26:1).

In that day Jehovah shall visit with His sword. In that day ye shall answer to it, A vineyard of unmixed wine (27:1, 2, 12, 13).

In that day shall Jehovah of hosts be for a crown of ornament, and for a diadem (28:5).

In that day shall the deaf hear the words of the book, and the eyes of the blind shall see out of darkness (29:18).

There shall be streams of waters in the day of the great slaughter, when the towers shall fall; and the light of the moon shall be as the light of the sun, in the day that Jehovah shall bind up the hurt of His people (30:25, 26).

In that day they shall cast away every man his idols of silver and of gold (31:7).

The day of Jehovah's vengeance, the year of His recompenses (34:8).

These two things shall come to thee in one day, the loss of children and widowhood (47:9).

My people shall know My name, and in that day that I am He that doth speak; behold it is I (52:6).

Jehovah hath anointed Me to proclaim the acceptable year of Jehovah, and the day of vengence of our God, to comfort all that mourn (61:1, 2).

The day of vengeance is in My heart, and the year of My redeemed is come (63:4).

In Jeremiah:

In those days ye shall say no more, The ark of the covenant of Jehovah. In that time they shall call Jerusalem the throne of Jehovah. In those days the house of Judah shall walk to the house of Israel (3:16-18).

In that day the heart of the king shall fail, and the heart of the princes, and the priests shall be appalled, and the prophets (4:9).

Behold the days come in which the land shall become a waste (7:32, 34).

They shall fall among them that fall, in the day of their visitation (8:12).

Behold the days come that I will visit all that is circumcised with what is uncircumcised (9:25).

In the time of their visitation they shall perish (10:15).

There shall be no remains to them, I will bring evil upon them in the year of their visitation (11:23).

Behold, the days come in which it shall no more be said (16:14).

I will look upon them in the nape, and not the faces, in the day of their destruction (18:17).

Behold, the days come in which I will give this place for a waste (19:6).

Behold, the days come that I will raise unto David a righteous off-shoot, who shall reign as king. In those days Judah shall be saved, and Israel shall dwell safely. Therefore, behold, the days come that they shall no more say . . . I will bring evil upon them in the year of their visitation. In the end of days ye shall understand intelligence (23:5, 6, 7, 12, 20).

Behold, the days come in which I will turn again. Alas! for that day is great, and none shall be like it. It shall come to pass in that day that I will break the yoke, and burst their bonds (30:3, 7, 8).

There shall be a day that the watchman upon Mount Ephraim shall cry, Arise ye, let us ascend Zion, unto Jehovah our God. Behold, the days come that I will make a new covenant. Behold, the days come that the city shall be built to Jehovah (31:6, 31, 38).

The days come that I will establish the good word. In those days, and at that time, will I make a righteous offshoot unto David. In those days shall Judah be saved (33:14-16).

I will bring words against this city for evil in that day. But I will deliver thee in that day (39:16, 17).

That day is to the Lord Jehovih of hosts a day of vengeance, that He will take vengeance of His enemies. The day of destruction has come upon them, the time of their visitation (46:10, 21).

Because of the day that cometh to lay waste (47:4).

I will bring upon him the year of visitation. Yet I will bring again his captivity in the end of days (48:44, 47)

I will bring destruction upon them in the time of their visitation. Her young men shall fall in the streets, and all the men of war shall be cut off in that day. In the end of days I will bring again their captivity (49:8, 26, 39).

In those days, and in that time, the sons of Israel and the sons of Judah shall come together, and shall seek Jehovah their God. In those days, and in that time, the iniquity of Israel shall be sought for, and there shall be none. Woe unto them, for their day is come, the time of their visitation (50:4, 20, 27, 31).

They are vanity, a work of errors, in the time of their visitation they shall perish (51:18).

In Ezekiel:

An end is come, the end is come, the morning cometh upon thee; the time is come, the day of tumult is near. Behold the day, behold it cometh, the morning hath gone forth, the rod hath blossomed, violence hath budded. The day is come, the time is come upon all the multitude thereof. Their silver and gold shall not deliver them in the day of the anger of Jehovah (7:6, 7, 10, 12, 19).

They said of the prophet, The vision that he seeth shall come to pass after many days; he prophesieth for times that are far off (12:27).

They shall not stand in the war in the day of the anger of Jehovah (13:5).

Thou, O deadly wounded wicked one, the prince of Israel, whose day is come, in the time of the iniquity of the end (21:25).

A city that sheddeth blood in the midst of her, that her time may come; and thou hast caused thy days to draw near, so that thou art come to thy years (22:3, 4).

Shall it not be in the day when I take from them their strength? In that day he that escapeth shall come unto thee to the instructing of thine ears. In that day shall thy mouth be opened together with him that is escaped (24:25-27).

In that day will I cause a horn to grow unto the house of Israel (29:21).

Howl ye, Woe worth the day! for the day is near, the day of Jehovah is near, a day of cloud; it shall be the time of the nations. In that day shall messengers go forth from Me (30:2, 3, 9).

In the day in which thou shalt go down into hell (31:15).

I will search for My flock in the day that he shall be in the midst of his flock; and I will deliver them out of all places whither they have been scattered, in the day of cloud and of thick darkness (34:11, 12).

In the day that I cleanse you from all your iniquities (36:33).

Prophesy and say, In that day when My people Israel shall sit securely, shalt thou not know it? In days to come I will lead thee into My land. In that day, even the day when Gog shall come upon the land. In My zeal, in the fire of Mine indignation, if not in this day, there shall be a great earthquake upon the land of Israel (38:14, 16, 18, 19).

Behold, it cometh, this day of which I have spoken. It shall come to pass in that day that I will give unto Gog a place for burial in the land of Israel, so that the house of Israel shall know that I am Jehovah their God, from that day and forward (39:8, 11, 22).

In Daniel:

God in the heavens hath revealed secrets, what shall be in days to come (2:28).

The time came that the saints possessed the kingdom (7:22).

Attend, for at the time of the end shall be the vision. And he said, Behold, I will make thee know what shall be in the last end of the anger, for at the time appointed shall the end be. The vision of the evening and the morning is truth; shut thou up the vision, for it shall be for many days (8:17, 19, 26).

I am come to make thee understand what shall befall thy people in the end of days; for the vision is yet for days (10:14).

The intelligent shall be proved to purge and cleanse them, even to the time of the end, because it is yet for the time appointed (11:35).

At that time shall Michael rise up, the great prince who standeth for the sons of thy people; and there shall be a time of trouble, such as never was since there was a nation. At that time thy people shall be delivered, every one that shall be found written in the book (12:1).

Thou, O Daniel, shut up the words, and seal the book, even to the time of the end. But from the time that the continual [burnt-offering] shall be taken away, and the abomination that maketh waste be set up, there shall be a thousand two hundred and ninety days. Thou shalt arise into thy lot at the end of the days (12:4, 11, 13).

In Hosea:

I will make an end of the kingdom of the house of Israel. In that day I will break the bow of Israel. Great shall be the day of Jezreel (1:4, 5, 11).

In that day thou shalt call Me, my Husband. In that day I will make a covenant for them. In that day I will hear (2:16, 18, 21).

The sons of Israel shall return, and seek Jehovah their God, and David their king, in the end of days (3:5).

Come, and let us return unto Jehovah; after two days He will revive us; in the third day He will raise us up, and we shall live before Him (6:1, 2).

The days of visitation are come; the days of retribution are come (9:7).

In Joel:

Alas for the day, for the day of Jehovah is at hand, and as a laying waste from Shaddai shall it come (1:15).

The day of Jehovah cometh, nigh is the day of darkness and of thick darkness, a day of cloud and of obscurity. The day of Jehovah is great and very terrible; and who can endure it? (2:1, 2, 11).

Upon the servants, and upon the handmaids in those days will I pour out My spirit. The sun shall be turned into darkness, and the moon into blood, before the great and terrible day of Jehovah is come (2:29, 31).

Behold, in those days, and in that time, which I will bring back, I will gather all nations. The day of Jehovah is near. It shall come to pass in that day that the mountains shall drop new wine (3:1, 2, 14, 18).

In Obadiah:

Shall I not in that day destroy the wise men out of Edom? Neither shouldst thou have rejoiced over them in the day of their destruction, in the day of their distress. For the day of Jehovah is near upon all the nations (verses 8, 12, 15).

In Amos:

He that is courageous in his heart shall flee away naked in that day (2:16).

In the day that I shall visit the transgressions of Israel upon him (3:14).

Woe unto you that desire the day of Jehovah! What to you is the day of Jehovah? it is one of darkness, and not of light. Shall not the day of Jehovah be darkness, and not light? even thick darkness, and no brightness in it (v. 18, 20).

The songs of the temple shall be howlings in that day. In that day I will cause the sun to go down at noon; and I will darken the earth in the day of light. In that day shall the beautiful virgins and the young men faint for thirst (8:3, 9, 13).

In that day I will raise up the tent of David that is fallen. Behold, the days come that the mountains shall drop new wine (9:11, 13).

In Micah:

In that day shall one lament, We be utterly laid waste (2:4).

In the end of days the mountain of the house of Jehovah shall be established at the head of the mountains. In that day will I gather her that halteth (4:1, 6).

In that day I will cut off thy horses and thy chariots (5:10).

The day of thy watchmen, and thy visitation, cometh. The day is at hand for building thy walls. In that day he shall come even to thee (7:4, 11, 12).

In Habakkuk:

The vision is yet for an appointed time, and at the end it shall speak; though it tarry, wait for it, because it will surely come, it will not delay (2:3).

O Jehovah, do Thy work in the midst of the years; in the midst of the years make known; God cometh (3:2, 3).

In Zephaniah:

The day of Jehovah is at hand. In the day of Jehovah's sacrifice I will visit upon the princes, and upon the king's sons. In that day there shall be the voice of a cry. At that time I will search Jerusalem with lamps. The great day of Jehovah is near. That day is a day of wrath, a day of trouble and distress, a day of wasteness and desolation, a day of darkness and thick darkness, a day of cloud and overclouding, a day of the trumpet and of sounding. In the day of Jehovah's wrath the whole land shall be devoured, and He shall make a speedy end of all them that dwell in the land (1:7, 8, 10, 12, 14-16, 18).

Before the day of Jehovah's anger has come upon us. It may be ye shall be hid in the day of Jehovah's anger (2:2, 3).

Wait ye upon Me until the day that I rise up to the prey, for it is My judgment. In that day shalt thou not be ashamed for all thy works. In that day it shall be said to Jerusalem, Fear thou not. At that time I will deal with thine oppressors. At that time will I bring you in, and at that time will I gather you; for I will make you a name, and a praise (3:8, 11, 16, 19, 20).

In Zechariah:

Many nations shall cleave to Jehovah in that day (2:11).

I will remove the iniquity of that land in one day. In that day shall ye cry every man to his companion under the vine and under the fig-tree (3:9, 10).

In those days ten men shall take hold of the skirt of a man that is a Jew (8:23).

Jehovah their God shall serve them in that day, as the flock of His people (9:16).

My covenant was broken in that day (11:11).

In that day will I make Jerusalem a stone of burden for all peoples. In that day I will smite every horse with astonishment. In that day will I make the leaders of Judah like a furnace of fire among the wood. In that day shall Jehovah defend the inhabitants of Jerusalem. In that day I will seek to destroy all nations. In that day shall there be a great mourning in Jerusalem (12:3, 4, 6, 8, 9, 11).

In that day there shall be a fountain opened to the house of David, and to the inhabitants of Jerusalem. It shall come to pass in that day I will cut off the names of the idols in the land. In that day the prophets shall be ashamed (13:1-4).

Behold, the day of Jehovah cometh. His feet shall stand in that day upon the Mount of Olives. In that day there shall not be light and brightness; but it shall be one day which shall be known unto Jehovah; not day, nor night, at evening time there shall be light. In that day living waters shall go out from Jerusalem. In that day there shall be one Jehovah, and His name one. In that day there shall be a great tumult from Jehovah. In that day shall there be upon the bells of the horses, Holiness unto Jehovah. In that day there shall be no more a Canaanite in the house of Jehovah (14:1, 4, 6-9, 13, 20, 21.)

In Malachi:

Who may abide the day of His coming, and who shall stand when He appeareth? They shall be Mine in the day wherein I do make a peculiar treasure. Behold, the day cometh that shall burn as an oven. Behold, I send you Elijah the prophet before the coming of the great and terrible day of Jehovah (3:2, 17; 4:1, 5).

In David:

In His days shall the righteous flourish, and abundance of peace, and He shall have dominion from sea to sea, and from the river unto the ends of the earth (Ps 72:7, 8). (Besides other places.)

5. In these passages by "day" and "time" is meant the advent of the Lord. By a "day" or "time" of darkness, of thick darkness, of gloom, of no light, of laying waste, of the end of iniquity, of destruction, is meant the advent of the Lord when He was no longer known, and when consequently there was no longer anything of the church left. By "a day" cruel, terrible, of wrath, of anger, of tumult, of visitation, of sacrifice, of recompense, of distress, of war, of a cry, is meant the advent of the Lord to judgment. By "the day" in which Jehovah alone shall be exalted, in which He shall be one and His name one, in which the offshoot of Jehovah shall be for beauty and glory, in which the righteous shall flourish, in which He shall vivify, in which He shall seek His flock, in which He shall make a new covenant, in which the mountains shall drop new wine, in which living waters shall go out from Jerusalem, in which they shall look unto the God of Israel, and many similar expressions, is meant the advent of the Lord to set up again a new church which will acknowledge Him as the Redeemer and Saviour.

6. To these passages may be added some which speak of the Lord's advent more openly:

The Lord Himself shall give you a sign: Behold a virgin shall conceive and bear a Son, and shall call His name GOD-WITH-US (Isa 7:14; Mt 1:22, 23).

Unto us a Child is born, unto us a Son is given, and the government shall be upon His shoulder; and His name shall be called Wonderful, Counselor, God, Hero, Father of eternity, Prince of peace. Of the increase of His government and peace there shall be no end, upon the throne of David, and upon his kingdom, to establish it in judgment and justice, from henceforth and even to eternity (Isa 9:6, 7).

There shall come forth a Rod out of the stem of Jesse, and a Shoot shall bear fruit out of his roots: and the spirit of Jehovah shall rest upon Him, the spirit of wisdom and understanding, the spirit of counsel and might. Righteousness shall be the girdle of His loins, and truth the girdle of His reins. Therefore it shall come to pass in that day, that the Root of Jesse, which standeth for an ensign of the peoples, shall the nations seek, and His rest shall be glory (11:1, 2, 5, 10).

Send ye the lamb of the ruler of the land, from the rock to the wilderness, to the mountain of the daughter of Zion. By mercy has the throne been established, and one shall sit upon it in truth, in the tabernacle of David, judging and seeking judgment, and hasting righteousness (16:1, 5).

It shall be said in that day, Lo, this is our God; we have waited for Him that He may save us: THIS IS JEHOVAH; we have waited for Him, we will rejoice and be glad in His salvation (25:9).

The voice of one crying in the wilderness, Prepare ye the way of JEHOVAH, make plain in the solitude a pathway for our God. For the glory of JEHOVAH shall be revealed, and all flesh shall see it together. Behold, the LORD JEHOVAH will come in strength, and His arm shall rule for Him; behold, His reward is with Him. He shall feed His flock like a shepherd (40:3, 5, 10, 11).

Mine elect, in whom My soul delighteth. I JEHOVAH have called Thee in righteousness, and I will give Thee for a covenant to the people, for a light to the nations, to open the blind eyes, to bring out the bound from the prison, and them that sit in darkness out of the prison house. I am JEHOVAH, this is My name, and My glory will I not give to another (42:1, 6-8).

Who hath believed our word, and to whom is the arm of Jehovah revealed? He hath no form; we have seen Him, but He hath no appearance. He hath borne our diseases, and carried our griefs (53:1, 2, 4, to end).

Who is this that cometh from Edom, with sprinkled garments from Bozrah, marching in the greatness of His strength? I that speak in righteousness, great to save: for the day of vengeance is in Mine heart, and the year of My redeemed is come. So He became their Saviour (63:1, 4, 8).

Behold, the days come that I will raise up to David a righteous offshoot, who shall reign as king, and shall prosper, and shall execute judgment and justice in the earth: and this is His name whereby they shall call Him, JEHOVAH OUR RIGHTEOUSNESS (Je 23:5, 6; 33:15, 16).

Rejoice greatly, O daughter of Zion; shout, O daughter of Jerusalem; behold, thy King cometh unto thee, He is just and saved. He shall speak peace to the nations; and His dominion shall be from sea to sea, and from the river even to the ends of the earth (Zech 9:9, 10).

Rejoice and be glad, O daughter of Zion; lo, I come, that I may dwell in the midst of thee; and many nations shall cleave to Jehovah in that day, and shall be My people (Zech 2:10, 11).

Thou Bethlehem Ephratah, little as thou art to be among the thousands of Judah, out of thee shall one come forth unto Me that is to be Ruler in Israel, and whose goings forth are from of old, from the days of eternity. He shall stand and feed in the strength of JEHOVAH (Micah 5:2, 4).

Behold, I send Mine Angel, who shall prepare the way before Me, and the LORD whom ye seek shall suddenly come to His temple, even the Angel of the covenant, whom ye have desired; behold, He cometh; but who shall abide the day of His coming? Behold, I send you Elijah the prophet, before the coming of the great and terrible day of Jehovah (Mal 3:1, 2; 4:5).

I saw, and behold, one like the Son of man came with the clouds of heaven; and there was given Him dominion, and glory, and a kingdom, that all peoples, nations, and languages may worship Him: His dominion is an everlasting dominion, which shall not pass away, and His kingdom that which shall not be destroyed; and all dominions shall worship Him, and obey Him (Da 7:13, 14, 27).

Seventy weeks are determined upon thy people, and upon thy

holy city, to consummate the transgression, and to seal up the vision and the prophecy, and to anoint the holy of holies. Know, therefore, and perceive, that from the going forth of the word to restore and build Jerusalem, unto Messiah the Prince, shall be seven weeks (Da 9:24, 25).

I will set his hand in the sea, and his right hand in the rivers: He shall cry unto Me, Thou art my Father, my God, and the rock of my salvation. I also will make him My first-born, higher than the kings of the earth. His seed also will I make to endure to eternity, and his throne as the days of the heavens (Ps 89:25-27, 29).

Jehovah said unto my Lord, Sit Thou at My right hand, until I make Thine enemies Thy footstool. Jehovah shall send the scepter of Thy strength out of Zion; rule Thou in the midst of Thine enemies. Thou art a priest to eternity after the manner of Melchizedek (Ps 110:1, 2, 4; Mt 22:44; Lu 20:42).

I have anointed My king upon Zion, the mountain of My holiness; I will declare for a statute, Jehovah hath said unto Me, Thou art My Son, this day have I begotten Thee; I will give the nations for Thine inheritance, and the uttermost parts of the earth for Thy possession. Kiss the Son, lest He be angry, and ye perish from the way; blessed are all they that put their trust in Him (Ps 2:6-8, 12).

Thou hast made him a little less than the angels, but hast crowned him with glory and honor; Thou hast made him to have dominion over the works of Thy hands; Thou hast put all things under his feet (8:5, 6).

Jehovah, remember David, who sware unto Jehovah, and vowed to the Mighty One of Jacob, If I shall enter within the tent of my house, if I shall go up upon my couch, if I shall give sleep to mine eyes, until I find out a place for Jehovah, a habitation for the Mighty One of Jacob. Lo, we heard of Him at Ephratah, we found Him in the fields of the forest. We will enter into His tabernacles, we will bow at His footstool. Let Thy priests be clothed with righteousness, and let Thy saints shout for joy (132:1, 7, 9).

The passages here cited, however, are but few.

7. All Holy Scripture has been written solely about the Lord. This will be more fully evident from what follows, especially from the things to be advanced in the small work on *The Sacred Scripture*. This is the one only source of the holiness of the Word, and is what is meant by the words

The testimony of Jesus is the spirit of prophecy (Rev 19:10).

II.

8. At the present day many persons believe that when it is said about the Lord that He fulfilled the law, the meaning is that He fulfilled all the commandments of the Decalogue, and thus became righteousness, and also justified the men of this world through this matter of faith. This however is not the meaning. The meaning is that the Lord fulfilled everything written about Himself in the Law and the Prophets, that is, in all Holy Scripture, because this treats solely of Him, as has been said in the foregoing article. The reason why many have believed differently, is that they have not searched the Scriptures and seen what is there meant by "the Law." The Law there means, in a restricted sense, the ten commandments of the Decalogue; in a wider sense, everything written by Moses in the five books; and in the widest sense, everything in the Word. It is well known that *by the Law in a restricted sense are meant the ten commandments of the Decalogue.*

9. *By the Law in a wider sense is meant everything written by Moses in his five books,* as is evident from the following passages.

In Luke:

Abraham said to the rich man in hell, They have Moses and the Prophets, let them hear them; if they hear not Moses and the Prophets, neither will they be persuaded though one rose from the dead (16:29, 31).

In John:

Philip said to Nathanael, We have found Him of whom Moses in the Law and the Prophets did write (1:45).

In Matthew:

Think not that I am come to destroy the Law and the Prophets; I am not come to destroy, but to fulfill (5:17).

All the Prophets and the Law prophesied until John (11:13).

In Luke:

The Law and the Prophets were until John; since then the Kingdom of God is evangelized (16:16).

In Matthew:

All things whatsoever that ye would that men should do to you, do ye even so to them, for this is the Law and the Prophets (7:12).

Jesus said, Thou shalt love the Lord thy God with all thy heart, and with all thy soul, and thou shalt love thy neighbor as thyself; on these two commandments hang all the Law and the Prophets 22:37, 39, 40).

In these passages, "Moses and the Prophets," and "the Law and the Prophets," mean all the things that have been written in the books of Moses and in the books of the prophets.

That "the Law" specifically means all the things that have been written by Moses, is further evident from the following passages.

In Luke:

When the days of her purification, according to the Law of Moses, were fulfilled, they brought Jesus to Jerusalem, to present Him to the Lord; as it is written in the Law of the Lord: Every male that openeth the womb shall be called holy to the Lord; and to offer a sacrifice, according to that which is said in the Law of the Lord: A pair of turtle doves, or two young pigeons. And the parents brought Jesus into the temple, to do for Him after the custom of the Law. And when they had performed all things according to the Law of the Lord. . . (2:22-24, 27, 39).

In John:

Moses in the Law commanded us that such should be stoned (8:5).

The Law was given by Moses (1:17).

From these passages it appears that where such things are spoken of as are written in the books of Moses, they are sometimes called "the Law," and sometimes "Moses."

(So also in Mt 8:4; Mk 10:2-4; 12:19; Lu 20:28, 37; Jn 3:14; 7:19, 51; 8:17; 19:7.)

Many things that were commanded are also called by Moses "the Law," as:

Concerning the burnt-offerings (Lev 6:9; 7:37).
Concerning the sacrifices (Lev 6:25; 7:1-11).
Concerning the meat-offering (Lev 6:14).
Concerning leprosy (Lev 14:2).
Concerning jealousy (Num 5:29, 30).
Concerning the Naziriteship (Num 6:13, 21).

And Moses himself calls his books "the Law:"

Moses wrote this Law, and delivered it to the priests, the sons of Levi, who bare the ark of the covenant of Jehovah; and he said to them, Take the Book of this Law, and put it at the side of the ark of the covenant of Jehovah (Dt 31:9, 11, 26).

It was placed at the side, because within the ark were the tables of stone, which in a restricted sense are the Law. Afterwards the books of Moses are called "The Book of the Law:"

And Hilkiah the high priest said unto Shaphan the scribe, I have found the Book of the Law in the house of Jehovah. And when the king had heard the words of the Book of the Law, he rent his garments (2 Kgs 22:8, 11; 23:24).

10. *In the widest sense, "the Law" means everything in the Word,* as is evident from these passages:

Jesus said. Is it not written in your Law, I said, Ye are gods? (Jn 10:34). (This is written in Ps 82:6).

The multitude answered Him, We have heard out of the Law, that the Christ abideth forever (Jn 12:34). (This is written in Ps 89:29; 110:4; and in Da 7:11, 14).

That the word might be fulfilled that is written in their Law, They hated Me without a cause (Jn 15:25). (This is written in Ps 35:19).

The Pharisees said, Have any of the rulers believed on Him? But this multitude that knoweth not the Law are cursed (Jn 7:48, 49).

It is easier for heaven and earth to pass than for one tittle of the Law to fall (Lu 16:17). (Here "the Law" means all Holy Scripture.)

11. The statement that the Lord fulfilled all things of the Law means that He fulfilled everything in the Word. This is evident from passages where it is said that the Scripture was fulfilled by Him, and that all things were consummated; as from the following:

Jesus went into the synagogue, and stood up to read, and there was delivered to Him the book of the prophet Isaiah, and He unrolled the book, and found the place where it is written, The Spirit of the Lord is upon Me, because He hath anointed Me, He hath sent Me to preach the gospel to the poor, to heal the broken-hearted, to preach deliverance to the captives, and recovering of sight to the blind, to preach the acceptable year of the Lord. And He rolled up the book and said, This day is this Scripture fulfilled in your ears (Lu 4:16-21).

Search the Scriptures, for they testify of Me (Jn 5:39).

That the Scripture may be fulfilled, He that eateth bread with Me hath lifted up his heel against Me (Jn 13:18).

None of them is lost, but the son of perdition, that the Scripture might be fulfilled (Jn 17:12).

That the word might be fulfilled which He spake, Of them whom Thou gavest Me have I lost none (Jn 18:9).

Jesus said to Peter, Put up again thy sword into its place. How then shall the Scriptures be fulfilled, that thus it must be? But all this was done that the Scriptures of the Prophets might be fulfilled (Mt 26:52, 54, 56).

The Son of Man goeth as it is written of Him, that the Scriptures be fulfilled (Mk 14:21, 49).

Thus the Scripture was fulfilled which saith, He was accounted among the transgressors (Mk 15:28; Lu 22:37).

That the Scripture might be fulfilled, which saith, They divided My garments among them, and upon my under-vesture did they cast a lot (Jn 19:24).

After this, Jesus knowing that all things were now consummated, that the Scripture might be fulfilled (verse 28).

When Jesus had received the vinegar, He said, It is consummated, that is, fulfilled (verse 30).

These things were done, that the Scripture might be fulfilled, A bone of Him shall not be broken. And again another Scripture saith, They shall look on Him whom they pierced (verses 36, 37).

There are other places where passages are adduced from the Prophets, without its being at the same time said that the Law, or the Scripture, was fulfilled.

The whole Word has been written about the Lord, and He came into the world to fulfill it. This He also taught His disciples before His departure, in these words:

Jesus said to His disciples, O fools, and slow of heart to believe all that the prophets have spoken. Ought not the Christ to suffer these things, and to enter into His glory? And beginning at Moses and all the Prophets, He expounded unto them in all the Scriptures the things concerning Himself (Lu 24:25-27).

Jesus said to His disciples, These are the words which I spake unto you while I was yet with you, that all things must be fulfilled which were written in the Law of Moses, and in the Prophets, and in the Psalms, concerning Me (verse 44).

That in the world the Lord fulfilled the whole Word, even to the smallest details of it, is evident from His own words:

Verily I say unto you, Till heaven and earth pass, one jot or one tittle shall not pass from the law, till everything be accomplished (Mt 5:18).

From these passages it may now be clearly seen that by its being said that the Lord fulfilled everything in the Law is not meant that He fulfilled all the commandments of the Decalogue, but that He fulfilled everything in the Word.

III.

12. It is known in the church that the Lord conquered death, by which is meant hell, and that He afterwards ascended in glory into heaven; but as yet it has not been known that it was by means of combats which are temptations that the Lord conquered death or hell, and at the same time by means of them glorified His Human; and that the passion of the cross was the final combat or temptation by means of which He effected this conquest and this glorification. About these temptations many things are said in the Prophets and in the Psalms; but not so many in the Evangelists. In the latter, the temptations which He endured from childhood are summarily described by His temptations in the wilderness, followed by those from the "devil"; and the last of them by the things He suffered at Gethsemane and on the cross.

(Concerning His temptations in the wilderness, and by the devil, see (Mt 4:1-11; Mk 1:12, 13; and Lu 4:1-13).

By these temptations, however, are meant all His temptations even to the last. He revealed no more about them to His disciples; for it is said in Isaiah:

He was oppressed, yet He opened not His mouth: as a lamb that is brought to the slaughter, and as a sheep before her shearers is dumb, so He opened not His mouth (53:7).

(Concerning His temptations at Gethsemane, see Mt 26:36-44; Mk 14:32-42; and Lu 22:39-46. And concerning the temptations on the cross, see Mt 27:33-50; Mk 15:22-37; Lu 23:33-49; and Jn 19:17-34).

Temptations are nothing else than combats against the hells.*

13. That the Lord fully conquered the hells by the passion of the cross, He Himself teaches in John:

Now is the judgment of this world; now shall the prince of this world be cast out (12:31).

The Lord said this when the passion of the cross was at hand:

The prince of this world is judged (16:11).
Be of good cheer, I have overcome the world (verse 33).

In Luke:

Jesus said, I beheld Satan as lightning fall from heaven (10:18).

The "world," the "prince of the world," "Satan," and "the devil," mean hell.
By the passion of the cross the Lord also fully glorified His Human, as He teaches in John:

When Judas was gone out, Jesus said, Now is the Son of man glorified, and God is glorified in Him; if God be glorified in Him, God will also glorify Him in Himself, and will straightway glorify Him (13:31, 32).
Father, the hour is come, glorify Thy Son, that Thy Son also may glorify Thee (17:1).
Now is My soul troubled; and He said, Father, glorify Thy name. Then came there a voice from heaven, saying, I have both glorified it, and I will glorify it again (12:27, 28).

In Luke:

Ought not the Christ to suffer this, and to enter into His glory? (24:26).

These things are said of the Passion. Glorification is the

---

* Concerning the Lord's temptations or combats, see the small work on *The New Jerusalem and its Heavenly Doctrine*, published in London, nn. 201 and 302; and concerning temptations in general, nn. 187-200.

unition of the Divine and the Human; and therefore it is said, "and God will glorify Him in Himself."

14. The Lord came into the world to reduce into order all things in heaven, and derivatively on earth. This was effected by means of combats against the hells, which were then infesting every man that came into the world and that went out of the world; and He thereby became Righteousness, and saved men, who otherwise could not have been saved. All this is foretold in many passages in the Prophets, of which only a few shall be cited.

[2] In Isaiah:

Who is this that cometh from Edom, with sprinkled garments from Bozrah; this that is glorious in His apparel, marching in the greatness of His strength? I that speak in righteousness, mighty to save. Wherefore art Thou red in Thine apparel, and Thy garments like Him that treadeth in the wine-press? I have trodden the wine-press alone, and of the people there was not a man with Me; wherefore I have trodden them in Mine anger, and trampled them in My wrath; therefore their victory is sprinkled upon My garments; for the day of vengeance is in Mine heart, and the year of My redeemed is come. Mine own arm brought salvation unto Me; and I brought down their victory to the earth. He said, Lo, they are My people, sons; therefore He was their Saviour; in His love, and in His pity, He redeemed them (63:1-9).

These things are said of the Lord's combats against the hells. The "apparel" in which He was "glorious," and which was "red," means the Word, to which violence had been done by the Jewish people. The actual combat against the hells, and the victory over them, are described by its being said that He "trod them in His anger, and trampled them in His wrath." That He fought alone, and from His own power, is described by, "of the people there was not a man with Me; Mine own arm brought salvation unto Me; I brought down their victory to the earth." That He thereby effected salvation and redemption, is described by, "therefore He was their Saviour; in His love and in His pity He redeemed them." This was the reason for His advent, described by, "the day of vengeance is in Mine heart, and the year of My redeemed is come."

[3] In Isaiah again:

He saw that there was not any one, and He was amazed that there was none to interpose; therefore His own arm brought salvation unto Him; and His righteousness, it upheld Him; therefore He put on righteousness as a coat of mail, and a helmet of salvation upon His head; and He put on garments of vengeance, and clad Himself with zeal as a cloak: then came the Redeemer to Zion (59:16, 17, 20).

These words also treat of the Lord's combats against the hells while He was in the world. That He fought against them from His own power, is meant by, "He saw that there was not any one, therefore His own arm brought salvation unto Him." "His righteousness, it upheld Him, whence He put on righteousness as a coat of mail" means that He thereby became righteousness. That He thus effected redemption is meant by "then came the Redeemer to Zion."

[4] In Jeremiah:

They are dismayed, their strong ones were beaten down, they are fled apace, and look not back: that day is to the Lord Jehovih of hosts a day of vengeance, that He may take vengeance of His enemies, and the sword shall devour, and be sated (46:5, 10).

The Lord's combat with the hells, and His victory over them, are described by its being said that they are dismayed, and that their strong ones being beaten down are fled apace, and looked not back. Their "strong ones," and "enemies," are the hells, for all there feel hatred against the Lord. His advent into the world for this purpose is meant by, "that day is to the Lord Jehovih of hosts a day of vengeance, that He may take vengeance of His enemies."

[5] In Jeremiah:

Her young men shall fall in the streets, and all the men of war shall be cut off in that day (49:26).

In Joel:

Jehovah hath uttered His voice before His army; the day of Jehovah is great and very terrible; who therefore can endure it? (2:11).

In Zephaniah:

In the day of the sacrifice of Jehovah I will visit upon the princes, upon the king's sons, upon all who are clothed with strange apparel. That day is a day of distress, a day of the trumpet and of sounding (1:8, 15, 16).

In Zechariah:

Jehovah shall go forth, and fight against the nations, as when He fought in the day of battle. And His feet shall stand in that day upon the Mount of Olives, which is eastward from Jerusalem. Then shall ye flee into the valley of My mountains. In that day there shall not be light and brightness. And Jehovah shall be king over all the earth; in that day there shall be one Jehovah, and His name one (14:3-6, 9).

These passages also treat of the Lord's combats. "That day" means His advent. The Mount of Olives that was eastward from Jerusalem, was where the Lord was wont to tarry. (See Mk 13:3; 14:26; Lu 21:37; 22:39; Jn 8:1; and elsewhere.)

[6] In David:

The cords of death compassed me about, the cords of hell encompassed me, the snares of death forestalled me; therefore He sent out His arrows, and many lightnings, and discomfited them. I will pursue Mine enemies, and catch them, neither will I turn until I have consumed them. I will smite them that they shall not be able to rise. Thou hast girded me with strength unto the war, and Thou shalt put mine enemies to flight; I will beat them small as dust before the faces of the wind, as the mire of the streets I will enfeeble them (Ps 18:5, 14, 37-40, 42).

The "cords" and "snares of death" that encompassed and forestalled, signify temptations, which, being from hell, are called also "the cords of hell." These and all other things in this whole Psalm treat of the Lord's combats and victories; and therefore it is added, "Thou wilt make me the head of the nations; a people that have not known shall serve me" (verse 43).

[7] In the Psalms of David again:

Gird Thy sword upon Thy thigh, O Mighty one; Thine arrows are sharp, the people shall fall under Thee, from the heart of the king's enemies. Thy throne is for ever and to eternity: Thou hast loved righteousness, wherefore God hath anointed Thee (45:3, 5-7).

These words also treat of combat with the hells, and of their subjugation; for this whole Psalm treats of the Lord, that is to say, of His combats, His glorification, and the salvation of the faithful by Him. In the Psalms:

A fire shall go before Him, it shall burn up His enemies round about; the earth shall see and shall fear; the mountains shall melt like wax before the Lord of the whole earth. The heavens shall declare His righteousness, and all the people shall see His glory (97:3-6).

This Psalm likewise treats of the Lord, and of the like things. [8]Again:

Jehovah said unto my Lord, Sit Thou at My right hand until I make Thine enemies Thy footstool; rule Thou in the midst of Thine enemies. The Lord at Thy right hand hath smitten kings in the day of His anger; He hath filled with dead bodies, He hath smitten the head over much land (110:1, 2, 5, 6).

That these words are said of the Lord, is evident from His own words in Mt 22:44; Mk 12:36; and Lu 20:42. To "sit at the right hand," means omnipotence; the "enemies" signify the hells; "kings," those there who are in falsities of evil. To "make them His footstool," "smite them in the day of anger," and "fill with dead bodies," mean to destroy their power; and to "smite the head over much land," signifies to destroy all.

[9] As the Lord alone conquered the hells, without the aid of any angel, He is called Hero, and a Man of wars (Isa 42:13); The King of Glory, Jehovah strong and mighty; a Hero of war (Ps 24:8, 10); The Mighty One of Jacob (132:2); and in many places, Jehovah Zebaoth, that is, Jehovah of the hosts of war. His advent is also called The Day of Jehovah terrible, cruel, of indignation, of wrath, of anger, of vengeance, of destruction, of war, of the sounding of the trumpet, of tumult, as may be seen from the passages quoted above, in n. 4.

[10] As the last judgment executed by the Lord when He was in the world was effected by means of combats with the hells, and by their subjugation, this coming judgment is treated of in many passages. As in the Psalms of David:

Jehovah cometh to judge the earth; He shall judge the world in righteousness, and the people in truth (96:13).

And so in many other passages. These are from the prophetical parts of the Word.

[11] In its historical parts like things are represented by the wars of the sons of Israel with various nations; for everything that is written in the Word, whether in prophecy or history, is written about the Lord; and this is why the Word is divine. Many arcana of the Lord's glorification are contained in the rituals of the Israelitish Church, as for example in its burnt-offerings and sacrifices, in its sabbaths and feasts, and in the priesthood of Aaron and the other Levites; as they are also in all those other things in Moses which are called laws, judgments, and statutes; and this is what is meant by the Lord's words to His disciples:

That He must needs fulfill all things which are written in the law of Moses concerning Him (Lu 24:44);

and by His saying to the Jews that Moses "wrote of Him" (John 5:46).

[12] From all this it is evident that the Lord came into the world to subjugate the hells, and to glorify His Human; and that the passion of the cross was the final combat, by which He fully conquered the hells, and fully glorified His Human. But more will be seen on this subject in the following small work on *The Sacred Scripture*, where are collected together all the passages from the prophetical Word that treat of the Lord's combats with the hells and His victories over them; or, what is the same, that treat of the last judgment executed by Him when He was in the world; and also those which treat of His passion, and of the glorification of His Human, which are so numerous that if quoted they would fill pages.

IV.

BY THE PASSION OF THE CROSS THE LORD DID NOT TAKE AWAY
SINS, BUT BORE THEM.

15. Some persons within the church believe that by the passion of the cross the Lord took away sins, and made satisfaction to the Father, and so effected redemption; and some, that He transferred to Himself, bore, and cast into the "depths of the sea" (that is, into hell), the sins of those who have faith in Him. They confirm themselves in these notions by the words of John concerning Jesus:

Behold the Lamb of God, that taketh away the sins of the world (Jn 1:29);

and by the Lord's words in Isaiah:

He hath borne our diseases, and carried our sorrows: He was wounded for our transgressions, He was bruised for our iniquities, the chastisement of our peace was upon Him, and by His wound has health been given us. Jehovah hath made to fall on Him the iniquities of us all. He was oppressed and He was afflicted, yet He opened not His mouth; He is led as a lamb to the slaughter. He was cut off out of the land of the living for the transgression of My people, to whom the stroke was due, that He might deliver the wicked into their sepulchre, and the rich into their deaths; He shall see of the labor of His soul, and shall be satisfied. By His knowledge shall He justify many; in that He hath borne their iniquities. He hath poured out His soul unto death, and He was numbered with the transgressors, and He bare the sins of many, and made intercession for the transgressors (53:4 to end).

Both these passages speak of the Lord's temptations and passion; and by His taking away sins and diseases, and by the iniquities of all being made to fall on Him, is meant the like as by His bearing sorrows and iniquities.

[2] Therefore it shall first be stated what is meant by bear-

29

ing iniquities, and afterwards what by taking them away. To bear iniquities means to endure grievous temptations; and also to suffer the Jews to treat Him as they had treated the Word, which they did because He was the Word. For the church as it then existed among the Jews was utterly devastated, and it was devastated by their having perverted all things of the Word, so that there was not any truth remaining; and therefore they did not acknowledge the Lord. This was meant and signified by all things of the Lord's passion. The prophets were treated in a similar way, because they represented the Lord as to the Word, and derivatively the Lord in respect to the church; and the Lord was *the* Prophet.

[3] That the Lord was *the* Prophet is evident from the following passages:

Jesus said, A prophet is not without honor, save in his own country, and in his own house (Mt 13:57; Mk 6:4; Lu 4:24).

Jesus said, It cannot be that a prophet perish out of Jerusalem (Lu 13:33).

They said of Jesus, This is that prophet of Nazareth (Mt 21:11; Jn 7:40).

Fear took hold on all; and they praised God, saying that a great prophet is risen up among us (Lu 7:16).

That a prophet should be raised up out of the midst of their brethren, whose words they shall obey (Dt 18:15-19).

The prophets underwent similar treatment, as is evident from the things which follow.

[4] In order that he might represent the state of the church, the prophet Isaiah was commanded

To loose the sackcloth from off his loins, and to put off the shoe from his foot, and to walk naked and barefoot three years, for a sign and a wonder (Isa 20:2, 3).

In order that he might represent the state of the church, the prophet Jeremiah was commanded

To buy for himself a girdle, and put it upon his loins, and not put it in water, and to hide it in a hole of the rock near the river Euphrates, and after many days he found it rotten (Je 13:1-7).

The same prophet represented the state of the church by

His not taking a wife in that place, nor entering into the house of mourning, neither going away to lament, nor entering into the house of feasting (16:2, 5, 8).

[5] In order that he might represent the state of the church, the prophet Ezekiel was commanded

To cause a barber's razor to pass upon his head, and upon his beard, and afterwards to divide it, and to burn the third part of it in the midst of the city, to smite a third part with a sword, and to scatter a third part in the wind: and that he should bind a few hairs in his skirts, and at last cast them into the midst of the fire, and burn them (5:1-4).

In order that he might represent the state of the church, the same prophet was commanded

To make vessels of wandering, and to wander to another place in the eyes of the sons of Israel, and to bring forth the vessels by day, and go forth in the evening through a hole dug in the wall, and cover his face so that he should not see the earth; and that so he should be for a wonder to the house of Israel, and should say, I am your sign; like as I have done, so shall it be done unto you (12:3-7, 11).

[6] In order that he might represent the state of the church, the prophet Hosea was commanded

To take to himself a harlot for a wife; and he took her, and she bare him three sons, one of whom he called "Jezreel"; the second, "That hath not obtained mercy"; and the third, "Not my people" (Hosea 1:2-9).

And again he was commanded

To go and love a woman beloved of her companion and an adulteress, whom he also bought for fifteen pieces of silver (3:1, 2).

[7] In order that he might represent the state of the church, the prophet Ezekiel was commanded

To take a tile, and engrave upon it Jerusalem, and to lay siege to it, and build a rampart and a mount against it, and to put an iron pan between himself and the city, and to lie on his left side three hundred and ninety days, and afterwards, on his right side, forty days. Also to take wheat, barley, lentils, millet, and spelt, and make bread thereof, which he should then eat by measure. And also that he should make for himself a barley cake with the dung of man; and because he prayed that it might not be so, he was commanded to make it with cow's dung (Ezek 4:1-15).

The prophets represented other things besides; as, for instance, Zedekiah, by

The horns of iron that he made for himself (1 Kgs 22:11).

And another prophet, by being

Smitten and wounded, and by putting ashes upon his eyes (1 Kgs 20:35-38).

[8] In general, the prophets represented the Word in its outermost sense, which is the sense of the letter, by a garment of hair (Zech 13:4); and therefore Elijah

Was clad in such a coat, and was girt about his loins with a leathern girdle (2 Kgs 1:8).

and in like manner John the Baptist,

Who had his raiment of camel's hair, and a leathern girdle about his loins, and ate locust and wild honey (Mt 3:4).

From these things it is clear that the prophets represented the state of the church, and also the Word; for he who represents the one represents the other, because the church is from the Word, and is according to the reception of it in life and faith. Therefore prophets, wherever mentioned in both Testaments, signify the doctrine of the church from the Word; and by the Lord, as the Grand Prophet, is signified the church itself, and the Word itself.

16. The state of the church from the Word thus represented in the Prophets, is what is meant by bearing the iniquities and sins of the people. That such is the case is evident from the things said of Isaiah the prophet:

That he went naked and barefoot three years, for a sign and a wonder (Isa 20:3).

Of the prophet Ezekiel:

That he brought forth vessels of wandering, and covered his face so that he should not see the earth, and that so he was for a portent to the house of Israel, and also said, I am your portent (Ezek 12:6, 11).

[2] That this was for them to bear iniquities, is plainly evident in Ezekiel, where that prophet is commanded to lie three hundred and ninety, and forty, days, upon his left side and upon his right, against Jerusalem, and to eat a barley cake made with cow's dung. As we read:

Lie thou upon thy left side, and lay the iniquity of the house of Israel upon it, according to the number of the days that thou shalt lie upon it, thou shalt bear their iniquity. For I have laid upon thee the years of their iniquity, according to the number of the days, three hundred and ninety days, that thou bear the iniquity of the house of Israel. And when thou hast accomplished them, thou shalt lie upon thy right side, so that thou bear the iniquity of the house of Judah forty days (4:4-6).

[3] By his having thus borne the iniquities of the house of Israel and of the house of Judah, the prophet did not take them away, and thus expiate them, but only represented and showed them. This is evident from what follows:

Thus saith Jehovah, The sons of Israel shall eat their unclean bread among the nations whither I will drive them. Behold, I will break the staff of bread in Jerusalem, that they may lack bread and water, and be desolate a man and his brother, and consume away for their iniquity (verses 13, 16, 17).

[4] So when the same prophet showed himself, and said,

Behold, I am your portent, it is added, as I have done, so shall it be done unto them (12:6, 11).

The meaning is therefore the same where it is said of the Lord:

> He hath borne our diseases, and carried our sorrows: Jehovah hath made to light on Him the iniquities of us all; by His knowledge hath He justified many, in that He hath borne their iniquities (Isa 53:4, 6, 11);

where, in this whole chapter, the Lord's passion is treated of.

[5] That the Lord Himself, as the Grand Prophet, represented the state of the church in respect to the Word, is evident from all the details of His passion; as that He was betrayed by Judas; that He was taken and condemned by the chief priests and elders; that they buffeted Him; that they smote Him on the head with a reed; that they put on Him a crown of thorns; that they divided His garments, and cast lots for His under-vesture; that they crucified Him; that they gave Him vinegar to drink; that they pierced His side; that He was buried; and that He rose again the third day.

[6] That He was betrayed by Judas, signified that He was betrayed by the Jewish nation, among whom at that time was the Word, for Judas represented that nation. That He was taken and condemned by the chief priests and elders, signified that He was so treated by the whole Jewish Church. That they scourged Him, spat in His face, buffeted Him, and smote Him on the head with a reed, signified that they had done the like to the Word in respect to its divine truths, all of which treat of the Lord. That they put on Him a crown of thorns, signified that they had falsified and adulterated those truths. That they divided His garments, and cast lots for His under-vesture, signified that they had dispersed all the truths of the Word, but not its spiritual sense, which His under-vesture signified. That they crucified Him, signified that they had destroyed and profaned the whole Word. That they offered Him vinegar

to drink, signified that everything had become falsified and false; and therefore He did not drink it, and then said, It is finished. That they pierced His side, signified that they had completely extinguished all the truth of the Word, and all its good. That He was buried, signified the rejection of the residue of the maternal human. That He rose again the third day, signified His glorification.

[7] Similar things are signified by these things as foretold in the Prophets and in the Psalms of David. It was for the same reason that, after He had been scourged and brought out wearing the crown of thorns and the purple robe put on Him by the soldiers, He said, Behold the Man! (John 19:1, 5). This He said because by "man (*hominem*)" is signified the church; for by "Son of man" is signified the truth of the church, thus the Word. It is evident then from these things, that to bear iniquities means to represent and effiy in one's self the sins against the divine truths of the Word. That the Lord endured and suffered such things as the Son of man, and not as the Son of God, will be seen in what follows; for "the Son of man" signifies the Lord as the Word.

17. Something shall now be said of what is meant by taking away sins. To take away sins means the same as to redeem man, and to save him; for the Lord came into the world to render salvation possible to man. Without His advent no mortal could have been reformed and regenerated, and so saved. But this became possible after the Lord had deprived the devil (that is, hell) of all his power; and had glorified His Human, that is, had united it to the Divine of His Father. If these things had not been done, no man would have been capable of permanently receiving any divine truth, still less any divine good; for the "devil," whose power was previously the stronger, would have plucked it out of his heart.

[2] From what has been said it is evident that the Lord

did not take away sins by the passion of the cross; but that He takes them away, that is, removes them, in those who believe in Him by living according to His commandments; as He also teaches in Matthew:

Think not that I am come to relax the law and the prophets. Whosoever shall relax the least of these commandments, and shall teach men so, shall be called the least in the kingdom of the heavens; but whosoever shall do and teach them shall be called great in the kingdom of the heavens (5:17, 19).

[3] Who cannot see from reason alone, provided he is in some enlightenment, that sins cannot be taken away from a man except by actual repentance, which consists in his seeing his sins, imploring the Lord's help, and desisting from them? To see, believe, and teach otherwise, is not from the Word, nor from sound reason, but from greed and a depraved will, which are peculiar to man, and from this comes the debasement of his intelligence.

V

18. It is believed in the church that the Lord was sent by the Father to make an atonement for the human race, and that this was effected by His fulfilling the law, and by the passion of the cross; and that in this way He took away condemnation, and made satisfaction; and that without this expiation, satisfaction, and propitiation, the human race would have perished in eternal death, and this on account of justice which by some is called vengeful justice. It is true that without the Lord's advent all in the world would have perished; but how it is to be understood that the Lord fulfilled all the things of the law, and why He suffered the cross, may be seen above, in chapters II and III, which show that it was not on account of any vengeful justice, because this is not a divine attribute. Divine attributes are justice, love, mercy, and good; and God is justice itself, love itself, mercy itself, and good itself; and where these are, there is not anything of vengeance, and therefore no vengeful justice.

[2] As the fulfilling of the law, and the passion of the cross, have heretofore been understood by many to mean that by these two things the Lord made satisfaction for mankind, and took away the condemnation that had been foreseen or appointed, there has followed from the connection, and also from the idea that man is saved by mere faith that it is so, the dogma of the imputation of the Lord's merit by our receiving, in satisfaction, these two things that belong to His merit. But this dogma is refuted by what has been said about the fulfilling of the law by the Lord, and

37

about His passion of the cross. At the same time we can see that "imputation of merit" is a phrase destitute of significance, unless it means the remission of sins after repentance. For nothing of the Lord can be imputed to man; but salvation can be awarded him by the Lord after he has performed repentance, that is, after he has seen and acknowledged his sins, and has then desisted from them, by the Lord's help. Then salvation is awarded him: not that he is saved by his own merit or righteousness, but by the Lord, who alone has fought and conquered the hells, and who alone still fights for man, and conquers the hells for him.

[3] These things are the Lord's merit and righteousness, and they never can be imputed to man; for if they were, the Lord's merit and righteousness would be imputed to man as if they were his; and this is never done, nor can it be done. If imputation were possible, an impenitent and wicked man could impute the Lord's merit to himself, and so think himself justified; and yet this would be to defile what is holy with things profane, and to blaspheme the Lord's name; for it would be to keep the thought fixed on the Lord, and the will in hell, and yet the will is the whole man. There is faith from God, and faith from man; those have faith from God who perform repentance; and those have faith from man who do not perform repentance, and yet think of imputation; and faith from God is a living faith, while faith from man is a dead faith.

[4] The Lord Himself, and His disciples, preached repentance and the remission of sins, as is evident from the following passages:

Jesus began to preach, and to say, Repent, for the kingdom of the heavens is at hand (Mt 4:17).

John said, Bring forth fruits worthy of repentance; and now is the axe laid to the root of the trees; every tree that bringeth not forth good fruit is hewn down, and cast into the fire (Lu 3:8, 9).

Jesus said, Except ye repent, ye shall all perish (13:3, 5).

Jesus came preaching the Gospel of the kingdom of God, saying, The time is fulfilled, and the kingdom of God is at hand; repent ye, and believe the Gospel (Mk 1:14, 15).

Jesus sent out the disciples, who went forth and preached that men should repent (6:12).

Jesus said to the apostles that they must preach in His name repentance and the remission of sins among all nations, beginning at Jerusalem (Lu 24:47).

John preached the baptism of repentance for the remission of sins (Lu 3:3; Mk 1:4).

By "baptism" is meant spiritual washing, which is a washing from sins, and is called regeneration.

[5] Repentance and the remission of sins are thus described by the Lord in John:

He came unto His own, but His own received Him not; but to as many as received Him to them gave He power to become the sons of God, even to them that believe in His name; who were born, not of bloods, nor of the will of the flesh, nor of the will of man, but of God (1:11-13).

By "His own," are meant those who were then of the church, where was the Word; by "the sons of God," and "those who believe in His name," are meant those who believe in the Lord, and who believe the Word; by "bloods," are meant falsifications of the Word, and confirmations of falsity thereby; "the will of the flesh," is man's selfhood pertaining to the will, which in itself is evil; "the will of man," is man's selfhood pertaining to the understanding, which in itself is falsity; those "born of God," are those who have been regenerated by the Lord. From these things it is evident that those are saved who are in the good of love and in the truths of faith from the Lord, and not those who are in what is their own.

VI.

19. In the church, the Son of God is supposed to be the second person of the Godhead, distinct from the Person of the Father, whence comes the belief about the Son of God born from eternity. As this belief has been universally received, and as it relates to God, no one has had any opportunity or permission to think about it from any understanding; not even as to what it is to be born from eternity; for any one who thinks about it from the understanding must needs say to himself, "This transcends my understanding; but still I say it because others say it, and I believe it because others believe it." Be it known, then, that there is no Son from eternity; but that the Lord is from eternity. When it is known what the Lord is, and what the Son, it will be possible, and not before, to think with understanding of the Triune God.

[2] That the Lord's Human, conceived of Jehovah the Father and born of the virgin Mary, is the Son of God, is plainly evident from the following passages. In Luke:

The angel Gabriel was sent from God unto a city of Galilee named Nazareth, to a virgin betrothed to a man whose name was Joseph, of the house of David; and the virgin's name was Mary. And the angel entered in to her, and said, Hail, thou that art highly favored, the Lord is with thee, blessed art thou among women. And when she saw, she was troubled at his word, and cast in her mind what manner of salutation this might be. And the angel said unto her, Fear not, Mary; for thou hast found grace with God. And behold, thou shalt conceive and bear a Son, and shalt call His name Jesus. He shall be great, and shall be called THE SON OF THE MOST HIGH. But Mary said unto the angel, How shall this be, seeing I know not a man? And the angel answered and said unto her, The Holy Spirit

40

shall come upon thee, and the power of the Most High shall over-shadow thee, wherefore also that HOLY THING which shall be born of thee shall be called THE SON OF GOD (1:26-35).

It is here said, "Thou shalt conceive and bear a Son; He shall be great, and shall be called THE SON OF THE MOST HIGH;" and further, "that Holy Thing which shall be born of thee shall be called THE SON OF GOD;" from which it is evident that the Human conceived of God, and born of the virgin Mary, is what is called "the Son of God."

[3] In Isaiah:

The Lord Himself shall give you a sign: Behold, a virgin shall conceive and bear a Son, and shall call His name GOD-WITH-US (7:14).

That the Son born of the virgin, and conceived of God, is He who is called "God-with-us," thus is He who is the Son of God, is evident. That this is the case is confirmed also by Mt 1:22, 23.

[4] In Isaiah:

Unto us a Child is born, unto us a Son is given; and the govern-ment shall be upon His shoulder; and His name shall be called Wonderful, Counselor, God, Hero, FATHER OF ETERNITY, Prince of peace (9:6).

The burden is the same here; for it is said, "Unto us a Child is born, unto us a Son is given," who is not a Son from eternity, but a Son born in the world, as is also evident from the words of the prophet in the next verse, which are similar to those of the angel Gabriel to Mary in Luke 1:32, 33.

[5] In the Psalms: of David

I will make an announcement concerning a statute, Jehovah hath said, Thou art My Son; this day have I begotten Thee. Kiss the Son, lest He be angry, and ye perish in the way (2:7, 12).

A Son from eternity is not meant here either but a Son born in the world; for it is a prophecy concerning the Lord who was to come; and therefore it is called "a statute concerning which Jehovah has made an announcement" to David. "This day," is not from eternity, but is in time.
[6] In the Psalms again:

I will set His hand in the sea. He shall call Me, Thou art My Father. I will make Him My First-born (89:25-27).

This whole Psalm treats of the Lord who was to come, and therefore He is meant by Him who "shall call Jehovah His Father," and who shall be the "First-born," thus who is the Son of God. [7] And so in other places, where He is called

A rod out of the stem of Jesse (Isa 11:1);
An Offshoot of David (Je 23:5);
The seed of the woman (Ge 3:15);
The Only-begotten (Jn 1:18);
A Priest to eternity, and the Lord (Ps 110:4, 5).

[8] In the Jewish Church there was understood by the Son of God the Messiah whom they had expected, and of whom they knew that He was to be born at Bethlehem. That they understood the Messiah by "the Son of God" is evident from the following passages. In John:

Peter said, We believe and know that Thou art THE CHRIST, THE SON OF THE LIVING GOD (6:69).

In the same Evangelist:

Thou art THE CHRIST THE SON OF GOD, who should come into the world (11:27).

In Matthew:

The chief priest asked Jesus whether He was THE CHRIST THE SON OF GOD. Jesus said, I am (26:63, 64; Mk 14:62).

In John:

These things are written, that ye might believe that Jesus is THE CHRIST THE SON OF GOD (20:31; also Mk 1:1).

"Christ" is a Greek word, and means "the Anointed," as also does "Messiah" in the Hebrew language; and therefore John says:

We have found the Messiah, which is, being interpreted, THE CHRIST (Jn 1:41).

And in another place:

The woman said, I know that MESSIAS cometh, who is called CHRIST (4:25).

[9] It has been shown in the first chapter that the Law and the Prophets, that is, the whole Word of the Old Testament, is concerning the Lord, and therefore by the Son of God who was to come, nothing else can be meant than the Human which the Lord assumed in the world. From this it follows that the Human was what was meant, when Jesus, at His baptism, was called by Jehovah, in a voice from heaven, His Son:

This is MY BELOVED SON, in whom I am well pleased (Mt 3:17; Mk 1:11; Lu 3:22).

It was His Human that was baptized. And when He was transfigured:

This is MY BELOVED SON, in whom I am well pleased, hear ye Him (Mt 17:5; Mk 9:7; Lu 9:35).

And in other places also, as Mt 8:29; 14:33; Mk 3:11; 15:39; Jn 1:34, 49; 3:18; 5:25; 10:36; 11:4.

20. As "the Son of God" means the Lord as to the Human which He assumed in the world, which is the Divine Human, it is evident what is meant by the Lord's so frequently saying that He was sent by the Father into the world, and that He came forth from the Father. His being sent by the Father into the world means that He was conceived from Jehovah the Father. That nothing else is meant by being sent, and sent by the Father, is evident from all the pas-

sages where it is said that He did the will of the Father
and His works, which were that He conquered the hells,
glorified His Human, taught the Word, and set up* a new
church, which could not have been done except by means
of a Human conceived from Jehovah and born of a virgin,
that is, unless God had been made Man. Examine the passages where "sent" occurs, and you will see; as, for instance,
Mt 10:40; 15:24; Mk 9:37; Lu 4:43; 9:48; 10:16; Jn 3:17,
34; 4:34; 5:23, 24, 36-38; 6:29, 39, 40, 44, 57; 7:16, 18, 28,
29; 8:16, 18, 29, 42; 9:4; 11:42; 12:44, 45, 49; 13:20; 14:24;
15:21; 16:5; 17:3, 8, 21, 23, 25; 20:21; and also the passages
where the Lord calls Jehovah "Father."

21. At the present day many think of the Lord no otherwise than as of a common man like themselves, because
they think solely of His Human, and not at the same time
of His Divine, when yet His Divine and His Human cannot
be separated. For the Lord is God and Man, and God and
Man in the Lord are not two, but one Person, yes, altogether one, just as soul and body are one man, according to
the doctrine received in the whole Christian world which
was formulated by Councils, and is called the doctrine of
the Athanasian Creed. Therefore, lest any one should in
future separate in his thought the Divine and the Human
in the Lord, I pray him to read the passages from Luke
quoted above, and also the following in Matthew:

The birth of Jesus Christ was on this wise. When His Mother
Mary had been betrothed to Joseph, before they came together, she
was found with child of the Holy Spirit. And Joseph her betrothed,
being a just man, and not willing to make her a public example,
was minded to put her away privily. But while he thought on these
things, behold, an angel of the Lord appeared unto him in a dream,
saying, Joseph, thou son of David, fear not to take unto thee Mary
thy betrothed, for that which is begotten in her is of the Holy
Spirit. And she shall bring forth a son, and thou shalt call His

---

* Latin *instaurare*, to set up, not originally, but in restoration and repair.
[Tr.]

name Jesus; for He shall save His people from their sins. And Joseph, being awakened from sleep, did as the angel of the Lord commanded him, and took unto him his betrothed, but knew her not till she had brought forth her first-born son; and he called His name Jesus (1:18-25).

From these words, and from those written in Luke concerning the Lord's nativity, and from others adduced above, it is evident that the "Son of God" is Jesus conceived of Jehovah the Father, and born of the virgin Mary, of whom all the Prophets and the Law prophesied until John.

22. He who knows *what* in the Lord is called "the Son of God," and what in Him is called "the Son of man," is able to see many of the secret things of the Word; for at one time the Lord calls Himself "the Son," at another "the Son of God," and at another "the Son of man," everywhere according to the subject that is being treated of. When His divinity, His oneness with the Father, His divine power, faith in Him, life from Him, are being treated of, He calls Himself "the Son," and "the Son of God." As, for instance, in John 5:17-26, and elsewhere. But where His passion, judgment, His advent, and, in general, redemption, salvation, reformation, and regeneration, are treated of, He calls Himself "the Son of Man;" the reason being that He is then meant as to the Word. In the Word of the Old Testament, the Lord is designated by various names, being there named Jehovah, Jah, Lord, God, the Lord Jehovih, Jehovah Zebaoth, the God of Israel, the Holy One of Israel, the Mighty One of Jacob, Shaddai, the Rock, and also Creator, Former, Saviour, Redeemer, everywhere according to the subject that is being treated of. The same is true in the Word of the New Testament, where He is named Jesus, Christ, the Lord, God, the Son of God, the Son of man, the Prophet, the Lamb, with other names, also everywhere according to the subject there treated of.

23. Having stated on what grounds the Lord is called

"the Son of God," we will now state those on which He is called "the Son of man." The Lord is called "the Son of man" where the subject treated of is His passion, judgment, His advent, and, in general, redemption, salvation, reformation, and regeneration. The reason is that "the Son of man" is the Lord as the Word; and as the Word He suffered, judges, came into the world, redeems, saves, reforms, and regenerates. That such is the case is evident from what now follows.

24. *That the Lord is called "the Son of man" when His passion is treated of,* is evident from these passages:

Jesus said to His disciples, Behold, we go up to Jerusalem, and the Son of man shall be delivered unto the chief priests and scribes, and they shall condemn Him to death, and shall deliver Him to the nations, and they shall scourge Him, and spit on Him, and shall kill Him; but on the third day He shall rise again (Mk 10:33, 34). (And so in other places where He foretells His passion, as in (Mt 20:18, 19; Mk 8:31; Lu 9:22.)

Jesus said to His disciples, Behold, the hour is at hand, and the Son of man is betrayed into the hands of sinners (Mt 26:45).

The angel said to the women that came to the sepulchre, Remember how He spake unto you, that the Son of man must be delivered into the hands of sinful men, and be crucified, and the third day rise again (Lu 24:6, 7).

The reason the Lord then called Himself "the Son of man," is that He suffered Himself to be treated in the same way as they had treated the Word, as has been shown above very fully.

25. *That the Lord is called "the Son of man" when the judgment is treated of,* is evident from these passages:

When the Son of man shall come in His glory, then shall He sit upon the throne of His glory, and He shall set the sheep on His right hand, and the goats on the left (Mt 25:31, 33).

When the Son of man shall sit on the throne of His glory, He shall judge the twelve tribes of Israel (Mt 19:28).

The Son of man shall come in the glory of His Father, and shall render to every one according to his deeds (16:27).

Watch ye at every season, that ye may be accounted worthy to stand before the Son of man (Lu 21:36).

In such an hour as ye think not, the Son of man cometh (Mt 24:44; Lu 12:40).

The Father judgeth no one, but hath given all judgment to the Son, because He is the Son of man (Jn 5:22, 27).

The reason why the Lord calls Himself "the Son of man" when judgment is treated of, is that all judgment is effected according to the divine truth which is in the Word. That this judges every one, is said by the Lord Himself in John:

If any one hear My words, and believe not, I judge him not, for I came not to judge the world. The Word that I have spoken, the same shall judge him in the last day (12:47, 48).

The Son of man has not come to judge the world, but that through Him it might be saved; he that believeth in Him is not judged; but he that believeth not is judged already, because he hath not believed in the name of the Only-begotten Son of God (3:17, 18).

(That the Lord judges no one to hell, and casts no one into hell, but that an evil spirit casts himself in, may be seen in the work on *Heaven and Hell,* nn. 545-550, 574.) By "the name" of Jehovah, of the Lord, of the Son of God, is meant the divine truth, and therefore also the Word, which is from Him, and about Him, and therefore is Himself.

26. *That the Lord is called "the Son of man" when His advent is treated of,* is evident from these passages:

The disciples said to Jesus, What shall be the sign of Thy coming, and of the consummation of the age? [And then the Lord foretold the successive states of the church down to its end; and of its end He said], Then shall appear the sign of the Son of man, and they shall see the Son of man coming in the clouds of heaven with power and glory (Mt 24:3, 30; Mk 13:26; Lu 21:27).

"The consummation of the age," means the last time of the church; His "coming in the clouds of heaven with glory," means the opening of the Word, and the making manifest that the Word has been written about Him alone. In Daniel:

I saw and behold one like the Son of man came with clouds of the heavens (7:13).

In the Apocalypse:

Behold, He cometh with clouds, and every eye shall see Him (1:7);

which is also said of the Son of man, as is evident from verse 13. In another place:

I saw and behold a white cloud, and upon the cloud one sat like unto the Son of man (14:14).

[2] By "the Son of God" the Lord meant one thing in Himself, and by "the Son of man" another. This is evident from His reply to the chief priest:

The high priest said unto Jesus, I adjure Thee by the living God that Thou tell us whether Thou be the Christ, the Son of God. Jesus said unto him, Thou hast said: nevertheless, I say unto you, Hereafter shall ye see the Son of man sitting at the right hand of power, and coming in the clouds of heaven (Mt 26:63, 64).

Here He first confessed that He was the Son of God, and afterwards said that they should see the Son of man sitting at the right hand of power, and coming in the clouds of heaven, by which is meant that after the passion of the cross He would possess the divine power of opening the Word and setting up the church anew, which could not be effected before, because He had not then conquered hell and glorified His Human. (What is signified by sitting upon the clouds of heaven, and coming in glory, has been set forth in the work on *Heaven and Hell*, n. 1.)

27. *The Lord is called "the Son of man" when Redemption, Salvation, Reformation, and Regeneration are treated of.* This is shown in these passages:

The Son of man came to give His life a redemption for many (Mt 20:28; Mk 10:45).

The Son of man is come to save, and not to destroy (Mt 18:11; Lu 9:56).

The Son of man is come to seek and save that which was lost (Lu 19:10).

The Son of man is come that the world through Him may be saved (Jn 3:17).

He that soweth the good seed is the Son of man (Mt 13:37).

Redemption and salvation are here treated of, and as the Lord effects these by means of the Word, He here calls Himself "the Son of man." The Lord says,

That the Son of man has power to forgive sins (Mk 2:10; Lu 5:24) (that is, to save). And also,

That He is the Lord of the Sabbath, because He is the Son of man (Mt 12:8; Mk 2:28; Lu 6:5) (*i.e.* because He is the Word, which He is Himself then teaching).

He says, further, in John:

Labor not for the meat which perisheth, but for that meat which endureth unto everlasting life, which the Son of man shall give unto you (6:27).

By "meat" is meant all truth and good of doctrine from the Word, thus from the Lord; and this is also meant there by manna, and by the bread which came down from heaven; and also by the following in the same chapter:

Except ye shall eat the flesh of the Son of man, and drink His blood, ye have no life in you (verse 53).

"Flesh," or "bread," is the good of love from the Word; "blood," or "wine," is the good of faith from the Word, both from the Lord.

[2] The like is signified by "the Son of man" in other passages where He is mentioned, as in the following:

The foxes have holes, and the birds nests, but the Son of man hath not where to lay His head (Mt 8:20; Lu 9:58).

By this is meant that the Word would have no place among the Jews, as also the Lord said in John 8:37; and also that they had it not abiding in them, because they had not acknowledged Him (John 5:38). In the Apocalypse also "the Son of man" means the Lord in respect to the Word:

In the midst of the seven lampstands I saw one like unto the Son of man, clothed with a garment down to the foot, and girt about the paps with a golden girdle (1:13, etc.).

Here, in various ways, the Lord is represented as the Word, and He is therefore called "the Son of man." In the Psalms:

Let Thy hand be upon the man of Thy right hand, upon the Son of man whom Thou hast made strong for Thyself: so will not we go back from Thee; quicken us (80:17, 18).

"The man of Thy right hand," also means the Lord in respect to the Word; and so does "the Son of man." He is called "the man of the right hand," because the Lord has power from the divine truth, which also the Word is; and He had divine power when He had fulfilled the whole Word: and therefore He had said

That they should see the Son of man sitting at the right hand of the Father, with power (Mk 14:62).

28. *"The Son of man" means the Lord as to the Word, and this was the reason why the prophets also were called sons of man.* The reason why the prophets were called sons of man, was that they represented the Lord as to the Word, and consequently signified the doctrine of the church from the Word. In heaven nothing else is understood by "prophets" as mentioned in the Word; for the spiritual meaning of "prophet," as well as of "son of man," is *the doctrine of the church from the Word;* and, when predicated of the Lord, "prophet" means *The Word* itself.

That the prophet Daniel is called "son of man" may be seen in Daniel 8:17.

The prophet Ezekiel is also called "son of man" as in Ezek 2:1, 3, 6, 8; 3:1, 3, 4, 10, 17, 25; 4:1, 16; 5:1; 6:2; 7:2; 8:5, 6, 8, 12, 15; 11:2, 4, 15; 12:2, 3, 9, 18, 22, 27; 13:2, 17; 14:3, 13; 15:2; 16:2; 17:2; 20:3, 4, 27, 46; 21:2, 6, 9, 12, 14, 19, 28; 22:18, 24; 23:2, 36; 24:2, 16, 25; 25:2; 26:2; 27:2; 28:2, 12, 21; 29:2, 18; 30:2, 21; 31:2; 32:2, 18; 33:2, 7, 10, 12, 24, 30; 34:2; 35:2; 36:1, 17; 37:3, 9, 11, 16; 38:2, 14; 39:1, 17; 40:4; 43:7, 10, 18; 44:5. From what has been said it is now evident that the Lord as to the Divine Human is called "the Son of God," and in respect to the Word, "the Son of man."

VII.

29. The doctrine of the church that is received in the whole Christian world is:

Our Lord Jesus Christ, the Son of God, is God and Man, who, although He is God and Man, yet He is not two, but one Christ; one, by the taking of the manhood into God; one altogether, by unity of person; for as the reasonable soul and flesh is one man, so God and man is one Christ.

These words are taken from the *Athanasian Creed*, which has been received in the whole Christian world; and they are what is essential in it concerning the unition of the Divine and the Human in the Lord. What is said further in that *Creed* about the Lord will be explained in its own chapter. From these words it is quite evident that it is in accordance with *The Faith of the Christian Church* that the Divine and the Human in the Lord are not two, but one, as the soul and body are one man, and that the Divine in Him assumed the Human.

[2] From this it follows that the Divine cannot be separated from the Human, nor the Human from the Divine, for this would be like separating the soul from the body. That this is so must be admitted by every one who reads what is cited above (nn. 9, 21) from two of the evangelists (namely, Lu 1:26-35, and Mt 1:18-25) concerning the Lord's birth; from which it is manifest that Jesus was conceived of Jehovah God, and born of the virgin Mary; so that the Divine was in Him, and was His soul. As therefore His soul was the very Divine of the Father, it follows that His body, or Human, must also have become Divine; for where

the one is Divine, the other must be so too. In this way
and in no other are the Father and the Son one, and the
Father in the Son and the Son in the Father, and all things
of the Son the Father's, and all things of the Father the
Son's, as the Lord Himself teaches in His Word.

[3] But how this unition was effected, is shown in the
following order:

i. The Lord from eternity is Jehovah.

ii. The Lord from eternity, or Jehovah, assumed the Human to
save men.

iii. He made Divine the Human from the Divine in Himself.

iv. He made Divine the Human by means of temptations admitted
into Himself.

v. The full unition of the Divine and the Human in Him was
effected by means of the passion of the cross, which was the last
temptation.

vi. By successive steps He put off the human taken from the
mother, and put on a Human from the Divine within Him, which is
the Divine Human, and is the Son of God.

vii. That thus God became Man, as in firsts, so also in lasts.

30. i. *That the Lord from eternity is Jehovah,* is known
from the Word; for the Lord said to the Jews,

Verily I say unto you, before Abraham was, I am (Jn 8:58).

And He says in another place,

Glorify Thou Me, O Father, with the glory which I had with Thee
before the world was (Jn 17:5).

By this is meant the Lord from eternity, and not a Son
from eternity; for "the Son" is His Human that was conceived of Jehovah the Father, and born of the virgin Mary,
in time, as has been shown above.

[2] That the Lord from eternity is Jehovah Himself, is
evident from many passages in the Word, of which at
present there shall be cited only these few:

It shall be said in that day, THIS IS OUR GOD; we have waited for

Him that He may deliver us; THIS IS JEHOVAH, we have waited for Him; we will rejoice and be glad in His salvation (Isa 25:9).

It is evident from the following also that Jehovah God Himself was awaited:

The voice of one crying in the wilderness, Prepare ye the way of JEHOVAH, make plain in the solitude a path for OUR GOD. The glory of JEHOVAH shall be revealed, and all flesh shall see it together. Behold, THE LORD JEHOVIH shall come in strength (Isa 40:3. 5, 10; Mt 3:3; Mk 1:3; Lu 3:4).

Here, too, the Lord is called Jehovah, who should come.

[3] I Jehovah will give thee for a covenant to the people for a light of the nations. I Jehovah, this is My name; and My glory will I not give another (Isa 42:6-8).

"A covenant to the people," and "a light of the nations," is the Lord as to the Human; and as this is from Jehovah, and has become one with Jehovah, it is said, *I Jehovah, this is My name, and My glory will I not give to another,* that is, not to another than Himself. To give glory, means to glorify, or to unite to Himself.

[4] THE LORD whom ye seek, shall suddenly come to His temple (Mal 3:1).

By the "temple" is meant the temple of His body (Jn 2:19, 21).

THE DAY-SPRING FROM ON HIGH hath visited us (Lu 1:78).

"The day-spring from on high" also is Jehovah, or the Lord from eternity.

From what has been said it is evident that by the Lord from eternity is meant His Divine as Source which in the Word is "Jehovah." But from the passages to be quoted below, it will be evident that by Lord, and also by Jehovah, after His Human was glorified, is meant the Divine and the Human together, as a one; and that by the Son, alone, is meant the Divine Human.

31. ii. *The Lord from eternity, or Jehovah, assumed the Human to save men.* This has been confirmed from the Word in preceding chapters; and that man could not have been saved in any other way, will be shown elsewhere. That He assumed a Human, is evident from the passages in the Word where it is said that He went forth from the Father, descended from heaven, and was sent into the world; as from these:

I went out from the Father, and am come into the world (Jn 16:28).

I went out and am come from God; neither came I of Myself, but He sent Me (8:42).

The Father loveth you, because ye have believed that I came out from God (16:27).

No one hath ascended into heaven, but He that came down from heaven (3:13).

The bread of God is He that cometh down from heaven, and giveth life unto the world (6:33, 35, 41, 50, 51).

He that cometh from above is above all; He that cometh from heaven is above all (3:31).

I know the Father because I am from Him, and He hath sent Me (7:29).

(That to be "sent by the Father into the world" means to assume the Human, may be seen above, at n. 20.)

32. iii. *That the Lord made His Human Divine from the Divine in Himself,* is evident from many passages of the Word, of which those shall be here cited which confirm:

1. *This was done by successive steps:*

Jesus grew and waxed strong in spirit and in wisdom, and the grace of God was upon Him (Lu 2:40).

Jesus increased in wisdom, in age, and in grace with God and men (verse 52).

[2] 2. *The Divine operated through the Human, as the soul does through the body:*

The Son can do nothing from Himself, but what He seeth the Father doing (Jn 5:19).

I do nothing of Myself, but as My Father hath taught Me, I speak these things; and He that hath sent Me is with Me; He hath not left Me alone (8:28, 29; 5:30).

I have not spoken of Myself, but the Father who sent Me, He hath given Me a commandment, what I should say, and what I should speak (12:49).

The words that I speak unto you I speak not of Myself, but the Father that dwelleth in Me, He doeth the works (14:10).

I am not alone, because the Father is with Me (16:32).

[3] 3. *That the Divine and Human operated unanimously:*

What things soever the Father doeth, these also doeth the Son likewise (Jn. 5:19).

As the Father raiseth up the dead and quickeneth them, even so the Son quickeneth whom He will (verse 21).

As the Father hath life in Himself so hath He given to the Son to have life in Himself (verse 26).

Now they have known that all things which Thou hast given Me, are of Thee (17:7).

[4] 4. *That the Divine was united to the Human, and the Human to the Divine:*

If ye had known Me ye would have known My Father also; and ye have seen Him. He said to Philip, who desired to see the Father, Have I been so long time with you, and yet hast thou not known Me, Philip? He that hath seen Me, hath seen the Father. Believest thou not that I am in the Father, and the Father in Me? Believe Me, that I am in the Father, and the Father in Me (Jn 14:7-11).

If I do not the works of My Father, believe Me not; but if I do, believe the works; that ye may know and believe that the Father is in Me, and I in the Father (10:37, 38).

That they all may be one, as Thou, Father, art in Me, and I in Thee (17:21).

At that day ye shall know that I am in My Father (14:20).

No one is able to pluck the sheep out of My Father's hand; I and the Father are one (10:29, 30).

The Father loveth the Son, and hath given all things into His hand (3:35).

All things that the Father hath are Mine (16:15).

All Mine are Thine, and Thine are Mine (17:10).

Thou hast given the Son power over all flesh (verse 2).

All power is given unto Me in heaven and on earth (Mt 28:18).

[5] 5. *The Divine Human is to be looked to,* as is evident from these passages:

That all may honor the Son, even as they honor the Father (Jn 5:23).
If ye had known Me, ye would have known My Father also (8:19).
He that seeth Me, seeth Him that sent Me (12:45).
If ye had known Me, ye would have known My Father also; and from henceforth ye know Him, and have seen Him (14:7).
He that receiveth Me, receiveth Him that sent Me (13:20).

The reason for all this is that no one can see the Divine Itself which is called "the Father;" but the Divine Human can be seen; for the Lord says,

No one hath seen God at any time; the Only-begotten Son who is in the bosom of the Father, He hath set Him forth (Jn 1:18).
Not that any one hath seen the Father, save He that is with the Father; He hath seen the Father (6:46).
Ye have not heard the Father's voice at any time, nor seen His shape (5:37).

[6] 6. *As the Lord made His Human Divine from the Divine in Himself, and as the Human is to be approached, and is the Son of God, we must put our faith in the Lord, who is both Father and Son.* This is evident from these passages:

Jesus said, As many as received Him, to them gave He power to be the sons of God, even to them that believe in His name (Jn 1:12).
That whosoever believeth in Him should not perish, but have eternal life (3:15).
God so loved the world He gave His Only-begotten Son, that whosoever believeth in Him should have eternal life (verse 16).
He that believeth in the Son is not judged; but he that believeth not hath been judged already, because he hath not believed in the name of the Only-begotten Son of God (verse 18).

He that believeth in the Son hath eternal life; but he that believeth not the Son, shall not see life, but the wrath of God abideth on him (verse 36).

The bread of God is He that cometh down from heaven, and giveth life unto the world. He that cometh to Me shall never hunger, and he that believeth in Me shall never thirst (6:33, 35).

This is the will of Him that sent Me, that every one who seeth the Son, and believeth in Him, may have eternal life, and I will raise him up at the last day (verse 40).

They said to Jesus, What shall we do that we may work the works of God? Jesus answered, This is the work of God, that ye believe in Him whom He hath sent (verses 28, 29).

Verily I say unto you, He that believeth in Me hath eternal life (verse 47).

Jesus cried, saying, If any one thirst let him come unto Me and drink; he that believeth in Me, as the Scripture hath said, out of his belly shall flow rivers of living water (7:37, 38).

Unless ye believe that I am, ye shall die in your sins (8:24).

Jesus said, I am the resurrection and the life; he that believeth in Me, though he were dead, shall live; and whosoever liveth and believeth in Me shall never die (11:25, 26).

Jesus said, I am come a light into the world, that whosoever believeth in Me should not abide in darkness (12:46; 8:12).

While ye have the light, believe in the light, that ye may become sons of light (12:36).

Verily I say unto you, that the dead shall hear the voice of the Son of God, and they that hear shall live (5:25).

Abide in Me, and I in you. I am the vine, ye are the branches; he that abideth in Me, and I in him, the same bringeth forth much fruit; for without Me ye can do nothing (15:4, 5).

That they should abide in the Lord, and the Lord in them (14:20; 17:23).

I am the way, the truth, and the life; no one cometh unto the Father but by Me (14:6).

[7] In these and all other passages where "the Father" is mentioned, the Divine which was in the Lord from conception is meant. According to the Doctrine of Faith of the Christian world, this relationship was like that of the soul in the body with man. The Human itself from this Divine is the Son of God. Now as this Human was made Divine, therefore, in order to prevent man from approaching the

Father only, and thereby in thought, faith, and thence in worship, separating the Father from the Lord in whom the Father is, after the Lord had taught that He and the Father are one; that the Father is in Him, and He in the Father; that all should abide in Him; and that no one cometh to the Father but by Him, He taught also that we must believe in Him, and that man is saved by a faith directed to Him.

[8] Many in Christendom can form no idea of the fact that the Human in the Lord was made Divine, the chief reason of which is that they think of a man from his material body, and not from his spiritual body. And yet the truth is that all the angels (who are spiritual) are also men in a complete form; and, what is more, the whole Divine which proceeds from Jehovah God, from its firsts in heaven, down to its lasts in this world, has a tendency to the human form.*

33. iv. *The Lord made His Human Divine by means of temptations admitted into Himself, and by means of continual victories in them.* This has been treated of above, nn. 12-14; to which shall be added only this: Temptations are nothing but combats against evils and falsities; and as evils and falsities are from hell, temptations are combats against hell. Moreover with those who are undergoing spiritual temptations, there are present evil spirits from hell, who induce them. The individual is unaware that evil spirits induce the temptations; yet that they do so has been granted me to know from much experience.

[2] This is the reason why man is drawn out of hell and elevated into heaven when from the Lord he conquers in temptations; and this again is why man becomes spiritual, and therefore an angel, by means of temptations, or com-

---

* That angels are human forms, and that everything Divine has a tendency to the human form, may be seen in the work on *Heaven and Hell* (nn. 73-77, 453-460), and more fully in the works which follow this present one, which will be from Angelic Wisdom concerning the Lord.

bats against evils. The Lord, however, fought from His own power against all the hells, and completely mastered and subjugated them; and as He at the same time glorified His Human, He holds them so to eternity.

[3] For before the Lord's advent the hells had grown up to such a height that they were beginning to infest the very angels of heaven, and also every man that came into the world and went out of it. The cause of such a high growth of the hells was the complete devastation of the church, and the consequent prevalence of idolatries which caused the men of this world to be in mere falsities and evils; for the hells are from men. Hence it was that no man could have been saved unless the Lord had come into the world.

[4] Of these combats of the Lord the Psalms of David and the Prophets treat much, but the Evangelists little. It is these combats which are meant by the temptations that the Lord endured, the last of which was the passion of the cross. And it is on account of them that the Lord is called Saviour and Redeemer. This is so far known in the church as to lead them to say that the Lord conquered death or the "devil" (that is, hell), and that He rose again victorious; and also that without the Lord there is no salvation. That the Lord also glorified His Human, and thereby became the Saviour, Redeemer, Reformer, and Regenerator to eternity, will be seen in what follows.

[5] By means of these combats or temptations the Lord has become our Saviour, as is evident from the passages quoted above in nn. 12-14; and also from this one in Isaiah:

The day of vengeance is in Mine heart, and the year of My redeemed is come; I have trampled them in Mine anger, I have brought down their victory to the earth; so He became their Saviour (63:4, 6, 8). [This chapter treats of the Lord's combats.]

Also from this passage in the Psalms of David:

Lift up your heads, ye gates; and be ye lifted up, ye doors of the world, that the King of glory may come in. Who is this King of glory? Jehovah mighty and a hero, Jehovah a Hero of war (Ps 24:7, 8).

These words also treat of the Lord.

34. v. *The full unition of the Divine and the Human in the Lord was effected by means of the passion of the cross, which was the last temptation.* This has been established above in its proper chapter, where it has been shown that the Lord came into the world to subjugate the hells and glorify His Human, and that the passion of the cross was the last combat, by means of which He fully conquered the hells, and fully glorified His Human. Now as by the passion of the cross the Lord fully glorified His Human (that is, united it to His Divine, and thus made His Human also Divine), it follows that He is Jehovah and God as to both the Divine and the Human. And therefore in many passages in the Word He is called Jehovah, God, and the Holy One of Israel the Redeemer, Saviour, and Former.

[2] As in the following:

Mary said, My soul doth magnify THE LORD, and my spirit hath exulted in GOD MY SAVIOUR (Lu 1:46, 47).

The angel said to them: Behold, I bring you good tidings of great joy, which shall be to all people; there is born this day, in the city of David, a Saviour, who is Christ the Lord (2:10, 11).

They said, This is indeed the Christ, the Saviour of the world (Jn 4:42).

I Jehovah God will help thee, and thy Redeemer is the Holy One of Israel (Isa 41:14).

Thus saith Jehovah thy Creator, O Jacob; and thy Former, O Israel; for I have redeemed thee. I am Jehovah thy God, the Holy One of Israel, thy Saviour (43:1, 3).

Thus saith Jehovah your Redeemer, the Holy One of Israel: I am Jehovah your Holy One, the Creator of Israel, your King (verses 14, 15).

Thus saith Jehovah, the Holy One of Israel, and his Former (45:11).

Thus saith Jehovah thy Redeemer, the Holy One of Israel (48:17).

That all flesh may know that I Jehovah am thy Saviour and thy Redeemer, the Mighty One of Jacob (49:26).

Then shall the Redeemer come to Zion (59:20).

That thou mayest know that I Jehovah am thy Saviour and thy Redeemer, the Mighty One of Jacob (60:16).

Jehovah thy Former from the womb (49:5).

Jehovah my Rock, and my Redeemer (Ps 19:14).

They remembered that God was their Rock, and the High God their Redeemer (78:35).

Thus saith Jehovah thy Redeemer, and thy Former from the womb (Isa 44:24).

As for our Redeemer, Jehovah of Hosts is His name, the Holy One of Israel (47:4).

With mercy of eternity will I have mercy on thee, saith Jehovah thy Redeemer (54:8).

Their Redeemer is strong, Jehovah of Hosts is His name (Je 50:34).

Let Israel hope in Jehovah, for with Jehovah there is mercy, and with Him is plenteous redemption; and He shall redeem Israel from all his iniquities (Ps 130:7, 8).

Jehovah is my rock and my fortress; the horn of my salvation, my Saviour (2 Sa 22:2, 3).

Thus saith Jehovah, the Redeemer of Israel, His Holy One, Kings shall see and stand, because of Jehovah who is faithful, the Holy One of Israel, who hath chosen thee (Isa 49:7).

Surely God is in thee, and there is none else, there is no God. Verily Thou art a God that hidest Thyself, O God of Israel, the Saviour (45:14, 15).

Thus saith Jehovah, the King of Israel, and his Redeemer Jehovah of hosts, Besides Me there is no God (44:6).

I am Jehovah, and besides Me there is no Saviour (43:11).

Am not I Jehovah? and there is no God else besides Me; and a Saviour, there is none besides Me (45:21).

I am Jehovah thy God, and thou shalt know no God but Me, and besides Me there is no Saviour (Hosea 13:4).

Am not I Jehovah, and there is no other God besides Me; a just God and a Saviour, there is none besides Me: look unto Me and be ye saved, all the ends of the earth; for I am God, and there is none else (Isa 45:21, 22).

Jehovah of hosts is His name, and thy Redeemer the Holy One of Israel, the God of the whole earth shall He be called (54:5).

[3] From these passages it may be seen that the Lord's Divine called "the Father" (and here "Jehovah" and "God"), and the Divine Human called "the Son" (and here "the Redeemer" and "Saviour," and also "the Former," which means the Reformer and Regenerator), are not two, but one. For not only is mention made of Jehovah, God, and the Holy One of Israel the Redeemer and Saviour, but the expression "Jehovah the Redeemer and Saviour" is used, and even "I am Jehovah the Saviour, and there is none besides Me." From this it is very evident that the Divine and the Human in the Lord are one Person; and that the Human also is Divine. For the Redeemer and Saviour of the world is no other than the Lord in respect to the Divine Human, and this is what is called the Son. Moreover redemption and salvation are an attribute proper to His Human, which is called merit and righteousness; for it was His Human that endured temptations and the passion of the cross; and therefore it was by means of His Human that He effected redemption and salvation.

[4] As, therefore, after the unition of the Human with the Divine in Him, which was like that of the soul and body in man, they were no longer two but one Person (according to the Doctrine of the Christian world), it follows that the Lord is Jehovah and God as to both the Divine and the Human. And this therefore is why it is said on the one hand that Jehovah and the Holy One of Israel are the Redeemer and Saviour, and on the other that the Redeemer and Saviour are Jehovah, as may be seen from the passages that have been quoted. Thus it is said,

Christ the Saviour (Lu 2:11; Jn 4:42).

God and the God of Israel the Saviour and Redeemer (Lu 1:47; Isa 45:15; 54:5; Ps 78:35).

Jehovah the Holy One of Israel the Saviour and Redeemer (Isa 41:14; 43:3, 11, 14, 15; 48:17; 49:7; 54:5).

Jehovah the Saviour, Redeemer, and Former (44:6; 47:4; 49:26; 54:8; 63:16; 50:34; Ps 19:14; 130:7, 8; Sa 22:2,3).

Jehovah God the Redeemer and Saviour, and besides Me there is none else (Isa 43:11; 44:6; 45:14, 15, 21, 22; Hosea 13:4).

35. vi. *By successive steps the Lord put off the human taken from the mother, and put on a Human from the Divine within Him, which is the Divine Human, and is the Son of God.* It is known that in the Lord were the Divine and the Human, the Divine from Jehovah the Father, and the human from the virgin Mary. Hence He was God and Man, having a Divine essence and a human nature; a Divine essence from the Father, and a human nature from the mother; and therefore was equal to the Father as to the Divine, and less than the Father as to the human. It is also known that this human nature from the mother was not transmuted into the Divine essence, nor commingled with it, for this is taught in the *Doctrine of Faith* which is called the *Athanasian Creed.* For a human nature cannot be transmuted into the Divine essence, nor can it be commingled therewith.

[2] Our doctrine in accordance with the same creed is that the Divine assumed the Human, that is, united itself to it, as a soul to its body, so that they were not two, but one Person. From this it follows that the Lord put off the human from the mother, which in itself was like that of another man, and thus material, and put on the Human from the Father, which in itself was like His Divine, and thus substantial, so that the Human too became Divine. This is why in the Word of the Prophets the Lord even as to the Human is called Jehovah, and God; and in the Word of the Evangelists, Lord, God, Messiah or the Christ, and the Son of God in whom we must believe, and by whom we are to be saved.

[3] As from His birth the Lord had a human from the mother, and as He by successive steps put it off, it follows that while He was in the world He had two states, the one called the state of humiliation or emptying out and the

other the state of glorification or unition with the Divine called the Father. He was in the state of humiliation at the time and in the degree that He was in the human from the mother; and in that of glorification at the time and in the degree that He was in the Human from the Father. In the state of humiliation He prayed to the Father as to one who was other than Himself; but in the state of glorification He spoke with the Father as with Himself. In this latter state He said that the Father was in Him and He in the Father, and that the Father and He were one. But in the state of humiliation He underwent temptations, and suffered the cross, and prayed to the Father not to forsake Him. For the Divine could not be tempted, much less could it suffer the cross. From what has been said it is now evident that by means of temptations and continual victories in them, and by the passion of the cross which was the last of the temptations, the Lord completely conquered the hells, and fully glorified His Human, as has been shown above.

[4] The Lord put off the human taken from the mother, and put on a Human from the Divine in Himself called the Father, as is evident also from the fact that whenever He addressed His mother directly, He did not call her Mother, but Woman. Only three times in the Evangelists do we read that He thus addressed or spoke of her, twice calling her Woman, and once not recognizing her as His mother. Of the two occasions when He called her Woman we read in John:

The mother of Jesus said unto Him, They have no wine. Jesus saith unto her, Woman, what [belongs] to Me, and to Thee? Mine hour is not yet come (2:3, 4).

When from the cross, Jesus sees His mother, and the disciple standing by whom He loved, He saith to His mother, Woman, behold thy son; and then He saith to the disciple, Behold thy mother (19:26, 27).

And of the one occasion when He did not recognize her, in Luke:

It was told Jesus by certain who said, Thy mother and Thy brethren stand without, desiring to see Thee. Jesus answering said unto them, My mother and My brethren are these, who hear the Word of God, and do it (8:20, 21; Mt 12:46-49; Mk 3:31-35).

In other places Mary is called His "mother," but not from His own mouth.

[5] The same inference is confirmed by the fact that the Lord did not admit that He was the son of David. For we read in the Evangelists:

Jesus asked the Pharisees, saying, What think ye of the Christ? whose son is He? They say unto Him, The Son of David. He saith unto them, How then doth David in spirit call Him Lord, saying, The Lord said unto my Lord, Sit Thou on My right hand till I make Thine enemies Thy footstool? If then David calls Him Lord, how is He his son? And no one was able to answer Him a word (Mt 22:41-46; Mk 12:35-37; Lu 20:41-44; Ps 110:1).

From what has been said it is evident that in respect to the glorified Human the Lord was the son neither of Mary nor of David.

[6] The quality of His glorified Human He showed to Peter, James, and John when transfigured before them:

His face shone as the sun, and His raiment was like the light; and then a voice out of the cloud said, This is My beloved Son, in whom I am well pleased, hear ye Him (Mt 17:1-8; Mk 9:2-8; Lu 9:28-36).

The Lord was also seen by John as the sun shining in his strength (Apoc 1:16).

[7] That the Lord's Human was glorified, is evident from what is said about His glorification in the Evangelists:

The hour is come that the Son of Man should be glorified. Jesus said, Father, glorify Thy name: then came there a voice from heaven, saying, I both have glorified it and will glorify it again (Jn 12:23, 28).

As the Lord was glorified by successive steps, it is said "I both have glorified it, and will glorify it again." Again in the same Evangelist:

After Judas had gone out, Jesus said, Now is the Son of man glorified, and God is glorified in Him: God shall also glorify Him in Himself, and shall straightway glorify Him (13:31, 32).

Jesus said, Father, the hour is come; glorify Thy Son, that Thy Son may also glorify Thee (17:1, 5).

And in Luke:

Behooved it not the Christ to suffer this, and to enter into His glory? (24:26).

These things are said concerning His Human.

[8] The reason the Lord said "God is glorified in Him," and "God shall glorify Him in Himself," and also "Glorify Thy Son that Thy Son may also glorify Thee," is that the unition was reciprocal, being that of the Divine with the Human and of the Human with the Divine. On this account He said also, "I am in the Father, and the Father in Me" (John 14:10, 11); and "All Mine are Thine, and Thine are Mine" (John 17:10); so that the unition was plenary. It is the same with all unition—unless it is reciprocal, it is not full. Such therefore must also be the uniting of the Lord with man, and of man with the Lord, as He teaches:

In that day ye shall know that ye are in Me, and I in you (Jn 14:20).

Abide in Me, and I in you; he that abideth in Me, and I in him, the same bringeth forth much fruit (15:4, 5).

[9] As the Lord's Human was glorified, that is, made Divine, He rose again after death on the third day with His whole body, which does not take place with any man; for a man rises again solely as to the spirit, and not as to the body. In order that men may know, and no one doubt, that the Lord rose again with His whole body, He not only said so through the angels in the sepulchre, but also showed Himself to His disciples in His human body, saying to them when they believed that they saw a spirit:

See My hands and My feet, that it is I Myself; handle Me and see; for a spirit hath not flesh and bones as ye see Me have; and

when He had thus spoken, He showed them His hands and His feet
(Lu 24:39, 40; Jn 20:20).

And He said to Thomas, Reach hither thy finger, and behold My
hands; and reach hither thy hand, and thrust it into My side; and
be not faithless but believing; then said Thomas, My Lord and my
God (Jn 20:27, 28).

[10] In order to demonstrate still further that He was not
a spirit but a Man, the Lord said to His disciples,

Have ye here any meat? And they gave Him a piece of a broiled
fish, and of a honey-comb; and He took it and did eat before them
(Lu 24:41-43).

As His body was no longer material, but Divine substantial,
He came in to His disciples when the doors were shut
(Jn 20:19, 26); and after He had been seen He became
invisible (Lu 24:31). Being such, the Lord was then taken
up, and "sat at the right hand of God"; as we read:

It came to pass that while Jesus blessed His disciples, He was
parted from them, and carried up into heaven (Lu 24:51).

After He had spoken unto them, He was carried up into heaven,
and sat at the right hand of God (Mk 16:19).

To "sit at the right hand of God," signifies Divine
omnipotence.

[11] As the Lord ascended into heaven, and sat at the
right hand of God (by which is signified divine omnipotence) with the Divine and the Human united into a one,
it follows that His human substance or essence is just as is
His divine substance or essence. To think otherwise would
be like thinking that His Divine was taken up into heaven
and sat at the right hand of God, but not His Human together with it, which is contrary to Scripture, and also to
the Christian Doctrine, which is that in Christ God and
Man are like soul and body, and to separate these is contrary to sound reason. This unition of the Father with the
Son, or of the Divine with the Human, is meant also in the
following:

I came forth from the Father, and am come into the world; again I leave the world, and go to the Father (Jn 16:28).

I go away, and come to Him that sent Me (7:33; 16:5, 16; 17:11, 13; 20:17).

If then ye shall see the Son of man ascending where He was before (6:62).

No one hath ascended into heaven but He that came down from heaven (3:13).

Every man who is saved ascends into heaven, but not of himself. He ascends by the Lord's aid. The Lord alone ascended of Himself.

36. vii. *Thus God became Man, as in firsts so also in lasts.* That God is a Man, and that every angel and every spirit is a man from God, has been partially shown in the work on *Heaven and Hell,* and will be further shown in the works entitled *Angelic Wisdom.* From the beginning, however, God was a Man in firsts and not in lasts; but after He had assumed the Human in the world, He became a Man in lasts also. This follows from what has been already established—that the Lord united His Human to His Divine, and thus made His Human Divine. It is from this that the Lord is called the beginning and the end, the first and the last, the Alpha and the Omega:

I am the Alpha and the Omega, the beginning and the end, saith the Lord, who is, and who was, and who is to come, the Almighty (Apoc 1:8, 11).

[When John saw the Son of man in the midst of the seven lampstands,] he fell at His feet as dead; but He laid His right hand upon him, saying, I am the first and the last (verses 13, 17; 2:8; 21:6).

Behold, I come quickly, to give every one according to his work: I am the Alpha and the Omega, the beginning and the end, the first and the last (22:12, 13).

Thus saith Jehovah the King of Israel, and his Redeemer Jehovah of Hosts, I am the first and the last (Isa 44:6; 48:12).

VIII.

37. In chapter I, we undertook to show that all Holy Scripture treats of the Lord, and that the Lord is the Word. This shall now be further shown from passages of the Word in which the Lord is called "Jehovah," the "God of Israel and of Jacob," the "Holy One of Israel," the "Lord," and "God;" and also "King," "Jehovah's Anointed," and "David." I may first mention that I have been permitted to run through all the Prophets and the Psalms of David, and to examine each verse and see what it treats of, and I have seen that the only subjects treated of are: the church set up anew and to be set up anew by the Lord; the advent, combats, glorification, redemption, and salvation; of the Lord; heaven from Him; and, with these, their opposites. As all these are works of the Lord, it became evident that all Holy Scripture is about Him, and therefore that the Lord is the Word.

[2] However, this can be seen only by those who are in enlightenment from the Lord, and who also know the spiritual sense of the Word. All the angels of heaven are in this sense, and therefore when the Word is being read by a man, they so comprehend it. For spirits and angels are constantly with man, and as they are spiritual they understand spiritually all that a man understands naturally. That all Holy Scripture is about the Lord, may be obscurely seen, as though a glass darkly, from the passages of the Word already cited in chapter I (nn. 1-6), as also from those concerning the Lord now to be quoted, to show how frequently He is called the Lord [that is, Jehovah] and

God; and from which it is apparent that it is He who spoke through the prophets, by whom it is everywhere said, "Jehovah spake," "Thus saith Jehovah," "The saying of Jehovah."

[3] That the Lord existed before His advent into the world, is evident from the following:

[John the Baptist said concerning the Lord]: He it is who coming after me was before me, whose shoe's latchet I am not worthy to unloose. This is He of whom I said, After me cometh a man who was before me, for He was before me (Jn 1:27, 30).

They fell down before the throne (on which was the Lord) saying, We give Thee thanks, Lord God Almighty, who art, and who wast, and who art to come (Apoc 11:16, 17).

Thou Bethlehem Ephratah, though thou be little among the thousands of Judah, out of thee shall He go forth unto Me that shall be Ruler in Israel, whose goings forth have been from of old, from the days of eternity (Mic 5:2).

The same is evident from the Lord's words in the Evangelists: that He "was before Abraham," that He had glory with the Father "before the foundation of the world," that He "had gone forth from the Father," and that "the Word was from the beginning with God," that "God was the Word," and that this "was made flesh."

The Lord is called "Jehovah," the "God of Israel and of Jacob," the "Holy One of Israel," "God," and "Lord," and also "King," "Jehovah's Anointed," and "David," as is evident from what now follows.

38. *That the Lord is called "Jehovah,"* is evident from these passages:

Thus saith Jehovah thy Creator, O Jacob, and thy Former, O Israel, Fear not, for I have redeemed thee. I am Jehovah thy God, the Holy One of Israel, thy Saviour (Isa 43:1, 3).

I am Jehovah your Holy One, the Creator of Israel, your King (verse 15).

The Holy One of Israel, and his Former, O God of Israel, the Saviour (45:11, 15).

That all flesh may know that I Jehovah am thy Saviour and thy Redeemer, the Mighty One of Jacob (49:26).

That thou mayest know that I Jehovah am thy Saviour and thy Redeemer, the Mighty One of Jacob 60:16).

Jehovah thy Former from the womb (49:5).

Jehovah my Rock, and my Redeemer (Ps 19:14).

Thus saith Jehovah thy Maker and Former from the womb. Thus saith Jehovah the King of Israel, and his Redeemer, Jehovah of Hosts (Isa 44:2, 6).

As for our Redeemer, Jehovah of Hosts is His name, the Holy One of Israel (47:4).

With the mercy of eternity will I have mercy on thee, saith Jehovah thy Redeemer (54:8).

Their Redeemer is strong, Jehovah of Hosts is His name (Je 1:34).

Jehovah God, my Rock, my fortress, the horn of my salvation, my Saviour (2 Sa 22:2, 3).

Thus saith Jehovah your Redeemer, the Holy One of Israel (Isa 43:14; 48:17).

Thus saith Jehovah the Redeemer of Israel, his Holy One, Kings shall see (49:7).

I am Jehovah, and besides Me there is no Saviour (43:11).

Am not I Jehovah, and there is none besides Me, and there is no Saviour besides Me. Look unto Me and be ye saved all the ends of the earth (45:21, 22).

I am Jehovah thy God, and there is no Saviour besides Me (Hosea 13:4).

Thou hast redeemed me, O Jehovah God of truth (Ps 31:5).

Let Israel hope in Jehovah, for with Jehovah there is mercy, and with Him is plenteous redemption, and He shall redeem Israel from all his iniquities (130:7, 8).

Jehovah of Hosts is His Name, and thy Redeemer the Holy One of Israel, the God of the whole earth shall be called (Isa 54:5).

In these passages Jehovah is called the "Redeemer and Saviour;" and as the Lord alone is the Redeemer and Saviour, it is He who is meant by "Jehovah." That the Lord is Jehovah, that is, that Jehovah is the Lord, is evident also from the following:

There shall come forth a rod out of the stem of Jesse, and a shoot out of his roots shall bear fruit, and the Spirit of Jehovah shall rest upon Him (Isa 11:1, 2).

It shall be said in that day, Lo, this is our God; we have waited for Him, and He will save us; this is Jehovah, we have waited for Him; we will rejoice and be glad in His salvation (25:9).

The voice of him that crieth in the wilderness, Prepare ye the way of Jehovah, make plain in the solitude a pathway for our God. For the glory of Jehovah shall be revealed, and all flesh shall see it. Behold the Lord Jehovih shall come in strength, and His arm shall rule for Him (40:3, 5, 10).

I Jehovah will give thee for a covenant to the people, for a light of the nations. I am Jehovah, that is My name, and My glory will I not give to another (42:6, 8).

Behold the days come that I will raise unto David a righteous offshoot, who shall reign a King, and shall prosper, and shall execute judgment and justice in the earth; and this is His name whereby He shall be called, Jehovah our righteousness (Je 23:5, 6; 33:15, 16).

Thou Bethlehem Ephratah, out of thee shall He go forth unto Me that shall be a Ruler in Israel; He shall stand and feed [His flock] in the strength of Jehovah (Mic 5:2, 4).

Unto us a child is born, unto us a son is given, and the government shall be upon His shoulder, and His name shall be called God, Hero, the Father of eternity, upon the throne of David to establish and to found it in judgment and in justice, from henceforth and even to eternity (Isa 9:6, 7).

Jehovah shall go forth and fight against the nations; and His feet shall stand upon the Mount of Olives on the east of Jerusalem (Zech 14:3, 4).

Lift up your heads, O ye gates; and be ye lifted up, ye doors of the world, that the King of glory may come in. Who is this King of glory? Jehovah strong and a Hero, Jehovah a Hero of war (Ps 24:7-10).

In that day shall Jehovah of Hosts be for a crown of ornament, and for a diadem of beauty, unto the residue of His people (Isa 28:5).

I will send you Elijah the prophet, before the coming of the great day of Jehovah (Mal 4:5).

Not to mention other passages where mention is made of the great and near day of Jehovah; as (Ezek 30:3; Joel 2:11; Amos 5:18, 20; Zeph 1:14, 15, 18).

39. *The Lord is called "the God of Israel," and "the God of Jacob,"* as is evident from the following:

Moses took the blood and sprinkled it upon the people, and said, Behold the blood of the covenant which Jehovah hath made with you. And they saw the God of Israel, under whose feet was as it were a work of sapphire stone, and as it were the substance of heaven (Ex 24:8, 10).

The multitude wondered when they saw the dumb speaking, the lame walking, and the blind seeing; and they glorified the God of Israel (Mt 15:31).

Blessed be the Lord God of Israel, for He hath visited and wrought deliverance for His people Israel, when He raised up a horn of salvation for us in the house of David (Lu 1:68, 69).

I will give thee the treasures of darkness, and hidden riches of secret places, that thou mayest know that I Jehovah, who have called thee by thy name, am the God of Israel (Isa 45:3).

O house of Jacob, who swear in the name of Jehovah, and of the God of Israel; for they are called of the city of holiness, and stay themselves upon the God of Israel, Jehovah of Hosts is His name (48:1, 2).

Jacob shall see his children in the midst of him, they shall sanctify My name, and they shall sanctify the Holy One of Jacob, they shall fear the God of Israel (29:23).

In the end of the days many people shall go and say, Come ye and let us go up to the mountain of Jehovah, to the house of the God of Jacob, who shall teach us of His ways, that we may walk in His paths (2:2, 3; Mic 4:1, 2).

That all flesh may know that I Jehovah am thy Saviour and thy Redeemer, the Mighty One of Jacob (Isa 49:26).

I Jehovah am thy Saviour and thy Redeemer, the Mighty One of Jacob (60:16).

Thou art in pain, O earth, before the Lord, before the God of Jacob (Ps 114:7).

David sware to Jehovah, he vowed to the Mighty One of Jacob, Surely I will not come into the tent of my house, until I find out a place for Jehovah, a habitation for the Mighty One of Jacob; we have heard of Him at Ephratah (Bethlehem) (132:2, 3, 5, 6).

Blessed be the God of Israel; the whole earth shall be filled with His glory (72:18, 19).

Not to quote those passages in which the Lord is called the God of Israel the Redeemer and Saviour; as Lu 1:47; Isa 45:15; 54:5; Ps 78:35.

Besides many other passages, in which He is called the God of Israel only; as Isa 17:6; 21:10, 17; 24:15; 29:23; Je 7:3; 9:15; 11:3; 13:12; 16:9; 19:3, 15; 23:2; 24:5; 25:15, 27; 29:4, 8, 21, 25; 30:2; 31:23; 32:14, 15, 36; 33:4; 34:2, 13; 35:13, 17, 18, 19; 37:7; 38:17; 39:16; 42:9, 15, 18; 43:10; 44:2, 7, 11, 25; 48:1; 50:18;

51:33; Ezek 8:4; 9:3; 10:19, 20; 11:22; 43:2; 44:2; Zeph 2:9; Ps 41:13; 59:5; 68:8.

40. *The Lord is called "the Holy One of Israel,"* as is evident from these passages:

The angel said to Mary, That Holy Thing which shall be born of thee shall be called the Son of God (Lu 1:35).

I saw in the visions, and behold, a Watcher and a Holy One came down from heaven (Da 4:13, 23).

God came from Teman, and the Holy One from Mount Paran (Hab 3:3).

I am Jehovah your Holy One, the Creator of Israel, your King (Isa 43:15).

The Holy One of Israel, and his Former (45:11).

Thus saith Jehovah, the Redeemer of Israel, His Holy One (49:7).

I am Jehovah thy God, the Holy One of Israel thy Saviour (43:3).

As for our Redeemer, Jehovah of hosts is His name, the Holy One of Israel (47:4).

Thus saith Jehovah your Redeemer, the Holy One of Israel (43:14; 48:17).

Jehovah of Hosts is His name, and thy Redeemer the Holy One of Israel (54:5).

They tempted God, and the Holy One of Israel (Ps 78:41).

They have forsaken Jehovah, and have provoked the Holy One of Israel (Isa 1:4).

They have said, Cause the Holy One of Israel to cease from our faces, wherefore thus saith the Holy One of Israel (30:11, 12).

Who say, Let Him hasten His work that we may see, and let the counsel of the Holy One of Israel draw nigh and come (5:19).

In that day they shall stay upon Jehovah, the Holy One of Israel, in truth (10:20).

Cry out and shout, O daughter of Zion, for great is the Holy One of Israel in the midst of thee (12:6).

Saith Jehovah of the God of Israel, In that day shall a man look to his Maker, and his eyes shall have respect to the Holy One of Israel (17:6, 7).

The meek shall increase their joy in Jehovah, and the needy among men shall rejoice in the Holy One of Israel (29:19; 41:16).

Nations shall run unto thee because of Jehovah thy God, and because of the Holy One of Israel (55:5).

The isles shall confide in Me, to bring thy sons from far, unto the name of Jehovah of hosts, and to the Holy One of Israel (60:9).

The land is full of guilt against the Holy One of Israel (Je 51:5).

Babylon hath been proud against Jehovah, against the Holy One of Israel (1:29).

(Besides many other passages.)

By "the Holy One of Israel" is meant the Lord as to the Divine Human; for the angel Gabriel said to Mary, "That Holy Thing which shall be born of thee shall be called the Son of God" (Lu 1:35). That Jehovah and the Holy One of Israel, although distinctively mentioned, are one and the same, is evident from the passages here quoted, in which it is said that Jehovah is that Holy One of Israel.

41. *That the Lord is called "Lord" and "God,"* is evident from so many passages that if quoted they would fill pages. Let these few suffice:

When by the Lord's command Thomas had seen His hands and touched His side, he said, My Lord and my God (Jn 20:27, 28).

They remembered that God was their Rock, and the High God their Redeemer (Ps 78:35).

Jehovah of Hosts is His name, and thy Redeemer the Holy One of Israel, the God of the whole earth shall He be called (Isa 54:5).

[The same is evident from the fact that they adored Him, and fell upon their faces before Him: Mt 9:18; 14:33; 15:25; 28:9; Mk 1:40; 5:22; 7:25; 10:17; Lu 17:15, 16; Jn 98:38).]

So in the Psalms of David:

We heard of Him at Ephratah; we will enter into His dwelling places, and will bow ourselves at His footstool (Ps 132:6, 7).

And it is the same in heaven:

I was in the spirit, and behold a throne was set in heaven, and one sat on the throne like a jasper and sardine stone, and there was a rainbow round about the throne, in sight like unto an emerald. And the four and twenty elders fell down before Him that sat on the throne, and adored Him that liveth for ever and ever, and cast their crowns before the throne (Apoc 4:2, 3, 10).

I saw in the right hand of Him that sat upon the throne a book sealed within and on the back side, sealed with seven seals, and no one was able to open the book. Then one of the elders said, Behold the Lion of the tribe of Judah, the root of David, hath prevailed to open the book, and to loose the seven seals thereof; and I beheld in the midst of the throne a Lamb standing, and He came and took the book, and they fell down before the Lamb, and worshipped Him that liveth for ever and ever (5:1, 3, 5-8, 14).

42. *The reason why the Lord is called "King" and "the Anointed,"* is that He was the Messiah, or Christ; and "Messiah" or "Christ" means the king and the anointed. This is why, in the Word, the Lord is meant by "king," and also by "David," who was king over Judah and Israel. That the Lord is called "king" and "Jehovah's anointed," is evident from many passages in the Word:

The Lamb shall overcome them; for He is Lord of lords and King of kings (Apoc 17:14).
He that sat upon the white horse had on His vesture a name written, King of kings and Lord of lords (19:16).

It is from the Lord's being called a "king," that heaven and the church are called His "kingdom," and that His advent in the world is called "the Gospel of the kingdom." That heaven and the church are called His kingdom, may be seen in Mt 12:28; 16:28; Mk 1:14, 15; 9:1; 15:43; Lu 1:33; 4:43; 8:1, 10; 9:2, 11, 60; 10:11; 16:16; 19:11; 21:31; 22:18; 23:51. And in Daniel:

God shall set up a kingdom which shall never be destroyed; it shall break in pieces and consume all these kingdoms, and it shall stand forever (2:44).
I saw in the night visions, and behold one like the Son of man came with the clouds of the heavens. And there was given Him dominion, and glory, and a kingdom, that all peoples, nations, and languages should worship Him; His dominion is an everlasting dominion, and His kingdom that which shall not be destroyed (7:13, 14, 27).

That His advent is called "the Gospel of the kingdom," may be seen in Mt 4:23; 9:35; 24:14.

43. *That the Lord is called "David,"* is evident from these passages:

In that day they shall serve Jehovah their God, and David their king, whom I will raise up to them (Je 30:8, 8).

Afterwards the sons of Israel shall return, and shall seek Jehovah their God, and David their king, and shall come with fear to Jehovah, and to His goodness in the end of days (Hosea 3:5).

I will raise up one shepherd over them, who shall feed them; My servant David, he shall feed them, and he shall be their shepherd: and I Jehovah will be their God, and My servant David a prince in the midst of them (Ezek 34:23, 24).

That they may be My people, and that I may be their God; and David My servant shall be king over them, that they may all have one shepherd; then shall they dwell upon the land, they and their sons and their sons' sons, even to eternity; and David shall be their prince to eternity; and I will make a covenant of peace, and it shall be a covenant of eternity with them (37:23-26).

I will make a covenant of eternity with you, the sure mercies of David: behold, I have given him for a witness to the people, a prince and a lawgiver to the nations (Isa 55:3, 4).

In that day I will raise up the tent of David that is fallen, and close up the breaches thereof; I will restore his ruins, and will build it as in the days of eternity (Amos 9:11).

The house of David shall be as God, as the angel of Jehovah before them (Zech 12:8).

In that day there shall be a fountain open to the house of David (13:1).

44. He who knows that the Lord is meant by David, may know why David so frequently wrote of the Lord in his Psalms while writing about himself; as in these words:

I have made a covenant with My chosen, I have sworn unto David My servant; thy seed will I establish to eternity, and will build up thy throne to generation and generation; and the heavens shall confess thy wonder, thy truth also in the congregation of the saints. Thou spakest in vision to Thine holy one and saidst, I have laid help upon one that is mighty, I have exalted One chosen out of the people, I have found David My servant, with My holy oil have I anointed Him, with whom My hand shall be established, Mine arm also shall strengthen Him, My truth and My mercy shall be with Him, and in My name shall His horn be exalted, I will set His hand in the sea, and His right hand in the rivers. He shall cry unto Me, Thou art My Father, My God, and the rock of My salvation. I will also make Him My first-born, higher than the kings of the earth; My covenant shall stand fast with Him; His seed will I make to endure to eternity, and His throne as the days of the heavens. Once have I sworn by My holiness that I will not lie unto David; His seed shall endure to eternity, and His throne as the sun before Me; it shall be established to eternity as the moon, and a faithful witness in the heavens (Ps 89:3-5, 19-21, 24-29, 35-37).

And so in other Psalms, as 45:1-17; 122:4, 5; 132:8-18.

GOD IS ONE, AND THE LORD IS THAT GOD.

45. From the numerous passages quoted from the Word in the preceding chapter, it is evident that the Lord is called Jehovah, the God of Israel and of Jacob, the Holy One of Israel, Lord, and God, and also King, the Anointed, and David, from which it may be seen, as yet however as through a glass, darkly, that the Lord is God Himself, from and about whom is the Word. Now it is known in the whole world that God is one, and no man possessed of sound reason denies it. It remains therefore to confirm this from the Word; and, in addition, that the Lord is that God.

i. *That God is one,* is confirmed by these passages of the Word:

Jesus said, The first of all the commandments is, Hear, O Israel, The Lord our God is one Lord; therefore thou shalt love the Lord thy God with all thy heart, and with all thy soul (Mk 12:29, 30).

Hear, O Israel, Jehovah our God is one Jehovah; and thou shalt love Jehovah thy God with all thy heart, and with all thy soul (Dt 6:4, 5).

One came unto Jesus and said, Good Master, what good thing shall I do that I may have eternal life? Jesus said unto him, Why callest thou Me good? There is none good but the one God (Mt 19:6, 17).

That all the kingdoms of the earth may know that Thou alone art Jehovah (Isa 37:20).

I am Jehovah and there is none else; there is no God besides Me: that they may know from the rising of the sun, and from the west, that there is no God besides Me: I am Jehovah and there is none else (45:5, 6).

O Jehovah of hosts, God of Israel, that dwellest on the cherubim, Thou art the God, even Thou alone, over all the kingdoms of the earth (37:16).

Is there a God besides Me? and a Rock? I know not any (44:8).

Who is God save Jehovah? and who is a Rock save our God? (Ps 18:31).

ii. *The Lord is that God,* as is confirmed by these passages of the Word:

Surely God is in thee, and there is none else, there is no God. Verily Thou art a God that hidest Thyself, O God of Israel, the Saviour (Isa 45:14, 15).

Am not I Jehovah? and there is no God else besides Me, a just God and a Saviour, there is none besides Me. Look unto Me that ye may be saved, all the ends of the earth; for I am God, and there is none else (45:21, 22).

I am Jehovah, and besides Me there is no Saviour (48:11).

I am Jehovah thy God, and thou shalt acknowledge no God but Me; for there is no Saviour besides Me (Hosea 13:4).

Thus saith Jehovah the King of Israel, and his Redeemer Jehovah of hosts, I am the First and I am the Last, and besides Me there is no God (Isa 44:6).

Jehovah of Hosts is His name, and thy Redeemer the Holy One of Israel; the God of the whole earth shall He be called (54:5).

In that day Jehovah shall be king over all the earth; in that day there shall be one Jehovah, and His name One (Zech 14:9).

As the Lord alone is the Saviour and the Redeemer, and as it is said that Jehovah is that Saviour and Redeemer, and that there is none besides Him, it follows that the one God is no other than the Lord.

X.

46. Jesus has said in Matthew:

All power is given unto Me in heaven and on earth; go ye therefore and make disciples of all nations, baptizing them into the name of the Father, and the Son, and of the Holy Spirit; teaching them to observe all things whatsoever I have commanded you; and lo I am with you all the days even to the consummation of the age (28:18-20).

It has already been shown that the Divine called "the Father," and the Divine called "the Son," are a one in the Lord; and it shall now be shown that "the Holy Spirit" is the same as the Lord.

[2] The reason why the Lord said that they were to baptize into the name of the Father and of the Son and of the Holy Spirit, is that there is in the Lord a Trine or Trinity; for there is the Divine called the Father, the Divine Human called the Son, and the proceeding Divine called the Holy Spirit. The Divine called the Father, and the Divine called the Son, are the Divine as Source of all things and the proceeding Divine is the Divine as Instrument or Communicator. That the Divine which proceeds from the Lord is no other than the Divine which is Himself, may be seen in the treatise on the *Divine Providence* for it is a matter of deep investigation.

[3] That there is a Trine in the Lord may be illustrated by comparison with an angel, who has a soul and a body, and also a proceeding. That which proceeds from him is himself outside of him. I have been permitted to learn many things about this proceeding, but this is not the place to present them.

82

[4] After death the first thing the angels teach every man who looks to God is that the Holy Spirit is not any other than the Lord; and that "to go forth" and "to proceed" is nothing else than to enlighten and teach by the presence, which is according to the reception, of the Lord. The result is that after death very many people put away the idea they had formed in this world about the Holy Spirit, and receive the idea that it is the Lord's presence with man through angels and spirits, by and according to which the man is enlightened and taught.

[5] Moreover, it is usual in the Word to name two Divines, and sometimes three, which yet are one; as Jehovah and God, Jehovah and the Holy One of Israel, Jehovah and the Mighty One of Jacob, and also God and the Lamb. And as these are one, it is said in other places, Jehovah alone is God, Jehovah alone is holy, and He is the Holy One of Israel, and there is none besides Him; and also instead of God it is sometimes said the Lamb, and instead of the Lamb, God; this is done in Apocalypse; the other expressions occur in the Prophets.

[6] That it is the Lord only who is meant by the Father, Son, and Holy Spirit in Mt 28:19, is evident from what there precedes and what follows. In the preceding verse the Lord says, "All power is given unto Me in heaven and on earth," and in the following verse He says, "Lo, I am with you all the days, even to the consummation of the age;" thus He speaks of Himself only, so that He spoke in that manner [about the Father, Son, and Holy Spirit] to make His disciples aware that there is a Trinity in Him.

[7] In order that it may be known that the Holy Spirit is not a Divine other than the Lord Himself, consider what is meant by "spirit" in the Word. By "spirit" is meant:

i. Man's life in general.

ii. As man's life varies according to his state, by "spirit" is meant the varying affection of life in man.

iii. Also the life of one who is regenerate, which is called spiritual life.

iv. But where "spirit" is said of the Lord, His Divine life is meant, thus the Lord Himself.

v. Specifically, the life of His wisdom, which is called the divine truth.

vi. Jehovah Himself, that is, the Lord, spoke the Word through the prophets.

47. i. *By "spirit" is meant man's life in general.* This is evident from ordinary discourse, in which it is said that a man, when he dies, yields up his spirit, so that by "spirit" in this sense is meant the life of the respiration, and in fact the term "spirit" is derived from the respiration, and this is why, in the Hebrew language, there is one word for both "spirit" and "wind." There are in man two fountains of life, one is the pulsation of the heart, and the other is the respiration of the lungs. The life from the respiration of the lungs is what is properly meant by "spirit" and also by "soul." This acts as one with the man's thought from the understanding, and the life from the heart's pulsation acts as one with his will's love. This will be seen in its own place. That man's life is meant in the Word by "spirit," is evident from these passages:

Thou gatherest in their breath (*spiritum*), they expire, and return into dust (Ps 104:29).

He remembered that they were flesh, a wind (*spiritus*) that passeth away, and cometh not again (78:39).

When his breath has gone forth, he will return into earth (146:4).

Hezekiah lamented that the life of his spirit should go forth (Isa 38:16).

The spirit of Jacob revived (Ge 45:27).

A molten image is falsehood, and there is no breath in it (Je 51:17).

The Lord Jehovah said to the dry bones, I will cause breath to enter into you, that ye may live. Come from the four winds O breath, and breathe upon these slain, and they shall live; and the breath came into them, and they revived (Ezek 37:5, 6, 9, 10).

Jesus took the daughter [of Jairus] by the hand, and her spirit returned, and she rose up immediately (Lu 8:54, 55).

48. ii. *As man's life varies according to his state, by "spirit" is meant the varying affection of life in man.* As,

1: *The life of wisdom:*

Bezaleel was filled with the spirit of wisdom, intelligence, and knowledge (Ex 31:3).

Thou shalt speak unto all that are wise-hearted, whom I have filled with the spirit of wisdom (28:3).

Joshua was filled with the spirit of wisdom (Dt 34:9).

Nebuchadnezzar said of Daniel [in whom is the spirit of the holy gods. The queen said] that an excellent spirit of knowledge, intelligence, and wisdom was in him (Da 4:8; 5:12).

They that erred in spirit shall know intelligence (Isa 29:24).

2. *The excitation of life:*

Jehovah hath stirred up the spirit of the kings of Media (Je 51:11).

Jehovah hath stirred up the spirit of Zerubbabel, and the spirit of all the remnant of the people (Hag 1:14).

I will put a spirit in the king of Assyria, that he may hear a rumor, and shall return into his own land (Isa 37:7).

Jehovah hardened the spirit of Sihon the king (Dt 2:30).

That which cometh up upon your spirit shall not be at all (Ezek 20:32).

3. *Freedom of life:*

[It is said of] the four living creatures (which were cherubs) seen by the prophet, Withersoever the spirit was to go, they went (Ezek 1:12, 20).

4. *Life in fear, pain or grief, and anger:*

That every heart may melt, and all hands be let down, and every spirit be faint (21:7).

My spirit hath failed upon me; my heart is amazed in the midst of me (Ps 142:3; 143:4).

My spirit is consumed (143:7).

As for me Daniel, my spirit was grieved (Da 7:15).

The spirit of Pharaoh was troubled (Ge 41:8).

Nebuchadnezzar said, My spirit was troubled (Da 2:3).
I went in sadness in the heat of my spirit (Ezek 3:14).

5. *A life of various evil affections:*

Provided that in his spirit there is no guile (Ps 32:2).
Jehovah hath mingled a spirit of perversities in the midst thereof (Isa 19:14).
He said to the foolish prophets that go away after their own spirit (Ezek 13:3)
The prophet is a fool, the man [that hath a] spirit is mad (Hosea 9:7).
Take ye heed to your spirit, and deal not treacherously (Mal 2:16).
The spirit of whoredoms hath led them astray (Hosea 4:12).
The spirit of whoredoms is in the midst of them (5:4).
When the spirit of jealousy hath passed upon him (Num 5:14).
A man who wandereth in spirit and chattereth a lie (Mic 2:11).
A generation whose spirit was not steadfast with God (Ps 78:8).
Jehovah hath poured out upon you the spirit of deep sleep (Isa 29:10).
Ye shall conceive chaff, ye shall bring forth stubble; as for your spirit, fire shall devour you (33:11).

6. *Infernal life:*

I will cause the unclean spirit to pass out of the land (Zech 13:2).
When the unclean spirit is gone out of a man, he walketh through dry places, and he afterwards joineth to himself seven spirits worse than himself, and they enter in and dwell there (Mt 12:43-45).
Babylon is become the hold of every foul spirit (Apoc 18:2).

7. *Besides the infernal spirits themselves by whom men are troubled:*

Mt 8:16; 10:1; 12:43-45; Mk 1:23-27; 9:17-29; Lu 4:33, 36; 6:17, 18, 7:21; 8:2, 29; 9:39, 42, 55; 11:24-26; 13:11; Apoc 13:15; 16:13,14.

49. iii. *By "spirit" is meant the life of one who is regenerate, which is called spiritual life:*

Jesus said, Except a man be born of water and of the spirit, he cannot enter into the kingdom of God (Jn 3:5).

I will give you a new heart, and a new spirit. I will put My spirit within you, and cause you to walk in My statutes (Ezek 36:26, 27).

To give a new heart and a new spirit (11:19).

Create in me a clean heart, O God, and renew a steadfast spirit within me. Restore unto me the joy of Thy salvation, and let a willing spirit uphold me (Ps 51:10, 12).

Make you a new heart, and a new spirit; for why will ye die, O house of Israel (Ezek 18:31).

Thou sendest forth Thy spirit, they are created, and Thou renewest the faces of the earth (Ps 104:30).

The hour cometh, and now is, when the true worshipers shall worship the Father in spirit and in truth (Jn 4:23).

Jehovah God giveth breath (*animam*) to the people, and spirit to them that walk therein (Isa 42:5).

Jehovah formeth the spirit of man in the midst of him (Zech 12:1).

With my soul have I awaited Thee in the night; with my spirit in the midst of me have I awaited Thee in the morning (Isa 26:9).

In that day shall Jehovah be for a spirit of judgment to him that sitteth in judgment (28:5, 6).

My spirit hath rejoiced in God my Saviour (Lu 1:47).

They have quieted my spirit in the land of the north (Zech 6:8).

Into Thy hand I commend my spirit; Thou hast redeemed me (Ps 31:5).

Did not He make one, and the rest in whom was spirit? (Mal 2:15).

After three days and a half the spirit of life from God entered into the two witnesses that had been killed by the beast (Apoc 11:11).

I Jehovah the former of the mountains, and the creator of the wind (*spiritus*) (Amos 4:13).

O God, the God of the spirits as to all flesh (Num 16:22; 27:18).

I will pour upon the house of David, and upon the inhabitant of Jerusalem, the spirit from on high (Zech 12:10).

Until He hath poured upon us the spirit from on high (Isa 32:15).

I will pour waters upon him that is thirsty, and brooks upon the dry [ground], I will pour My spirit upon thy seed (44:3).

I will pour My spirit upon all flesh, also upon the servants and the handmaids; in those days will I pour out My spirit (Joel 2:28, 29). (To pour out the spirit means to regenerate; as does also to give a new heart and a new spirit.)

[2] *By "spirit" is meant spiritual life in those who are in humiliation:*

I dwell in a contrite and humble spirit, and to revive the spirit of the humble, and to revive the heart of the contrite ones (Isa 57:15).

The sacrifices of God are a broken spirit, a broken and contrite heart, O God, Thou wilt not depise (Ps 51:17).

He will give the oil of joy for mourning, and the garment of praise for the spirit of heaviness (Isa 61:3).

A woman forsaken and grieved in spirit (54:6).

Blessed are the poor in spirit, for theirs is the kingdom of the heavens (Mt 5:3).

50. iv. *Where "spirit" is said of the Lord, there is meant His Divine life, thus the Lord Himself.* This is evident from these passages:

He whom the Father hath sent speaketh the words of God, for God hath not given the spirit by measure unto Him; the Father loveth the Son, and hath given all things into His hand (Jn 3:34, 35).

There shall go forth a rod out of the stem of Jesse, and the spirit of Jehovah shall rest upon Him, the spirit of wisdom and intelligence, the spirit of counsel and might (Isa 11:1, 2).

I have put My spirit upon Him, He shall bring forth judgment to the nations (42:1).

When the enemy shall come as a pent-up stream, the spirit of Jehovah shall lift up a standard against him; then shall the Redeemer come to Zion (59:19, 20).

The spirit of the Lord Jehovih is upon Me; Jehovah hath anointed Me to preach good tidings to the poor (61:1; Lu 4:18).

Jesus knowing in His spirit that they so reasoned within themselves (Mk 2:8).

Jesus exulted in spirit, and said (Lu 10:21).

Jesus was troubled in His spirit (Jn 13:21).

Jesus sighed in His spirit (Mk 8:12).

[2] *"Spirit" as used for Jehovah Himself, that is, the Lord:*

God is a Spirit (Jn 4:24).

Who hath directed the Spirit of Jehovah, or who is a man of His counsel? (Isa 40:13).

The Spirit of Jehovah led them by the hand of Moses (63:12, 14).

Whither shall I go from Thy Spirit, and whither shall I flee? (Ps 139:7).

Jehovah said, Not by might, but by My Spirit shall he do it (Zech 4:6).

They provoked the Spirit of His holiness, therefore He was turned to be their enemy (Isa 63:10; Ps 106:33, 40).

My Spirit shall not strive with man for ever, for he is flesh (Gen 6:3).

I will not contend to eternity, for the Spirit should fail before Me (Isa 57:16).

The blasphemy against the Holy Spirit shall not be forgiven; but he who shall speak a word against the Son of man, it shall be forgiven (Mt 12:31, 32; Mk 3:28-30; Lu 12:10).

"Blasphemy against the Holy Spirit," is blasphemy against the Lord's Divine; "a word against the Son of man," is something said against the Word by wrongly interpreting its meaning; for "the Son of man" is the Lord in respect to the Word, as has been shown above.

51. v. *"Spirit," when said of the Lord, specifically means the life of His wisdom, which is divine truth:*

I tell you the truth, it is expedient for you that I go away, for if I go not away the Comforter will not come unto you, but if I go away I will send Him unto you (Jn 16:7).

When He, the Spirit of Truth, is come, He will lead you into all truth. He shall not speak from Himself; but whatsoever He shall hear, that shall He speak (16:13).

He shall glorify Me, for He shall receive of Mine, and shall declare it unto you: all things that the Father hath are Mine; therefore said I that He shall receive of Mine and shall declare it unto you (16:14, 15).

I will ask the Father, that He may give you another Comforter, the Spirit of Truth, whom the world cannot receive, because it seeth Him not, neither knoweth Him; but ye know Him, for He abideth with you, and shall be in you: I will not leave you orphans, I come to you, and ye shall see Me (14:16-19).

When the Comforter is come, whom I will send unto you from the Father, even the Spirit of Truth, He shall testify of Me (15:26).

Jesus cried, saying, If any one thirst let him come unto Me and drink; he that believeth in Me, as the Scripture hath said, out of his belly shall flow streams of living water. This He said of the spirit which they that believe in Him should receive. For the Holy Spirit was not yet, because Jesus was not yet glorified (7:37-39).

Jesus breathed on His disciples, and said, Receive ye the Holy Spirit (20:22).

[2] That by the "Comforter," the "Spirit of Truth," and the "Holy Spirit," the Lord meant Himself, is evident from His words that "the world did not as yet know Him," for they did not as yet know the Lord. And when He said that He "would send it," He added, "I will not leave you orphans, I come to you, and ye shall see Me" (Jn 14:16-19, 26, 28); and in another place, "Lo I am with you all the days, even to the consummation of the age" (Mt 28:20); and when Thomas said, "We know not whither Thou goest," Jesus said, "I am the way and the truth" (Jn 14:5, 6).

[3] As the "Spirit of Truth" or "Holy Spirit" is the same as the Lord, who is the Truth itself, it is said, "the Holy Spirit was not yet, because Jesus was not yet glorified" (Jn 7:39); for after His glorification or complete unition with the Father, which was effected by the passion of the cross, the Lord was divine wisdom and divine truth itself, thus the Holy Spirit. The reason why the Lord breathed on the disciples and said, "Receive ye the Holy Spirit," was that all the breathing of heaven is from the Lord. For angels as well as men have breathing and beating of the heart; their breathing being according to their reception of wisdom from the Lord, and their beating of the heart or pulse being according to their reception of divine love from the Lord. That this is so will be seen in its own place.

[4] That "the Holy Spirit" is divine truth from the Lord, is further evident from these passages:

When they bring you to the synagogues, be not anxious as to what ye shall say; for the Holy Spirit shall teach you in the same hour what ye ought to say (Lu 12:11, 12; 21:14; Mk 13:11).

Jehovah said, My spirit that is upon thee, and My words which I have put in thy mouth, shall not depart out of thy mouth (Isa 59:21).

There shall go forth a Rod out of the stem of Jesse, and He shall smite the earth with the rod of His mouth, and with the breath (*spiritu*) of His lips shall He slay the wicked, and truth shall be the girdle of His thighs (11:1, 4, 5).

Now with the mouth He hath commanded, and His spirit hath gathered them (34:16).

They who worship God must worship in spirit and in truth (Jn 4:24).

It is the spirit that quickeneth, the flesh profiteth nothing; the words that I speak unto you, they are spirit and they are life (6:63).

John said, I baptize you with water unto repentance; but He that cometh after me shall baptize you with the Holy Spirit and with fire (Mt 3:11; Mk 1:8; Lu 3:16).

To "baptize with the Holy Spirit and with fire," is to regenerate by means of the divine truth which is of faith and the divine good which is of love.

When Jesus was baptized, the heavens were opened, and He saw the Holy Spirit descending like a dove (Mt 3:16; Mk 1:10; Lu 3:21, 22; Jn 1:32, 33).

A dove is a representative of purification and regeneration by means of divine truth.

[5] As by "the Holy Spirit," where the Lord is treated of, is meant His Divine life, thus Himself, and, specifically, the life of His wisdom which is called divine truth, by the "spirit" mentioned in the writings of the prophets which is called also the "Holy Spirit," is meant divine truth from the Lord. Thus in the following passages:

The Spirit said unto the churches (Apoc 2:7, 11, 29; 3:1, 6, 13, 22).

The seven lamps of fire burning before the throne are the seven spirits of God (4:5).

In the midst of the elders a Lamb standing, having seven eyes, which are the seven spirits of God sent forth into all the earth (5:6).

"Lamps of fire," and the Lord's "eyes," signify divine truths, and "seven" signifies what is holy.

The Spirit said, that they may rest from their labors (14:13).
The Spirit and the bride say, Come (22:17).

They made their hearts adamant, that they should not hear the law or the words which Jehovah hath sent in His Spirit by the hand of the prophets (Zech 7:12).

The spirit of Elijah came upon Elisha (2 Kgs 2:15).

John went before in the spirit and power of Elijah (Lu 1:17).

Elisabeth was filled with the Holy Spirit and prophesied (1:41).

Zacharias, filled with the Holy Spirit, prophesied (1:67).

David said in the Holy Spirit, The Lord said to my Lord, Sit at My right hand (Mk 12:36).

The testimony of Jesus is the spirit of prophecy (Apoc 19:10).

As, therefore, by the "Holy Spirit" is meant, specifically, the Lord as to divine wisdom, and derivatively as to divine truth, it is evident why it is said that the Holy Spirit enlightens, teaches, inspires.

52. vi. *Jehovah Himself (that is, the Lord) spoke the Word through the prophets.* We read of the prophets that they were in vision, and that Jehovah spoke to them. When they were in vision they were not in the body, but in their spirit, in which state they saw things such as are in heaven. But when Jehovah spoke to them, they were in the body, and heard Him speaking. These two states of the prophets should be carefully distinguished. In their state of vision, the eyes of their spirit were opened, and those of their body shut, and they then seemed to themselves to be carried from place to place, the body remaining in its own place. In this state, at times, were Ezekiel, Zechariah, Daniel, and John when he wrote the Apocalypse; and it is then said that they were "in vision," or "in the spirit." Thus Ezekiel says:

The spirit lifted me up, and brought me into Chaldea to the captivity, in the vision of God, in the Spirit of God; thus went up above me the vision which I saw (11:1, 24).

He says too,

That the spirit took him up, and he heard behind him an earthquake, and other things (3:12, 14).

Also that the spirit lifted him up between the earth and the heaven, and brought him in the visions of God to Jerusalem, and he saw abominations (8:3, etc.) .

In like manner in the vision of God, or in the spirit, he saw

The four living creatures, which were cherubs (1 and 10).
And also the new earth and the new temple, and an angel measuring them (40 to 48).

That he was then in the visions of God, he says in 40:2; and that the spirit took him up, in 43:5.

The case was the same with Zechariah, in whom at the time there was an angel, when he saw:

A man riding among the myrtle trees (Zech 1:8, etc.).
Four horns, and afterwards a man who had a measuring line in his hand (1:18; 2:1).
Joshua the high priest (3:1, etc.).
A lampstand, and two olive-trees (4:2, 3).
A flying roll, and an ephah (5:1, 6).
Four chariots going out between two mountains, and horses (6:1, etc.).

In a similar state was Daniel, when he saw

Four beasts coming up out of the sea (Da 7:3).
The combats of the ram and the he-goat (8:1, etc.).

That he saw these things in visions, is stated in 7:1, 2, 7, 13; 8:2; 10:1, 7, 8. That the angel Gabriel was seen by him in vision, and spoke with him, is stated in 9:21, 22. The case was the same with John when he wrote the Apocalypse, who says,

That he was in the spirit on the Lord's day (1:10).
That he was carried away in the spirit into the wilderness (17:3).
Into a high mountain in the spirit (21:10).
That he saw horses in vision (9:17).
And elsewhere that he saw the things which he described, thus in spirit, or in vision (1:12; 4:1; 5:1; 6:1; and in every other chapter).

53. As to the Word itself, however, it is not said in the Prophets that they spoke it from the Holy Spirit, but that they spoke it from Jehovah, from Jehovah of Hosts, from the Lord Jehovih; for we read "the Word of Jehovah came unto me," "Jehovah said unto me," and very frequently "Jehovah said," and "the word (*dictum*) of Jehovah." And, as the Lord is Jehovah, as has been shown above, it follows that all the Word has been spoken by Him. That no one may doubt this to be the case, I will give the references, in Jeremiah only, to the places where these four expressions occur:—1:4, 7, 11-14, 19; 2:1-5, 9, 19, 22, 29, 31; 3:1, 6, 10, 12, 14, 16; 4:1, 3, 9, 17, 27; 5:11, 14, 18, 22, 29; 6:6, 9, 12, 15, 16, 21, 22; 7:1, 3, 11, 13, 19-21; 8:1, 3, 12, 13; 9:3, 7, 9, 13, 15, 17, 22, 24, 25; 10:1, 2, 18; 11:1, 6, 9, 11, 17, 21, 22; 12:14, 17; 13:1, 6, 9, 11-15, 25; 14:1, 10, 14, 15; 15:1-3, 6, 11, 19, 20; 16:1, 3, 5, 9, 14, 16, 17:5, 19, 20, 21, 24; 18:1, 5, 6, 11, 13; 19:1, 3, 6, 12, 15; 20:4; 21:1, 4, 7, 8, 11, 12; 22:2, 5, 6, 11, 16, 18, 24, 29, 30; 23:2, 5, 7, 12, 15, 24, 29, 31, 38; 24:3, 5, 8; 25:1, 3, 7-9, 15, 27-29, 32; 26:1, 2, 18; 27:1, 2, 4, 8, 11, 16, 19, 21, 22; 28:2, 12, 14, 16; 29:4, 8, 9, 16, 19-21, 25, 30-32; 30:1-5, 8, 10-12, 17, 18; 31:1, 2, 7, 10, 15-17, 23, 27, 28, 31-38; 32:1, 6, 14, 15, 25, 26, 28, 30, 36, 42; 33:1, 2, 4, 10-13, 17, 19, 20, 23, 25; 34:1, 2, 4, 8, 12, 13, 17, 22; 35:1, 13, 17-19; 36:1, 6, 27, 29, 30; 37:6, 7, 9; 38:2, 3, 17; 39:15-18; 40:1; 42:7, 9, 15, 18, 19; 43:8, 10; 44:1, 2, 7, 11, 24-26, 30; 45:1, 2, 5; 46:1, 23, 25, 28; 47:1; 48:1, 8, 12, 30, 35, 38, 40, 43, 44, 47; 49:2, 5-7, 12, 13, 16, 18, 26, 28, 30, 32, 35, 37-39; 50:1, 4, 10, 18, 20, 21, 30, 31, 33, 35, 40; 51:25, 33, 36, 39, 52, 58. These are from Jeremiah only. All the other prophets speak in the same way, and none say that the Holy Spirit has spoken, or that Jehovah has spoken to them by means of the Holy Spirit.

54. From all this then it is evident that Jehovah (who is the Lord from eternity) spoke through the prophets; and that where the Holy Spirit is mentioned, it is the Lord Himself. It follows that God is one in both person and essence, and that this God is the Lord.

XI.

55. The recognition by Christians of three divine persons, and thus as it were of three gods, has arisen from there being in the Lord a Trine, one of which is called the Father, the second the Son, and the third the Holy Spirit. This Trine is also referred to in the Word under distinct names; just as we refer by distinct names to soul, to body, and to that which proceeds from them, which, however, taken together, form a one. In the sense of the letter the Word is of such a nature that things which form a one it distinguishes from each other as if they did not form a one. This is why Jehovah (who is the Lord from eternity) is sometimes called "Jehovah," sometimes "Jehovah of hosts," sometimes "God," sometimes "the Lord;" and at the same time He is called "Creator," "Saviour," "Redeemer," and "Former," and even "Shaddai;" and His Human which He assumed in this world, "Jesus," "Christ," "Messiah," "Son of God," "Son of man;" and, in the Word of the Old Testament, "God," "Holy One of Israel," "Jehovah's Anointed," "King," "Prince," "Counselor," "Angel," "David."

[2] In consequence of this feature of the Word in the sense of the letter (that it speaks of as many those who really form a one) Christians, who at first were simple folk, and understood everything in accordance with the literal import of the words, discriminated the Divinity into three persons. On account of their simplicity this was permitted, but in such a manner that they should believe the Son to

be Infinite, Uncreate, Almighty, God, and Lord, altogether equal to the Father; and that they should also believe that these are not two, or three; but one in essence, majesty, and glory, and therefore in divinity.

[3] They who believe this in simplicity in accordance with doctrine, and do not confirm themselves in the idea of three gods but of the three make a one, after death are taught by the Lord by means of angels that He Himself is that one God, and that Trine. And this teaching is received by all who come into heaven; for no one can be admitted into heaven who thinks of three gods, however much he may say One; for the life of the whole heaven, and the wisdom of all the angels, are founded upon the acknowledgment and consequent confession of one God, and upon the faith that this one God is also Man, and that He is the Lord, who is at once both God and Man.

[4] From all this it is evident that it was of divine permission that Christians at first received the doctrine of three persons, provided that they at the same time received the idea that the Lord is God, infinite, almighty, and Jehovah. For unless they had received this too, it would have been all over with the church, because the church is the church from the Lord; and the eternal life of all is from the Lord, and from no other.

[5] That the church is the church from the Lord is evident from this alone, that the whole Word from beginning to end treats solely of the Lord, as was shown above; and that we must believe in Him, and that they who do not believe in Him have not eternal life, but that the anger of God abideth on them (Jn 3:36).

[6] Now as every one sees in himself that if God is one, He is one in both person and essence (for no one thinks differently, or can think differently, while thinking that God is one), I will here cite the whole of the *Creed* which takes its name from Athanasius, and will afterwards show that all

things said therein are true, provided that instead of a trinity of persons there is understood a trinity of Person.

56. The *Creed* is as follows

Whosoever will be saved, before all things it is necessary that he hold the Catholic (*other authorities say,* Christian) Faith, which faith, except every one do keep whole and undefiled, without doubt he shall perish everlastingly. And the Catholic (*others say,* Christian) Faith is this: That we worship one God in Trinity, and the Trinity in Unity, neither confounding the persons, nor dividing the substance (*others say,* essence). For there is one person of the Father, another of the Son, and another of the Holy Spirit; but the Godhead of the Father, of the Son, and of the Holy Spirit, is all one, the glory equal, the majesty coeternal. Such as the Father is, such is the Son, and such is the Holy Spirit. The Father uncreate, the Son uncreate, and the Holy Spirit uncreate. The Father infinite the Son infinite, and the Holy Spirit infinite. The Father eternal, the Son eternal, and the Holy Spirit eternal: and yet there are not three eternals, but One Eternal: as also there are not three infinites, nor three uncreates; but One Uncreate, and One Infinite. So likewise the Father is almighty, the Son almighty, and the Holy Spirit almighty; and yet there are not three almighties, but One Almighty. So the Father is God, the Son is God, and the Holy Spirit is God: and yet there are not three gods, but One God. So likewise the Father is Lord, the Son Lord, and the Holy Spirit Lord: and yet not three lords, but One Lord. For as we are compelled by the Christian verity to acknowledge every person by himself to be God and Lord, so are we forbidden by the catholic religion to say there be three gods or three lords (*others say,* still we cannot, according to the Christian faith, mention three gods or three lords). The Father is made of none, neither created, nor begotten (*natus*): the Son is of the Father alone, not made, nor created, but begotten (*natus*): the Holy Spirit is of the Father and of the Son, neither made, nor created, nor begotten (*natus*), but proceeding. So there is one Father, not three Fathers; one Son, not three Sons; one Holy Spirit, not three Holy Spirits. And in this Trinity none is before or after another; none is greater or less than another; but the whole three persons are coeternal together, and coequal. So that in all things, as is aforesaid, the Unity in Trinity and the Trinity in Unity is to be worshiped (*others say,* three persons in one Godhead, and one God in three persons, is to be worshiped). He therefore that will be saved, must thus think of the Trinity.

Furthermore, it is necessary to everlasting salvation that he also believe rightly the incarnation of our Lord Jesus Christ (*others say,* that he firmly believes that our Lord is very Man). For the right faith is that we believe and confess that our Lord Jesus Christ, the Son of God, is God and Man; God of the substance (*or* essence; *others,* nature) of the Father, begotten before the worlds; and Man of the substance (*others say,* nature) of his mother, born in the world; perfect God, and perfect Man, of a reasonable soul and human flesh (*corpore*) subsisting; equal to the Father as touching his Godhead, and inferior to the Father as touching his manhood. Who although He be God and Man, yet He is not two, but one Christ; one, not by conversion of the Godhead into flesh (*corpus*); but by taking of the manhood into God (*others say,* He is one, yet not that the Godhead was transmuted into manhood, but the Godhead took up the Manhood to itself); one altogether, not by confusion (*others say,* commingling) of substance, but by unity of person (*others say,* He is altogether One, not that the two natures are commixed, but he is one person). For as the reasonable soul and flesh (*corpus*) is one man, so God and man is one Christ, who suffered for our salvation, descended into hell, rose again the third day from the dead. He ascended into heaven, He sitteth on the right hand of the Father, God Almighty, from whence He shall come to judge the quick and the dead. At whose coming all men shall rise again with their bodies, and shall give account for their own works. And they that have done good shall go into life everlasting, and they that have done evil into everlasting fire.

57. All the statements of the Creed are true in so far as its verbal expressions are concerned, provided that instead of a trinity of persons there is understood a Trinity of Person. This may be seen if we transcribe it again, with this latter Trinity substituted in it. A Trinity of Person is this: THAT THE LORD'S DIVINE IS THE FATHER, THE DIVINE HUMAN THE SON, AND THE PROCEEDING DIVINE THE HOLY SPIRIT. When this Trinity is understood, the man can both think of and say One God; but who fails to see that otherwise he cannot but think of three gods? Athanasius himself saw this, and this is why there were inserted these words:

As we are compelled by the Christian verity to acknowledge every person by himself to be God and Lord; so are we forbidden by the catholic religion (or, by the Christian faith) to say (or name) three gods or three lords.

This amounts to saying, "Although it is allowable, by the Christian verity, to acknowledge, or think of, three gods and lords, yet it is not allowable, by the Christian faith, to say or name more than one God and one Lord." And yet it is acknowledgment and thought which conjoin man with the Lord and heaven, and not mere speech. Besides, no one can comprehend how the Divine, which is one, can be divided into three persons, each of whom is God, for the Divine is not divisible. And to make the three one through the essence or substance does not take away the idea of three gods, but merely conveys an idea of their unanimity.

58. In so far as its verbal expressions are concerned, everything in this Creed is true, provided that instead of a trinity of persons there is understood a Trinity of Person. This is evident from the same when rewritten in this form:

Whosoever will be saved, it is necessary that he hold this Christian Faith; and the Christian Faith is, that we worship one God in Trinity, and Trinity in Unity, not confounding the Trine of Person, nor dividing the Essence. The Trine of one Person is what is called the Father, Son, and Holy Spirit. The Divinity of the Father, Son, and Holy Spirit is one and the same, the glory and majesty equal. Such as the Father is, such is the Son, and such is the Holy Spirit. The Father is uncreate, the Son uncreate, and the Holy Spirit uncreate. The Father is infinite, the Son infinite, and the Holy Spirit infinite. And yet there are not three infinites, nor three uncreates, but one Uncreate, and one Infinite. So likewise the Father is Almighty, the Son Almighty, and the Holy Spirit Almighty; and yet there are not three almighties, but one Almighty. So the Father is God, the Son is God, and the Holy Spirit is God; and yet there are not three gods, but one God. So likewise the Father is Lord, the Son is Lord, and the Holy Spirit is Lord; and yet there are not three lords, but one Lord. For as by the Christian verity we acknowledge a trine in one Person, who is God and Lord, so by the Christian faith we can say one God and one Lord. The Father is made of none, neither created, nor born; the Son is of the Father alone, not made, nor created, but born; the Holy Spirit is of the

Father and of the Son, not made, nor created, nor born, but proceeding. So there is one Father, not three Fathers; one Son, not three Sons; one Holy Spirit, not three Holy Spirits. And in this Trinity none is greatest or least, but they are altogether equal. So that in all things, as is aforesaid, the Unity in Trinity, and Trinity in Unity, is to be worshiped.

59. So far in the *Creed* as to the Trinity and Unity of God. The Creed then treats of the Lord's assumption of the Human in the world, called the Incarnation. Everything said in the *Creed* on this point also is true, provided we make a clear distinction between the human from the mother in which the Lord was when in a state of humiliation or emptying out (*exinanitio*) [see Isa 53:12], as when He suffered temptations and the cross; and the Human from the Father, in which He was when in a state of glorification or unition. For in the world the Lord assumed a Human conceived of Jehovah (who is the Lord from eternity), and born of the virgin Mary; so that He had both a Divine and a human, a Divine from His Divine from eternity, and a human from the mother Mary in time; but this latter human He put off, and put on the Human that was Divine. This Human is what is called the Divine Human, and is meant in the Word by the "Son of God." When therefore the things first said in the *Creed* about the Incarnation are understood of the maternal human (in which the Lord was when in a state of humiliation), and the things that follow, of the Divine Human (in which He was when in a state of glorification), all things there are in agreement. With the maternal human (in which the Lord was when in a state of humiliation) agree the following statements, that come first in the *Creed:*

That Jesus Christ was God and Man, God of the Substance of the Father, and Man of the substance of the mother, born in the world; perfect God and perfect Man, of a rational soul and human body consisting; equal to the Father as touching the Godhead, but inferior to the Father as touching the manhood.

That this manhood was not converted into the Godhead, nor commixed therewith; it being put off, and the Divine Human assumed in its place.

With the Divine Human (in which He was when in a state of glorification, and is now to eternity) agree the following words in the *Creed:*

Although our Lord Jesus Christ, the Son of God, be God and Man, yet He is not two, but one Christ; yea, He is altogether one, for He is one person; for as the reasonable soul and body are one man, so God and Man are one Christ.

60. Thus in the Lord, God and Man (as is said in the *Creed*) are not two, but one Person, yea, altogether one, as soul and body are one. This is clear from many things said by the Lord Himself, as that the Father and He are one; that all things of the Father are His, and all His the Father's; that He is in the Father, and the Father in Him; that all things are given into His hand; that He has all power; that He is the God of heaven and earth; that whosoever believes in Him has eternal life; and further from its being said of Him that He was taken up into heaven as to both the Divine and the Human, and that, with respect to both, He sits on the right hand of God, which means that He is almighty: not to repeat many passages of the Word treating of His Divine Human which are copiously quoted above, and all of which bear witness that GOD IS ONE IN BOTH PERSON AND ESSENCE; THAT THE TRINITY IS IN HIM; AND THAT THIS GOD IS THE LORD.

61. The reason why these truths relative to the Lord are now for the first time made publicly known, is that it has been foretold in the Apocalypse (chapters 21 and 22) that a new church, in which this doctrine will hold the chief place, is to be instituted by the Lord at the end of the former church. It is this church which is meant by the "New Jerusalem," and no one can come into it who does not acknowledge the Lord alone as the God of heaven and earth. This I can declare—that the universal heaven acknowledges the Lord alone; and that no one who does not acknowledge Him is admitted into heaven; for heaven is heaven from the Lord. It is precisely this acknowledgment from love and faith which causes all there to be in the Lord and the Lord in them, as the Lord Himself teaches in John:

In that day ye shall know that I am in My Father, and ye in Me, and I in you (14:20).

Abide in Me, and I in you. I am the vine, ye are the branches; he that abideth in Me and I in him, the same bringeth forth much fruit, for without Me ye can do nothing; if any one abide not in Me, he is cast forth (15:4-6; 17:22, 23).

The reason why this has not been previously seen from the Word, is that if it had been it would not have been received, because the last judgment had not been effected. Before that event the power of hell prevailed over the power of heaven, and as man is in the midst between the two, it is evident that the devil (which is hell) would have plucked it out of men's hearts, and would also have profaned it. But this state of power on the part of hell was completely broken by the last judgment, which has now been executed. Since that judgment—thus now—every man who craves to be enlightened and wise can be so. (On this subject see the work on *Heaven and Hell*, nn. 589-596, 597-603; and also that on the *Last Judgment*, nn. 65-72, 73, 74).

XII.

by the "New Jerusalem" (spoken of in the Apocalypse) is meant a New Church.

62. In the Apocalypse, after a description of the state of the Christian Church as it would be at its end, and as it now is,° and after those of that church who are signified by the false prophet, the dragon, the harlot, and the beasts, are said to have been cast into hell, it is added:

I saw a new heaven and a new earth, for the former heaven and the former earth were passed away. And I John saw the Holy City New Jerusalem coming down from God out of heaven. And I heard a great voice out of heaven, saying, Behold, the tabernacle of God is with men, and He will dwell with them, and they shall be His people, and God Himself shall be with them, their God. And He that sat upon the throne said, Behold, I make all things new. And He said unto me, Write, for these words are true and faithful (21:1-3, 5).

By the "new heaven," and by the "new earth," which John saw, after the former heaven and the former earth had passed away, is not meant a new starry and atmospheric heaven such as appears before the eyes of men, nor a new earth such as that on which men dwell; but there is meant a newness of the church in the spiritual world, and a newness of the church in the natural world. As a newness of the church in both worlds, spiritual and natural, was effected by the Lord when He was in this world, a like prediction had been made in the Prophets, namely, that a new heaven and a new earth would then come into existence (as in Isa 65:17; 66:22, and elsewhere), which cannot possibly mean a heaven visible to the eyes, and an earth habitable by men. By *spiritual world* is meant the world

° That is, in 1763. [Tr.]

where angels and spirits dwell, and by *natural world* is meant the world where men dwell. A newness of the church in the spiritual world has been recently effected, and a newness of the church in the natural world will be effected, as has been partly shown in the little work on the *Last Judgment*, and will be shown more fully in the *Continuation* of that work.

63. By the "Holy City Jerusalem" is meant this New Church as to doctrine, and therefore it was seen coming down from God out of heaven, for the doctrine of genuine truth comes to us from the Lord through heaven, and from no other source. As the church in respect to doctrine is meant by the city New Jerusalem, it is said in the same chapter of the Apocalypse that the city was,

Prepared as a bride adorned for her Husband (verse 2);

and afterwards,

There came unto me one of the seven angels, and talked with me, saying, Come hither, I will show thee the bride, the Lamb's wife; and he carried me away in the spirit to a great and high mountain, and showed me that great city, the Holy Jerusalem, descending out of heaven from God (verses 9, 10).

That by "bride" and "wife" is meant the church, when the Lord is meant by "bridegroom" and "husband," is well known. The church is a "bride" when she is desirous to receive the Lord; and a "wife," when she does receive Him. That the Lord is meant by "her Husband" is evident; for it is said, "the bride the Lamb's wife."

64. The reason why "Jerusalem" means the church as to doctrine, is that there and at no other place in the land of Canaan were the temple and altar, the offering of sacrifices, and therefore divine worship; and for this reason the three yearly feasts were celebrated there, to which every male in the whole country was commanded to go. This is why "Jerusalem" signifies the church in regard to worship, and therefore as to doctrine—for worship is prescribed in doctrine, and is performed according to it. An additional reason is that the Lord was present in Jerusalem, and taught in its temple, and afterwards glorified His Human there. Besides, "city" in the spiritual sense of the Word signifies doctrine, and therefore "holy city" signifies the doctrine of divine truth from the Lord.

[2] That by "Jerusalem" is meant the church as to doctrine, is further evident from other passages in the Word, as from these:

> For Zion's sake I will not hold my peace, and for Jerusalem's sake I will not rest, until the righteousness thereof go forth as brightness, and the salvation thereof as a lamp that burneth. Then shall the nations see thy righteousness, and all kings thy glory; and thou shalt be called by a new name, which the mouth of Jehovah shall name; and thou shalt be a crown of ornament in the hand of Jehovah, and a kingdom's diadem in the hand of thy God; for Jehovah shall delight in thee, and thy land shall be married. Behold, thy salvation cometh; behold, His reward is with Him; and they shall call them the holy people, the redeemed of Jehovah; and thou shalt be called, A city sought out, not forsaken (Isa 62:1-4, 11, 12).

This whole chapter treats of the Lord's advent, and of a new church to be set up by Him. This new church is here meant by "Jerusalem called by a new name which the mouth of Jehovah shall name," and which shall be "a crown of ornament in the hand of Jehovah, and a kingdom's diadem in the hand of God," and in which Jehovah shall "delight," and which shall be called "a city sought out, not forsaken." These words cannot possibly mean the Jerusalem in which were the Jews at the time of the Lord's coming into the world, for that city was of a wholly contrary character, and might rather be called Sodom, as indeed it is called in Apoc 11:8; Isa 3:9; Je 23:14; Ezek 16:46, 48.

[3] Again in Isaiah:

> Behold, I create new heavens and a new earth, and the former shall not be remembered: be ye glad and rejoice to eternities in

that which I create; for behold I create Jerusalem a rejoicing, and
her people a gladness, that I may rejoice over Jerusalem, and be glad
over My people. Then shall the wolf and the lamb feed together;
they shall not do harm in all the mountain of My holiness
(65:17-19, 25).

This chapter also treats of the Lord's advent, and of a
church to be set up anew by Him. This church was not
set up anew among those who were in Jerusalem, but
among those outside of it, so that it is this church which
is meant by the Jerusalem that should be to the Lord a
rejoicing, and whose people should be to Him a gladness,
and where also the wolf and the lamb should feed together,
and where they should do no harm. Here, too, it is said,
just as in the Apocalypse that the Lord will "create a new
heaven and a new earth," the meaning being similar; and
it is added that He will "create Jerusalem."

[4] In another place in Isaiah:

Awake! awake! put on thy strength, O Zion; put on thy beautiful
garments, O Jerusalem, the holy city, for henceforth there shall no
more come into thee the uncircumcised and the unclean. Shake
thyself from the dust, arise, and sit down, O Jerusalem. My people
shall know My name in that day, for I am He that doth speak,
behold it is I. Jehovah hath comforted His people; He hath redeemed Jerusalem (52:1, 2, 6, 9).

This chapter also treats of the Lord's advent, and of the
church to be set up anew by Him; so that by the Jerusalem
into which the uncircumcised and the unclean should no
more come, and which the Lord should redeem, is meant
the church; and by "Jerusalem the holy city," the church
as to doctrine from the Lord.

[5] In Zephaniah:

Shout, O daughter of Zion; be glad with all the heart, O daughter
of Jerusalem; the King of Israel is in the midst of thee; fear evil
no longer: He will be glad over thee with joy, He will rest in thy
love, He will exult over thee with a shout: I will make you a name
and a praise to all the people of the earth (3:14-17, 20).

Here in like manner it treats of the Lord and of a church from Him, over which "the King of Israel" (who is the Lord) will be glad with joy, will exult with a shout, and in whose love He will rest, and whose members He will make a name and a praise to all people of the earth.

[6] In Isaiah:

Thus saith Jehovah thy Redeemer, and thy Former, saying to Jerusalem, Thou shalt be inhabited; and to the cities of Judah, Ye shall be built (44:24, 26).

In Daniel:

Know and perceive that from the going forth of the word even to the restoring and the building up of Jerusalem, even to Messiah the Prince, shall be seven weeks (9:25).

It is evident that here also "Jerusalem" means the church, because this was indeed restored and built by the Lord, but not the Jerusalem that was the residence of the Jews.

[7] "Jerusalem" means a church from the Lord in the following passages also. In Zechariah:

Thus saith Jehovah, I will return to Zion, and I will dwell in the midst of Jerusalem; whence Jerusalem shall be called the city of truth; and the mountain of Jehovah of hosts, the mountain of holiness (8:3, 20-23).

In Joel:

Then shall ye know that I am Jehovah your God, dwelling in Zion, the mountain of holiness; and Jerusalem shall be holiness: and it shall come to pass in that day that the mountains shall drop new wine, and the hills shall flow with milk, and Jerusalem shall abide from generation to generation (3:17-20).

In Isaiah:

In that day shall the shoot of Jehovah be for ornament and glory; and it shall come to pass that he that is left in Zion, and he that remaineth in Jerusalem shall be called holy; even every one that is written for life in Jerusalem (4:2, 3).

In Micah:

In the latter days it shall come to pass that the mountain of the house of Jehovah shall be established in the head of the mountains; for doctrine shall go forth out of Zion, and the word of Jehovah from Jerusalem: unto thee shall come the former kingdom, the kingdom of the daughter of Jerusalem (4:1, 2, 8).

In Jeremiah:

At that time they shall call Jerusalem the throne of Jehovah; and all nations shall be gathered to the name of Jehovah to Jerusalem; neither shall they walk any more after the confirmation of their evil heart (3:17).

In Isaiah:

Look upon Zion the city of our set feast; thine eyes shall see Jerusalem a quiet habitation, a tabernacle that shall not be scattered; not one of the stakes thereof shall ever be removed, neither shall any of the cords thereof be broken (33:20).

Besides other passages, as Isa 24:23; 37:32; 66:10-14; Zech 12:3, 6, 8, 9, 10; 14:8, 11, 12, 21; Mal 3:1, 4; Ps 122:1-7; 137:5, 6.

[8] In these passages "Jerusalem" means the church which was to be set up anew by the Lord, and which actually was set up anew by Him, and not the Jerusalem in the land of Canaan that was inhabited by the Jews. This is evident from those passages in the Word where it is said of the latter Jerusalem that it should utterly perish and be destroyed; as Jer 5:1; 6:6, 7; 7:17, 20, etc.; 8:5-7, etc.; 9:10, 11, 13, etc.; 13:9, 10, 14; 14:16; Lam 1:8, 9, 15, 17; Ezek 4:1 to end; 5:9 to end; 12:18, 19; 15:6-8; 16:1 to end; 23:1-49; Mt 23:33, 37, 39; Lu 19:41-44; 21:20-22; 23:28-30; and in many other places.

65. In the Apocalypse occur the words, "A new heaven and a new earth;" and afterwards, "Behold I make all things new," which mean nothing else than that in the church now to be set up anew by the Lord the doctrine will be new. This doctrine did not exist in the former church, the reason of which is that if it had, it would not have been received, because the last judgment had not then been executed, and previous to that judgment the power of hell prevailed over the power of heaven, so that if the doctrine had been given before, even from the Lord's mouth, it would not have remained with men; nor does it at this day remain except with those who approach the Lord alone, and acknowledge Him as the God of heaven and earth. (See above, at n. 61.) This same doctrine had indeed been given in the Word; but as not long after its setting up anew the church was turned into Babylon, and afterwards, with others, into Philistia, that doctrine could not be seen from the Word, for the church sees the Word from the principles of its religion and from its doctrine, and in no other way.

The new things contained in the present little work are, in general, as follows:

i. God is one in Person and Essence, and this God is the Lord.

ii. All Holy Scripture treats of Him alone.

iii. He came into the world to subdue the hells, and to glorify His Human; and He accomplished both by admitting temptations into Himself, and did so fully by the last of them which was the passion of the cross. Thereby He became the Redeemer and Saviour; and thereby merit and righteousness are His alone.

iv. The statement that He "fulfilled all things of the law" means that He fulfilled all things of the Word.

v. By the passion of the cross He did not take away sins, but bore them as the Prophet, that is to say, He suffered that there should be represented, in Himself, the church in respect to its maltreatment of the Word.

vi. The imputation of His merit is not anything at all unless thereby is meant the forgiveness of sins after repentance.

These things are contained in this little work. In those which follow it, which are to be *Doctrine of the Sacred Scripture, Doctrine of Life, Doctrine of Faith, and Divine Love and Wisdom,* still other new things will be seen.

THE DOCTRINE OF THE SACRED SCRIPTURE

THE NEW JERUSALEM

I.

THE SACRED SCRIPTURE OR THE WORD IS DIVINE TRUTH ITSELF.

1. It is in everybody's mouth that the Word is from God, is divinely inspired, and is therefore holy; and yet hitherto no one has known wherein it is divine. For in the letter the Word appears like a common writing, in a style that is strange, and neither so sublime nor so brilliant as apparently are the writings of the day. For this reason a man who worships nature as God, or in preference to God, and who consequently thinks from himself and what is his own, and not from the Lord through heaven, may easily fall into error in regard to the Word, and into contempt for it, and while reading it may say to himself, What is this? What is that? Can this be divine? Could God, whose wisdom is infinite, speak like this? What does its holiness consist in and where does it come from, except from religious feeling and its persuasiveness?

2. But one who thinks in this way does not consider that Jehovah Himself, the God of heaven and earth, spoke the Word through Moses and the prophets, and that it must therefore be divine truth itself, for what Jehovah Himself speaks can be nothing else. Nor does he consider that the Lord, who is the same as Jehovah, spoke the Word that is in the Gospels, much of it with His own mouth, and the rest from the spirit of His mouth, which is the Holy Spirit. This is why, as He Himself says, there is life in His words, that He is the light which enlightens, and that He is the truth.

[2] That the words which the Lord Himself spoke in the Gospels are life, is declared in John:

The words that I speak unto you, they are spirit, and they are life (6:63).

Jesus said to the woman at Jacob's well, If thou knewest the gift of God, and who it is that saith to thee, Give Me to drink, thou wouldst have asked of Him, and He would have given thee living water. Whosoever drinketh of the water that I shall give him shall never thirst; but the water that I shall give him shall be in him a well of water springing up into eternal life (4:6, 10, 14).

"Jacob's well" signifies the Word, as also in Dt 33:28. This is why the Lord sat there and conversed with the woman. And "water" signifies the truth that is in the Word.

[3] Again in John:

If any man thirst, let him come unto Me, and drink. He that believeth in Me, as the Scripture hath said, out of his belly shall flow rivers of living water (7:37, 38).

Peter said unto Jesus, Thou hast the words of eternal life (6:68).

And therefore the Lord says in Mark:

Heaven and earth shall pass away; but My words shall not pass away (13:31).

The reason the Lord's words are "life," is that He Himself is the "life" and the "truth," as He teaches in John:

I am the way, the truth, and the life (14:6).

In the beginning was the Word, and the Word was with God, and God was the Word; in Him was life; and the life was the light of men (1:1, 4).

"The Word" here means the Lord as to divine truth, in which alone there is life and there is light.

[4] It is on this account that the Word, which is from the Lord and which is the Lord, is called

A fountain of living waters (Je 2:13; 17:13; 31:9):
A fountain of salvation (Isa 12:3):
A fountain (Zech 13:1):
A river of the water of life (Apoc 21:1).

And it is said that

The Lamb that is in the midst of the throne shall feed them, and shall lead them unto living fountains of waters (7:17).

There are other passages where the Word is called the "sanctuary" and the "tabernacle" in which the Lord dwells with man.

3. But the natural man cannot be persuaded by these considerations to believe that the Word is divine truth itself wherein are divine wisdom and divine life; for he judges it by its style, and in this they do not appear. Yet the style of the Word is the divine style itself, with which no other style, however sublime and excellent it may seem, is at all to be compared; for every other style is as darkness is to light. The style of the Word is such that there is holiness in every sentence, and in every word, and in some places in even the very letters. This is why the Word conjoins man with the Lord, and opens heaven. From the Lord proceed two things: divine love, and divine wisdom (or, what is the same, divine good, and divine truth, for divine good is of His divine love, and divine truth is of His divine wisdom), and in its essence the Word is both of these; and as it conjoins man with the Lord, and opens heaven, it follows that the man who reads it from the Lord, and not from himself alone, is filled by it with the good of love and the truths of wisdom; his will with the good of love, and his understanding with the truths of wisdom. In this way man has life by means of the Word.

4. Therefore in order to remove all doubt as to such

being the character of the Word, the Lord has revealed to me the Word's internal sense. In its essence this sense is spiritual, and in relation to the external sense, which is natural, is as soul to body. This sense is the spirit which gives life to the letter; it can therefore bear witness to the divinity and holiness of the Word, and convince even the natural man, if he is willing to be convinced.

II.

This subject shall be considered in the following order:

i. What the spiritual sense is.

ii. This sense is everywhere in the Word and in every detail of it.

iii. It is from this sense that the Word is divinely inspired, and is holy in every word.

iv. Hitherto this sense has been unknown.

v. Henceforth it will be imparted only to him who from the Lord is in genuine truths.

5. i. *What the spiritual sense is.* The spiritual sense of the Word is not that meaning which shines forth from the sense of the letter while one is studying and unfolding the Word with intent to confirm some tenet of the church. This is the literal sense of the Word. The spiritual sense does not appear in the sense of the letter, being within it as the soul in the body, as thought in the eyes, and as affection in the face, which act as a one, like cause and effect. It is this sense chiefly which renders the Word spiritual, not for men only, but for angels also; and therefore by means of this sense the Word gives communication with the heavens.

6. From the Lord proceed the CELESTIAL, the SPIRITUAL, and the NATURAL, one after another. That is called the CELESTIAL which proceeds from His divine love, and is divine good; that is called the SPIRITUAL which proceeds from His divine wisdom, and is divine truth; the NATURAL is from both, being their complex in the outmost. The angels of the Lord's celestial kingdom, of whom is composed the third or highest heaven, are in that divine which proceeds from the Lord that is called the celestial, for they are in the good of love from the Lord. The angels of the

Lord's spiritual kingdom, of whom is composed the second or middle heaven, are in that divine which proceeds from the Lord that is called the spiritual, for they are in truths of wisdom from the Lord. But the men of the church on earth are in the divine natural, which also proceeds from the Lord. From this it follows that the divine in proceeding from the Lord to its ultimates descends through three degrees, and is named the celestial, the spiritual, and the natural. The divine which comes down from the Lord to men descends through these three degrees; and when it has come down, it holds these three degrees contained within it. Such is everything divine, so that when it is in its lowest or outermost degree it is in its fullness. Such is the Word: in its outmost sense it is natural, in its interior sense it is spiritual, and in its inmost sense it is celestial ; and in each sense it is divine. That such is the nature of the Word does not appear in the letter, which is natural, for the reason that hitherto the man of this world has known nothing about the heavens; and consequently has not known what the spiritual is, nor what the celestial is, nor therefore the distinction between them and the natural.

7. The distinction between these degrees cannot be known unless correspondence is known. For these three degrees are altogether distinct from each other, like end, cause, and effect, or like prior, posterior, and postreme; yet they make one by correspondences, for the natural corresponds to the spiritual, and also to the celestial. What correspondence is may be seen in the work *Heaven and Hell,* where the subject of the correspondence of all things of heaven with all things of man has been treated of (nn. 87-102); and also the correspondence of heaven with all things of the earth (nn. 103-115). The same will further appear below, from examples drawn from the Word.

8. As therefore the Word interiorly is spiritual and celestial, it is written exclusively by correspondences. And what is thus written is in its lowermost sense written in a style like that of the Prophets and Evangelists, which, although it may appear common, yet conceals within it divine and all angelic wisdom.

9. ii. *The spiritual sense is everywhere in the Word, and in every single particular of it.* This cannot be better seen than by examples, such as the following. John says in the Apocalypse:

I saw heaven opened, and behold a white horse, and He that sat upon him was called Faithful and True, and in righteousness He doth judge and make war. His eyes were as a flame of fire, and on His head were many crowns, and He had a name written that no man knew but He Himself, and He was clothed with a vesture dipped in blood, and His name is called THE WORD OF GOD. And His armies in heaven followed Him upon white horses, clothed in fine linen, white and clean. And He hath on His vesture and on His thigh a name written, KING OF KINGS AND LORD OF LORDS. And I saw an angel standing in the sun, and he cried with a loud voice, Come and gather yourselves together to the great supper, that ye may eat the flesh of kings, and the flesh of captains, and the flesh of mighty men, and the flesh of horses, and of them that sit on them, and the flesh of all men, both free and bond, and small and great (19:11-18).

What these things signify cannot be known except from the spiritual sense of the Word, and no one can know the spiritual sense except from a knowledge of correspondences, for all the above words are correspondences, and not one word there is without meaning. The knowledge of correspondences teaches what is signified by the white horse, by Him who sat thereon, by His eyes that were as a flame of fire, by the crowns that were upon His head, by His vesture dipped in blood, by the white linen in which they were clothed who were of His army in heaven, by the angel standing in the sun, by the great supper to which they should come and congregate, and by the flesh of kings, and captains, and others, which they should eat. The significa- tion of each of these things in the spiritual sense may be

seen in the little work *The White Horse*, where they are
explained, so that it is unnecessary to explain them further
here. In that little work it has been shown that the Lord
as the Word is here described; and that by His eyes which
were as a flame of fire, and by the crowns that were upon
His head, and by the name that no one knew but He Himself, is meant the spiritual sense of the Word, which no
one can know but the Lord Himself and he to whom He
wills to reveal it; and also that by His vesture dipped in
blood is meant the natural sense of the Word, or the sense
of its letter, to which violence has been done. That it is
the Word which is thus described is very evident, for it is
said "His name is called the Word of God;" and that it is
the Lord who is meant is equally clear, for it is said that
the name of Him who sat on the white horse was written,
King of kings and Lord of lords. At the end of the church
the spiritual sense of the Word is to be opened, as is signified not only by what is said of the white horse and of
Him who sat thereon, but also by the great supper to which
the angel standing in the sun invited all to come, and to eat
the flesh of kings and of captains, of mighty men, of horses,
and of them that sat on them, and of all both free and bond.
All these expressions would be empty words and devoid
of spirit and life, unless there were what is spiritual within
them, like soul in body.

10. In the Apocalypse chapter 21, the Holy Jerusalem is
thus described:

That there was a light in her like unto a stone most precious, as
it were a jasper stone, clear as crystal; that she had a wall great
and high, having twelve gates, and over the gates twelve angels, and
the names written thereon of the twelve tribes of the sons of Israel;
that the wall was a hundred and forty-four cubits, which is the
measure of a man, that is, of an angel; and that the structure of the
wall was of jasper, and its foundations of every precious stone, of
jasper, sapphire, chalcedony, emerald, sardonyx, sardius, chrysolite,
beryl, topaz, chrysoprase, jacinth, and amethyst; that the twelve
gates were twelve pearls; that the city itself was pure gold, like unto

pure glass; and that it was four-square; and that the length, the breadth, and the height thereof were equal, twelve thousand furlongs; with many other particulars.

All these things are to be understood spiritually, as is evident from the fact that by the Holy Jerusalem is meant a new church which is to be set up by the Lord. This has been shown in *Doctrine of the Lord* (nn. 62-65). And as the church is here signified by Jerusalem, it follows that everything said of it as a city—about its gates, its wall, the foundations of its wall, and their measures—contains a spiritual sense; for things that concern the church are spiritual. But what the different things signifiy has been explained in the work *The New Jerusalem and its Heavenly Doctrines,* published in London in the year 1758 (n. 1). I therefore refrain from a further explanation of them here. It is enough to know from that source that there is a spiritual sense in each particular of the description, like a soul in its body; and that without this sense nothing of the church would be understood in the things there written; such as that the city was of pure gold; that its gates were of pearls; its wall of jasper; the foundations of its wall of precious stones; that its wall was of a hundred and forty-four cubits, which is the measure of a man, that is, of an angel; and that the city itself was twelve thousand furlongs in length, breadth, and height; and so on. But whoever, from a knowledge of correspondences, has come to know the spiritual sense, will understand these particulars; as that the wall and its foundations signify doctrine from the literal sense of the Word; and that the numbers twelve, one hundred and forty-four, and twelve thousand, signify like things, namely, all the truths and goods of the church in one complex.

11. In the Apocalypse, chapter 7, it is said:

That there were sealed one hundred and forty-four thousand—twelve thousand of each tribe of Israel—of the tribe of Judah, of the tribe of Reuben, of Gad, of Asher, of Naphtali, of Manasseh, of Simeon, of Levi, of Issachar, of Zebulon, of Joseph, and of Benjamin.

The spiritual sense of these words is that all are saved in whom the church is from the Lord; for, in the spiritual sense, to be sealed on the forehead, or to be sealed, signifies to be acknowledged by the Lord and saved. The twelve tribes of Israel signify all of that church; twelve, twelve thousand, and a hundred and forty-four thousand, signify all; Israel signifies the church; and each tribe some specific thing pertaining to it. He who does not know this spiritual meaning may imagine that only this precise number are to be saved, and they solely from the Israelitish and Jewish nation.

12. In the Apocalypse, chapter 6, it is said:

That when the Lamb opened the first seal of the book, there went forth a white horse, and that He who sat thereon had a bow, and to Him was given a crown; that when He opened the second seal there went forth a red horse, and that to him who sat thereon was given a great sword; that when He opened the third seal there went forth a black horse, and that he who sat thereon had a pair of balances in his hand; and that when He opened the fourth seal there went forth a pale horse, and that the name of him who sat thereon was Death.

What these things mean can be unfolded solely by means of the spiritual sense; and it is completely unfolded when it is known what is signified by the opening of the seals, by a horse, and by the other things mentioned. By them are described the successive states of the church, from its beginning to its end, as to its understanding of the Word. The "opening of the seals of the book by the Lamb" signifies the manifestation by the Lord of those states of the church. A "horse" means the understanding of the Word; the "white horse," the understanding of truth from the Word in the first state of the church; the "bow" of him who sat upon that horse, the doctrine of charity and faith fighting against falsities; the "crown," eternal life the prize of victory. The "red horse" signifies the understanding of the Word destroyed in respect to good, in the second state of the church; the "great sword," falsity fighting against truth. The "black horse" means the understanding of the Word destroyed as to truth, in the third state of the church; the "pair of balances," the estimation of truth so small that there was scarcely any. The "pale horse" means the understanding of the Word annihilated by evils of life and the derivative falsities, in the fourth or last state of the church; and "Death" signifies eternal condemnation. It is not apparent in the literal or natural sense that such is the meaning of these things in the spiritual sense, so that unless the spiritual sense were at some time opened, the Word as to this and everything else in the Apocalypse would be so completely closed that at last no one would know wherein its divine holiness lies. It is equally so in regard to what is signified by the "four horses" and the "four chariots" that came forth from between two mountains of brass (Zech 6:1-8).

13. In the Apocalypse, chapter 9, we read:

The fifth angel sounded, and I saw a star fall from heaven unto the earth, and to him was given the key of the bottomless pit; and he opened the bottomless pit, and there went up a smoke out of the pit as the smoke of a great furnace; and the sun and the air were darkened by reason of the smoke of the pit; and there came out of the smoke locusts upon the earth, and unto them was given power as the scorpions of the earth have power. . . . The shapes of the locusts were like unto horses prepared for war, and on their heads were as it were crowns like gold; and their faces were as the faces of men; and they had hair as the hair of women; and their teeth were as the teeth of lions; and they had breastplates as of iron; and the sound of their wings was as the sound of chariots, of many horses running to war; and they had tails like scorpions; and there were stings in their tails; and their power was to hurt men five months. And they had a king over them, the angel of the bottomless pit, whose name in the Hebrew is Abaddon, but in the Greek he hath the name Apollyon (verses 1-3, 7-11).

These things could not be understood by any one unless the spiritual sense were revealed to him; for nothing here is said idly, but every single thing has its meaning. The subject here treated of is the state of the church when all knowledges of truth from the Word have been destroyed, and consequently man, having become sensuous, persuades himself that falsities are truths.

[2] The "star fallen from heaven," signifies the knowledges of truth destroyed; the "sun and air darkened," means the light of truth become thick darkness; the "locusts that came out of the smoke of the pit," signify falsities in the outermost things such as exist with those who have become sensuous, and who see and judge all things from fallacies; a "scorpion" means their persuasiveness. That the locusts appeared "like horses prepared for war," means their reasonings as it were from the understanding of truth; the locusts' having "crowns like gold upon their heads, and faces as the faces of men," means that they appeared to themselves as conquerors, and as wise; their having "hair as the hair of women," signifies that they appeared to themselves as if they were in the affection of truth; their having "teeth as the teeth of lions," means that sensuous things, which are the lowest things of the natural man, appeared to them as having power over all things.

[3] Their having "breastplates as breastplates of iron," means argumentations from fallacies by which they fight and prevail; that "the sound of their wings was as the sound of chariots running to war," signifies reasonings as if from the truths of doctrine from the Word for which they were to fight; their having "tails like scorpions," means persuasions; their having "stings in their tails," signifies their cunning arts of deceiving thereby; their having "power to hurt men five months," signifies that they induce a kind of stupor on those who are in the understanding of truth and perception of good; their having "a king over

them, the angel of the bottomless pit, whose name is Abaddon or Apollyon," signifies that their falsities were from hell, where dwell those who are merely natural and in self-intelligence.

[4] This is the spiritual sense of these words, of which nothing appears in the sense of the letter. Everywhere in the Apocalypse it is the same. In the spiritual sense all things hang together in a continuous connection, which is fitted together in such a manner by the force and meaning of all the words in the literal or natural sense, that if even a little word were taken out of it, the connection would be broken and the coherence lost. In order to prevent this, it is added at the end of this prophetical book, that not a word shall be taken away (chapter 22:19).

It is the same with the books of the prophets of the Old Testament: in order to prevent anything from being taken away from them, it came to pass of the Lord's divine providence that everything therein down to the very letters was counted. This was done by the Masorites.

14. In speaking to His disciples about the consummation of the age (which is the last time of the church), at the end of His predictions concerning the successive changes of state in the church, the Lord says,

Immediately after the affliction of those days shall the sun be darkened, and the moon shall not give her light, and the stars shall fall from heaven, and the powers of the heavens shall be shaken. And then shall appear the sign of the Son of man in heaven, and then shall all the tribes of the earth wail, and they shall see the Son of man coming in the clouds of heaven with power and much glory. And He shall send His angels with a trumpet and a great voice, and they shall gather together His elect from the four winds, from the end of the heavens even to the end of them (Mt 24:29-31).

[2] By these words, in the spiritual sense, is not meant that the sun and moon [of our earth] would be darkened, that the stars would fall from heaven, that the Lord's sign would appear in heaven, and that He would be seen in the

clouds together with angels with trumpets; but by every word is meant some spiritual thing pertaining to the church, concerning the state of which at its end these things were spoken. For, in the spiritual sense, the "sun, which shall be darkened," means the Lord as to love; the "moon, which shall not give her light," means the Lord as to faith; the "stars, which shall fall from heaven," mean the knowledges of what is good and true that would perish; the "sign of the Son of man in heaven," means the appearing of divine truth; the "tribes of the earth, which shall wail," means the lack of all truth that is of faith, and of all good that is of love; the "coming of the Son of man in the clouds of heaven with power and glory," means the Lord's presence in the Word, and revelation; "clouds" signify the sense of the letter of the Word, and "glory," the spiritual sense of the Word; the "angels with a trumpet and a great voice," signifies heaven whence comes divine truth; to "gather together the elect from the four winds, from the end of the heavens even to the end of them," signifies a newness of the church in respect to love and faith.

[3] A darkening of [our natural] sun and moon is not meant nor a falling of the stars to the earth, as is very evident from the Prophets, in which like things are said about the state of the church when the Lord should come into the world. As in Isaiah:

Behold the day of Jehovah cometh, cruel, with wrath and fierce anger; the stars of the heavens, and the constellations thereof, shall not give their light, the sun shall be darkened in his rising, and the moon shall not cause her light to shine: I will visit upon the world its wickedness (13:9-11; 24:21, 23).

In Joel:

The day of Jehovah cometh, a day of darkness and of thick darkness; the sun and the moon shall be blackened, and the stars shall withdraw their shining (2:1, 2, 10; 3:15).

In Ezekiel:

> I will cover the heavens, and blacken the stars; I will cover the sun with a cloud, and the moon shall not cause her light to shine; all the bright lights of heaven will I make dark over thee, and will set darkness upon thy land (32:7, 8).

"The day of Jehovah" means the Lord's advent, which took place when there was no longer anything good and true left in the church, and not any knowledge of the Lord.

15. In order that it may be seen that without the spiritual sense the prophetical parts of the Word of the Old Testament are in many passages not intelligible, I will cite a few, such as the following in Isaiah:

> Then shall Jehovah of hosts stir up a scourge against Asshur, according to the smiting of Midian at the rock of Oreb, and his rod shall be over the sea, which he shall lift up in the manner of Egypt. And it shall come to pass in that day that his burden shall be taken away from off thy shoulder, and his yoke from off thy neck. He shall come against Aiath; he shall pass to Migron; against Michmash he shall command his arms; they shall pass over Mebara; Gebah shall be a lodging to us; Ramah shall tremble; Gibeah of Saul shall flee. Wail with thy voice O daughter of Gallim; hearken O Laish, O wretched Anathoth. Madmenah shall be a fugitive; the inhibitants of Gebim shall gather themselves together. Is there as yet a day to stand in Nob? the mountain of the daughter of Zion, the hill of Jerusalem, shall shake her hand. Jehovah shall cut off the thickets of the forest with iron, and Lebanon shall fall by a mighty one (10:26-32, 34).

Here we meet with mere names, from which nothing can be drawn except by the aid of the spiritual sense, in which all the names in the Word signify things of heaven and the church. From this sense it is gathered that these words signify that the whole church has been devastated by memory-knowledges perverting all truth, and confirming falsity.

[2] In another place in the same Prophet:

> In that day the envy of Ephraim shall depart, and the enemies of Judah shall be cut off; Ephraim shall not envy Judah, and Judah shall not vex Ephraim; but they shall fly upon the shoulder of the

Philistines toward the sea, together shall they spoil the sons of the east; upon Edom and Moab shall they put forth their hand. Jehovah shall utter a curse against the tongue of the Egyptian sea, and with the vehemence of His spirit He shall shake His hand over the river, and shall smite it into seven streams, so that He shall make a way [to pass over it] with dry shoes. Then shall there be a highway for the remnant of His people, which remnant shall be from Asshur (11:13-16).

Here also no one would see anything divine except one who knows what is signified by the several names; and yet the subject treated of is the Lord's advent, and what shall then come to pass, as in plainly evident from verses 1 to 10. Who, therefore, without the aid of the spiritual sense, would see that by these things in their order is signified that they who are in falsities from ignorance, yet have not suffered themselves to be led astray by evils, will come to the Lord, and that the church will then understand the Word; and that falsities will then no longer harm them.

[3] The case is the same where there are no names, as in Ezekiel:

Thus saith the Lord Jehovih, Son of man, say unto the bird of every wing, and to every wild beast of the field, Assemble yourselves and come, gather yourselves from round about to My sacrifice which I sacrifice for you, even a great sacrifice upon the mountains of Israel, that ye may eat flesh and drink blood; ye shall eat the flesh of the mighty, and drink the blood of the princes of the earth; ye shall eat fat to satiety, and drink blood to drunkenness, of My sacrifice which I have sacrificed for you. Ye shall be sated at My table with the horse and the chariot, with the mighty man, and with every man of war. Thus will I set My glory among the nations (39:17-21).

One who does not know from the spiritual sense what is signified by a sacrifice, by flesh and blood, by a horse, a chariot, a mighty man, and a man of war, would suppose that such things were to be eaten and drunk. But the spiritual sense teaches that to "eat the flesh and drink the blood of the sacrifice which the Lord Jehovih will offer upon the mountains of Israel," signifies to appropriate to one's self divine good and divine truth from the Word; for the subject treated of is the calling together of all to the Lord's kingdom, and, specifically, the setting up anew of the church by the Lord among the nations. Who cannot see that by "flesh" is not here meant flesh, nor blood by "blood"? As that people should drink blood to drunkenness, and that they should be sated with horse, chariot, mighty man, and every man of war. So in a thousand other passages in the Prophets.

16. Without the spiritual sense no one would know why the prophet Jeremiah was commanded

to buy himself a girdle, and put it on his loins; and not to draw it through the waters, but to hide it in a hole of the rock by Euphrates (Je 13:1-7).

Or why the prophet Isaiah was commanded

to loose the sackcloth from off his loins, and put the shoe from off his foot, and go naked and barefoot three years (Isa 20:2, 3).

Or why the prophet Ezekiel was commanded

to pass a razor upon his head and upon his beard, and afterwards to divide the hairs, and burn a third part in the midst of the city, smite a third part with the sword, scatter a third part in the wind, and bind a few of them in his skirts, and at last throw them into the midst of the fire (5:1-4);

or why the same prophet was commanded

to lie upon his left side three hundred and ninety days, and upon his right side forty days, and to make himself a cake of wheat, and barley, and millet, and spelt, with the dung of an ox, and eat it; and in the meantime to raise a rampart and a mound against Jerusalem, and besiege it (4:1-15).

or why the prophet Hosea was twice commanded

to take himself a harlot to wife (Hosea 1:2-9; 3:2, 3);

and many like things. Moreover, without the spiritual sense who would know what is signified by all the things pertaining to the tabernacle, such as the ark, the mercy-seat, cherubim, lampstand, altar of incense, the bread of the Presence on the table, and its veils and curtains? Who without the spiritual sense would know what is meant by Aaron's garments of holiness, by his coat, cloak, ephod, urim and thummim, mitre, and other things? Who without the spiritual sense would know what is signified by all the things enjoined concerning the burnt-offerings, sacrifices, meat-offerings, and drink-offerings? and also concerning the sabbaths and feasts? The truth is that not the least thing was commanded concerning them that did not mean something of the Lord, heaven, and the church. From these few examples it may be clearly seen that there is a spiritual sense in all things of the Word and in every particular of it.

17. The Lord when in the world spoke by correspondences, thus spiritually while He spoke naturally. This is evident from His parables, in each and every word of which there is a spiritual sense. Take for example the parable of the ten virgins:

The kingdom of the heavens is like unto ten virgins, who took their lamps and went forth to meet the bridegroom: five of them were foolish, and five were wise; they that were foolish took their lamps, and took no oil, but the wise took oil in their lamps. While the bridegroom tarried they all slumbered and slept; and at midnight there was a cry made, Behold, the bridegroom cometh, go ye out to meet him. Then all those virgins awaked, and trimmed their lamps; and the foolish said unto the wise, Give us of your oil, for our lamps are gone out; but the wise answered, saying, Not so, lest there be not enough for us and you; but go ye rather to them that sell, and buy for yourselves. And while they went away to buy, the bridegroom came, and they that were ready went in with him to the wedding, and the door was shut. Afterwards came also the other virgins, saying, Lord, lord, open to us; but he answered and said, Verily I say unto you, I know you not (Mt 25:1-12).

[2] There is a spiritual sense in each and every one of these things, and a consequent divine holiness; but this

can be seen only by him who knows that a spiritual sense exists, and what is its nature. In the spiritual sense, the "kingdom of God" means heaven and the church; the "bridegroom," the Lord; the "wedding," the marriage of the Lord with heaven and the church by means of the good of love and of faith. "Virgins" signify those who are of the church; "ten," all; "five," some; "lamps," the truths of faith; "oil," the good of love; to "sleep," and to "awake," the life of man in this world which is natural life, and his life after death which is spiritual; to "buy," to procure for themselves; to "go to them that sell and buy oil," to procure for themselves the good of love from others after death; and as this can then be no longer procured, although they came with their lamps and the oil they had bought to the door where the wedding was, yet the bridegroom said to them, "I know you not." The reason is that after his life in this world a man remains such as he had lived in this world.

[3] From all this it is evident that the Lord spoke exclusively by correspondences, and this because He spoke from the divine that was in Him, and was His. That the "bridegroom" signifies the Lord; the "kingdom of the heavens," the church; a "wedding," the marriage of the Lord with the church by means of the good of love and of faith; "ten," all; "five," some; to "sleep," a natural state; [to "awake," a spiritual state]; to "buy," to procure for one's self; a "door," entrance into heaven; and "not to know them," when spoken by the Lord, not to be in His love, is evident from many passages in the prophetic Word where these expressions have a like signification. It is because "virgins" signify those who are of the church that the virgin and daughter of Zion, of Jerusalem, of Judah, and of Israel, are so often mentioned in the prophetic Word. And it is because "oil" signifies the good of love that all the holy things of the Israelitish Church were anointed with oil. It is the same with all the other parables, and

with all the words the Lord spoke, and that were written in the Gospels. This is why the Lord says that

His words are spirit and are life (Jn 6:63).

[4] It is the same with all the Lord's miracles, which were divine because they signified the various states of those with whom the church was to be set up anew by the Lord. Thus when the blind received sight, it meant that they who had been in ignorance of truth should receive intelligence; when the deaf received hearing, it signified that they who had previously heard nothing about the Lord and the Word should hearken and obey; when the dead were raised, it signified that they who otherwise would spiritually perish would become living; and so on. This is meant by the Lord's reply to the disciples of John, who sent them to ask whether He was the One that should come:

Tell John the things which ye do hear and see: the blind receive their sight, and the lame walk, the lepers are cleansed, and the deaf hear, the dead rise again, and the poor hear the Gospel (Mt. 11:3-5).

Moreover, all the miracles related in the Word contain in them such things as belong to the Lord, to heaven, and to the church. This makes these miracles divine, and distinguishes them from those which are not divine. These few examples are given in order to illustrate what the spiritual sense is, and to show that it is in all things of the Word and in every particular of it.

18. iii. *It is from the spiritual sense that the Word is divinely inspired, and is holy in every word.* It is said in the church that the Word is holy, because Jehovah God spoke it; but as its holiness is not apparent from the letter alone, he who on this account once doubts its holiness, afterwards confirms his doubt when reading the Word by many things in it, for he then thinks, Can this be holy? Can this be divine? Therefore lest such a thought should flow in with many, and should afterwards prevail, and thereby the conjunction of the Lord with the church, in which is the Word, should perish, it has now pleased the Lord to reveal the spiritual sense, in order that it may be known where in the Word this holiness lies hid.

[2] This again may be illustrated by examples. The Word treats sometimes of Egypt, sometimes of Asshur, sometimes of Edom, of Moab, of the sons of Ammon, of Tyre and Sidon, of Gog; and one who does not know that these names signify things of heaven and the church may be led into the error that the Word treats much of nations and peoples, and but little of heaven and the church; thus much of earthly, and little of heavenly things. But when he knows what is signified by them, or by their names, he can come out of error into truth.

[3] And so when he sees in the Word such frequent mention of gardens, groves, and forests, and also of the trees in them, as the olive, vine, cedar, poplar, oak; and also such frequent mention of the lamb, sheep, goat, calf, ox; and likewise of mountains, hills, valleys, and the fountains, rivers, and waters in them, and many like things, one who knows nothing about the spiritual sense of the Word must believe that these things only are meant. For he is not aware that a garden, grove, and forest, mean wisdom, intelligence, and knowledge; that an olive, vine, cedar, poplar, and oak, mean the celestial, spiritual, rational, natural, and sensuous good and truth of the church; that a lamb, sheep, goat, calf, and ox, mean innocence, charity, and natural affection; that mountains, hills, and valleys, mean higher, lower, and lowest things of the church; that Egypt signifies memory-knowledge,* Asshur reason, Edom the natural, Moab the adulteration of good, the sons of Ammon the adulteration of truth, Tyre and Sidon the knowledges of truth and good, and Gog external worship without internal. But when a man knows these things he is able to

* See foot-note on p. 133

consider that the Word treats solely of heavenly things, and that these earthly things are merely the subjects in which the heavenly things are.

[4] But let this also be illustrated by an example from the Word. We read in the Psalms of David:

> The voice of Jehovah is upon the waters; the God of glory maketh it to thunder; Jehovah is upon the great waters. The voice of Jehovah breaketh the cedars; yea, Jehovah breaketh in pieces the cedars of Lebanon. He maketh them also to skip like a calf, Lebanon and Sirion like a son of unicorns. The voice of Jehovah cutteth out as a flame of fire. The voice of Jehovah maketh the wilderness to tremble; it maketh the wilderness of Kadesh to tremble. The voice of Jehovah maketh the hinds to be in travail, and layeth bare the forests; but in His temple every one saith, Glory (Ps 29:3-9).

He who is not aware that everything here, even as to every single word, is divinely holy, may, if a merely natural man, say to himself, What is this—that Jehovah sitteth upon the waters, that by His voice He breaketh the cedars, maketh them skip like a calf, and Lebanon like a son of unicorns, and maketh the hinds to be in travail, and so on? For he knows not that in the spiritual sense the power of divine truth, or of the Word, is described by these things.

[5] In this sense, the "voice of Jehovah," here called "thunder," means the divine truth or the Word in its power. The "great waters," upon which Jehovah sits, mean the truths of the Word. The "cedars," and "Lebanon," which He "breaks," and "breaks in pieces," mean the false things of the rational man. The "calf," and a "son of unicorns," signify the false things of the natural and of the sensuous man. The "flame of fire," means the affection of what is false. The "wilderness," and the "wilderness of Kadesh," mean the church in which there is not anything true and good. The "hinds" which the voice of Jehovah causes to be in travail, mean the nations who are in natural good. And the "forests" which He lays bare, mean the knowledges

(*scientiae et cognitiones*)* which the Word opens to them. Therefore these words follow: "In His temple every one saith, Glory," which mean that there are divine truths in each and every thing of the Word. For the "temple" signifies the Lord, and therefore the Word, and also heaven and the church; and "glory" signifies divine truth. From all this it is evident that there is not a word in this passage that is not descriptive of the divine power of the Word against falsities of every kind in natural men, and of the divine power in reforming the nations.

19. There is a still more interior sense in the Word which is called celestial, and of which something has been said above (n. 6); but this sense can not easily be made plain, because it does not fall so much into the thought of the understanding as into the affection of the will. The reason there is in the Word this still more interior sense called celestial, is that there proceeds from the Lord divine good and divine truth, divine good from His divine love, and divine truth from His divine wisdom; and both are in the Word, for the Word is the Divine proceeding;** and it is for this reason that the Word gives life to those who devoutly read it. But this subject will be spoken of in the chapter in which it will be shown that there is a marriage of the Lord and the church, and a derivative marriage of good and truth, in each and every thing of the Word.

20. iv. *Heretofore the spiritual sense of the Word has been unknown.* It has been shown in the work on *Heaven and Hell* (nn. 87-105) that all the things of nature, and likewise of the human body, and also every single particular

* Note the careful distinction made by Swedenborg between those knowledges that are merely in the external memory, and those which a man has some real knowledge of by experience or in some other way, and which are therefore not mere matters of memory. The former he calls "memory-knowledges (*scientiae or scientifica*);" the latter simply "knowledges (*cognitiones*)." This distinction runs all through these works, and must not be lost sight of, the recognition of it being vital to the understanding of important doctrines. [TR.]

** That is, the Divine in the act of proceeding. See foot-note to *Doctrine of the Lord,* n. 2 (page 2 [TR]).

in them, correspond to spiritual things. Hitherto, however, it has not been known what correspondence is, although in the most ancient times this was very well known; for the knowledge of correspondences was then the knowledge of knowledges, and was so wide-spread that all writings and books were composed by means of correspondences.

[2] The book of *Job*, which is an ancient book, is full of correspondences. The hieroglyphics of the Egyptians, and also the myths of the most ancient times, were nothing else. All the ancient churches were churches representative of heavenly things; their rites, and also the ordinances according to which their worship was instituted, consisted exclusively of correspondences. So did everything pertaining the church among the sons of Jacob; their burnt-offerings and sacrifices, with each and every thing thereto pertaining, were correspondences; so was the tabernacle with all its contents; so were their feasts, the feast of unleavened things, the feast of tabernacles, and the feast of first-fruits; so was the priesthood of Aaron and the Levites, and also the holy garments of Aaron and his sons; besides all the ordinances and judgments that concerned their worship and their life.

[3] As divine things present themselves in the world by correspondences, the Word has been written exclusively by means of them. Therefore the Lord spoke by correspondences, because He spoke from His Divine, for that which is from the Divine, descending into nature, is turned into such things as correspond to divine things, and which then store up and conceal in their bosom the divine things that are called celestial and spiritual.

21. I have been instructed that the men of the Most Ancient Church (the church before the flood) were of a genius so heavenly that they spoke with angels of heaven, and that they were able to speak with them by means of correspondences. For this the state of their wisdom was such that whatever they saw in this world they thought about not only in a natural way, but spiritually also at the same time, so that they thought unitedly with angels. I have been instructed besides that Enoch (of whom mention is made in Genesis 5:21-24) together with his associates, collected correspondences from the lips of those men [of the Most Ancient Church], and transmitted the knowledge of them to posterity, and that in consequence of this the knowledge of correspondences was not only possessed but was also much cultivated in many kingdoms of Asia, especially in the land of Canaan, in Egypt, Assyria, Chaldea, Syria, Arabia, and also in Tyre, Sidon, and Nineveh; and that this knowledge was carried over from places on the sea-coast there into Greece, where it was turned into myths, as is evident from the earliest writers of that country.

22. However, in process of time the representative things of the church, which were correspondences, were converted into things idolatrous and also into magic, and then of the Lord's divine providence the knowledge of correspondences was gradually blotted out of remembrance, and among the Israelitish and Jewish people was altogether lost and annihilated. The worship of that nation did indeed consist exclusively of correspondences, and was consequently representative of heavenly things; but still they did not know what anything of it signified, for they were utterly natural men, and therefore were neither willing nor able to know anything about spiritual things, nor consequently about correspondences.

23. The reason why, in ancient times, the idolatries of the nations originated from the knowledge of correspondences, was that all things visible on the earth have a correspondence; not only trees, but also beasts and birds of every kind, and likewise fishes, and all other things. The ancients, possessing a knowledge of correspondences, made

for themselves images that corresponded to heavenly things, and delighted in them because they signified such things as belong to heaven, and therefore to the church. They therefore set them not only in their temples, but also in their houses, not to be worshiped, but to call to remembrance the heavenly things they signified. Consequently in Egypt and elsewhere there were images of calves, oxen, serpents, also of children, old men, maidens; because calves and oxen signified affections and powers of the natural man; serpents, the sagacity of the sensuous man; children, innocence and charity; old men, wisdom; and maidens, affections of truth; and so on. When the knowledge of correspondences had been blotted out of remembrance, their descendants began to worship as holy, and at last as deities, the images and emblems set up by the ancients, because they stood in and about their temples.

[2] It was so too with other nations; as, with the Philistines at Ashdod, the image of Dagon (concerning whom see 1 Sa 5:1 to end), whose upper part was like a man, and his lower like a fish, was so devised because a man signifies intelligence, and a fish knowledge, which make a one. It was also because they possessed a knowledge of correspondences that the ancients worshiped in gardens and groves, in accordance with the kinds of trees in them; and also upon mountains and hills. For gardens and groves signified wisdom and intelligence, and each particular tree something relating thereto; as the olive, the good of love; the vine, truth from that good; the cedar, rational good and truth. A mountain signified the highest heaven; and a hill, the heaven under it.

[3] The knowledge of correspondences survived among a number of the orientals, even until the Lord's advent, as is evident from the wise men of the east who came to the Lord at His birth; and this was why a star went before them, and why they brought with them as gifts, gold,

frankincense, and myrrh (Mt 2:1, 2, 9-11). For the "star that went before them" signified knowledge from heaven; "gold," celestial good; "frankincense," spiritual good; and "myrrh," natural good; from which three is all worship.

[4] Nevertheless there was no knowledge of correspondences whatever among the Israelitish and Jewish nation, although everything in their worship, and all the judgments and ordinances delivered them through Moses, and everything in the Word, were nothing but correspondences. The reason was that at heart they were idolaters, and of such a character that they were not even willing to know that anything of their worship signified what is celestial and spiritual; for they desired that all those things should be holy in themselves and in connection with *them;* so that if celestial and spiritual things had been disclosed to them, they would not only have rejected but would have profaned them. Therefore heaven was so closed toward them that they scarcely knew that there is a life eternal. This is clearly evident from the fact that they did not acknowledge the Lord, although all holy Scripture prophesied concerning Him, and foretold His advent; and they rejected Him for this sole reason—that He taught of a heavenly and not an earthly kingdom; for they wanted a Messiah who would exalt them above every other nation in the world, and not a Messiah who cared for their eternal salvation. For the rest, they affirm that the Word contains within it many arcana that are called mystical; but are unwilling to learn that these refer to the Lord; they however are quite willing to learn when it is said that the reference is to gold.

24. The reason why the knowledge of correspondences, which gives the spiritual sense of the Word, was not disclosed after those times, is that the Christians of the primitive church were so very simple that it could not be disclosed to them; for it would have been of no use to them, nor would it have been understood. After their day, because of the papal dominion, darkness came over all the Christian world; and they who are of that dominion, and have confirmed themselves in its falsities, neither can nor will apprehend anything spiritual, nor consequently the correspondence in the Word of natural things with spiritual. For thereby they would be convinced that by "Peter" is not meant Peter, but the Lord as a Rock; and they would also be convinced that the Word is divine even to its inmosts, and that a decree of the Pope is relatively of no account. On the other hand, after the Reformation, as men began to effect a separation between faith and charity, and to worship God in three persons—thus three gods, whom they conceived to be one—heavenly truths were hidden from them; and if they had been disclosed they would have falsified them and applied them to faith alone, and not one of them to charity and love. And thus they would have closed heaven against themselves.

25. The reason why the spiritual sense of the Word has been at this day disclosed by the Lord is that the doctrine of genuine truth has now been revealed; and this doctrine, and no other, is in accord with the spiritual sense of the Word. This sense, moreover, is signified by the appearing of the Lord in the clouds of heaven with glory and power (Mt 24:30, 31); which chapter treats of the consummation of the age, by which is meant the last time of the church. The opening of the Word as to its spiritual sense was also promised in the Apocalypse. It is there meant by the "white horse," and by the "great supper" to which all are invited (19:11-18). For a long time the spiritual sense will not be recognized, and this is owing entirely to those who are in falsities of doctrine, especially concerning the Lord, and who therefore do not admit truths. This is meant in the Apocalypse by the "beast," and by the "kings of the earth," who should make war with him that sat upon the white horse (19:19). By the "beast" are meant the Papists,

as in chapter 17:3; and by the "kings of the earth" are meant the Reformed who are in false things of doctrine.

26. v. *Henceforth the spiritual sense of the Word will be imparted only to him who from the Lord is in genuine truths.* The reason for this is that no one can see the spiritual sense except from the Lord alone, nor unless from Him he is in genuine truths. For the spiritual sense of the Word treats solely of the Lord and His kingdom; and this is the sense in which are His angels in heaven, for it is His divine truth there. To this sense a man can do violence if he has a knowledge of correspondences, and wishes by means of it and from self-intelligence to investigate the spiritual sense of the Word. For through some correspondences with which he is acquainted he could pervert the meaning of it, and even force it to confirm what is false, and this would be doing violence to divine truth, and also to heaven. And therefore if any one purposes to open that sense from himself and not from the Lord, heaven is closed; and then the man either sees nothing, or else becomes spiritually insane.

[2] Another reason is that the Lord teaches every one by means of the Word, and He teaches from those truths which the man already has, and not without a medium does He pour new truths in, so that unless man is in divine truths, or if he is only in a few truths and at the same time in falsities, he may from these falsify the truths, as it is well known is done by every heretic in regard to the Word's sense of the letter. Therefore in order to prevent anybody from entering into the spiritual sense of the Word, or from perverting the genuine truth that belongs to that sense, guards have been set by the Lord, which in the Word are meant by the cherubim.

[3] That guards have been set has been represented to me in the following manner:

It was granted me to see great purses, having the appearance of sacks, in which silver was stored up in great abundance. As the purses were open, it seemed as if any one might take out, and even pillage, the silver therein deposited; but near those purses sat two angels as guards. The place where the purses were laid appeared like a manger in a stable. In an adjoining apartment were seen modest maidens together with a chaste wife, and near the apartment stood two little children, and it was said that they might be played with, not in childish fashion, but wisely. After this there appeared a harlot, and also a horse lying dead.

[4] On seeing these things I was instructed that by them was represented the sense of the letter of the Word, in which is the spiritual sense. The large purses full of silver, signified knowledges of truth in great abundance. Their being open and yet guarded by angels, signified that every one may get knowledges of truth from the Word, but that care is taken lest any one should falsify the spiritual sense, in which are pure truths. The manger in a stable in which the purses lay, signified spiritual instruction for the understanding—a manger signifies this because the horse that feeds from it signifies the understanding. [5] The modest maidens seen in the adjoining apartment, signified affections of truth; and the chaste wife, the conjunction of good and truth. The little children signified the innocence of wisdom therein: they were angels from the third heaven, who all appear like little children. The harlot, together with the dead horse, signified the falsification of the Word by many at this day, whereby all understanding of truth perishes. The harlot signified falsification; and the dead horse, no understanding of truth.

III.

THE SENSE OF THE LETTER OF THE WORD IS THE BASIS, THE CONTAINANT, AND THE SUPPORT OF ITS SPIRITUAL AND CELESTIAL SENSES.

27. In every divine work there is a first, a middle, and a last; and the first passes through the middle to the last, and so comes into manifest being and subsists. Hence the last is the *basis*. But the first is in the middle, and through the middle in the last; so the last is the *containant*. And as the last is the containant and the basis, it is also the *support*.

28. The learned reader will comprehend that these three may be called end, cause, and effect; also *esse, fieri,* and *existere;*[*] and that the end is the *esse,* the cause the *fieri,* and the effect the *existere*. Consequently, in every complete thing there is a trine, which is called first, middle, and last; also end, cause, and effect; and also *esse, fieri,* and *existere*. When these things are comprehended, it is also comprehended that every divine work is complete and perfect in its last; and likewise that the whole is in the last, which is a trine, because the prior things are *together,* or simultaneously, in it.[**]

29. It is from this that by "three," in the Word, in the spiritual sense, is meant what is complete and perfect; and

---

[*] That is, *being, becoming,* and *coming forth*. The *being* of a thing is what we call its existence; and therefore it was said by the ancients that "in God we live, and move, and have our being" (Acts 17:28). Here our being means the inmost of our life (*Arcana Coelestia,* 5605e). The *becoming* of a thing is its being taking form. And the *coming forth* of a thing is the presentation or manifestation of that thing as an actual reality. Thus the Latin word *existere* has a very different meaning from the English *exist,* and cannot be translated by it without causing a complete misconception in the mind of the English reader. [TR.]

[**] That is, the two prior degrees are in the ultimate degree in simultaneous order; for a full explanation of which see below at n. 38, and also in *Divine Love and Wisdom* (nn. 205-207). [TR.]

also the whole simultaneously. And as this is the meaning of the number three, it is employed in the Word whenever any such thing is marked out for notice. As in the following passages:

Isaiah went naked and barefoot three years (Isa 20:3).

Jehovah called Samuel three times, and Samuel ran three times to Eli, and Eli understood him the third time (1 Sa. 3:1-8).

David said to Jonathan that he would hide himself in the field three days; and Jonathan afterwards shot three arrows at the side of the stone; and after that, David bowed himself down three times before Jonathan (1 20:5, 12-41).

Elijah stretched himself three times over the widow's son (1 Kgs 17:21.)

Elijah commanded that they should pour water on the burnt-offering three times (18:34).

Jesus said, The kingdom of the heavens is like unto leaven, which a woman took and hid in three measures of meal, till the whole was leavened (Mt 13:33).

Jesus said unto Peter that he should deny Him thrice (26:34).

The Lord said three times unto Peter, Lovest thou Me? (Jn 21:15-17).

Jonah was in the whale's belly three days and three nights (Jonah 1:17).

Jesus said, Destroy this temple, and in three days I will raise it up (Jn 2:19; Mt 26:61).

Jesus prayed three times in Gethsemane (verses 39-44).

Jesus rose again on the third day (28:1).

There are many other passages where the number "three" is mentioned; and it is mentioned wherever a finished and perfect work is treated of, because this is signified by that number.

30. These things are introduced with a view to those which follow, in order that they may be comprehended with understanding; and for the present purpose that it may be comprehended that the natural sense of the Word, or the sense of the letter, is the basis, the containant, and the support of its spiritual sense and of its celestial sense.

31. It has been said above (nn. 6, 19) that there are

three senses in the Word; and also that the celestial sense is its first, the spiritual sense its middle, and the natural sense its lowermost sense. From this the rational man may infer that the first of the Word, which is celestial, passes through its middle, which is spiritual, to its last, which is natural; and thus that its last is the *basis*. Furthermore that the first of the Word which is celestial, is within its middle which is spiritual, and through this in its last which is natural, and that consequently its last or literal sense is the *containant*. And as the literal sense is the basis and the containant, it is also the *support*.

32. How these things come to pass cannot be told in a few words. Indeed they are arcana in which the angels of heaven are, and which will be unfolded, so far as can possibly be done, in other treatises. For the present it is sufficient to conclude from what has been said above, that the Word—which in a special sense is a divine work for the salvation of mankind—as to its outermost sense which is natural and is called the sense of the letter, is the basis, the containant, and the support of the two interior senses.

33. From all this it follows that without the sense of the letter, the Word would be like a palace without a foundation, and thus like a palace in the air and not on the earth, which would be but the mirage of a palace, that would vanish away. Furthermore, without the sense of the letter the Word would be like a temple containing many holy things, and in its midst a sanctuary, but without roof and walls, which are its containants, and in the absence or loss of which its holy things would be plundered by thieves, or invaded by beasts of earth and birds of heaven, and thus be dispersed. Or it would be like the tabernacle (in the inmost of which was the ark of the covenant, and in its middle the golden lampstand, the golden altar for incense, and the table on which were the loaves of the shew (show)-bread, or bread of the Presence, which were its holy things)

without its externals, which were the curtains and veils. Nay, without the sense of the letter, the Word would be like a human body without its covering which is called skin, and without its supports which are called bones; lacking which supports and covering all the interior things of the body would fall apart; and it would be like the heart and lungs in the chest without their covering which is called the pleura, and their supports which are called the ribs; or like the brain without its covering which is called the dura mater, and without its general covering, containant, and support, which is called the skull. Such would be the Word without the sense of the letter; and therefore it is said in Isaiah:

Jehovah createth upon all the glory a covering (4:5).

34. So would it be with the heavens where angels are, without the world where men are. The human race is the basis, containant, and support of the heavens; and the Word is among men and in them. For all the heavens have been distinguished into two kingdoms, called the celestial kingdom and the spiritual kingdom; these two kingdoms are founded upon a natural kingdom, in which are men. And so is it therefore with the Word which is among men and within men. (That the angelic heavens have been distinguished into two kingdoms, the celestial, and the spiritual, may be seen in the work on *Heaven and Hell,* nn. 20-28).

35. It has been shown in the *Doctrine of the Lord* (n. 28), that the prophets of the Old Testament represented the Lord as to the Word, and thereby signified the doctrine of the church from the Word, and that for this reason they were called "sons of man." From this it follows that by means of the various things they suffered and endured, they represented the violence done by the Jews to the sense of the letter of the Word. Thus the prophet Isaiah was commanded to put off the sackcloth from off his loins, and to put off his shoe from off his foot, and to go naked and barefoot three years (Isa 20:2, 3).

And so

the prophet Ezekiel was commanded to pass a barber's razor upon his head and upon his beard, and to burn a third part in the midst of the city, to smite a third part with the sword, and to scatter a third part in the wind, and to wrap a few of the hairs in his skirts, and at last to cast them into the midst of the fire and burn them (Ezek 5:1-4).

[2] As the "prophets" represented the Word, and consequently signified the doctrine of the church from the Word, as said above, and as the "head" signifies wisdom from the Word, therefore the "hair" and "beard" signify the outmost expression of truth. By reason of this signification, it was a mark of deep mourning, and also a great disgrace, for any one to make himself bald, or to be seen bald. For this and no other reason it was that the prophet shaved off the hair of his head and his beard, that so he might represent the state of the Jewish Church in respect to the Word. For this and no other reason was it that the forty-two children who called Elisha bald were torn to pieces by two she-bears (2 Kgs 2:23, 24).

As before said a "prophet" represented the Word, and "baldness" signified the Word without its ultimate sense.

[3] It will be seen in the next chapter (n. 49) that the "Nazirites" represented the Lord in respect to the Word in its letter; and therefore it was an ordinance for them that they should let their hair grow, and shave off none of it. Moreover the term "Nazirite" in the Hebrew tongue means the hair of the head. It was also an ordinance for the high priest that he should not shave his head (Lev 21:10); Likewise for the head of a household (verse 5).

[4] This was why baldness was to them a great disgrace, as is evident from the following passages:

On all heads baldness, and every beard shaven (Isa 15:2; Je 48:37).

Shame upon all faces, and baldness upon all heads (Ezek 7:18).

Every head made bald, and every shoulder plucked (29:18).

I will cause sackcloth to come up upon all loins, and baldness upon every head (Amos 8:10).

Put on baldness, and shave thee on account of the sons of thy delights, and enlarge thy baldness, for they are gone into exile from thee (Mic 1:16).

To "put on baldness" and to "enlarge" it, here signifies to falsify the truths of the Word in its letter, for when these are falsified (as was done by the Jews) the whole Word is destroyed; for the literal sense of the Word is its prop and support; indeed, each word is a prop and a support to its celestial and spiritual truths. As the "hair" signifies truth in the outmosts, in the spiritual world all who despise the Word, and falsify its sense of the letter, appear bald; whereas they who honor and love it appear with becoming hair. On this subject see also below (n. 49).

36. The Word in its lowermost or natural sense, which is the sense of the letter, is signified also by the wall of the holy Jerusalem, the structure of which was of jasper; and by the foundations of the wall, which were precious stones; and likewise by the gates, which were pearls (Apoc 21:18-21); for Jerusalem signifies the church as to doctrine. But of these things more in the following chapter. From what has been cited it is evident now that the letter of the Word, which is the natural sense, is the basis, containant, and support of its interior senses, which are the spiritual and the celestial.

IV.

DIVINE TRUTH IN THE SENSE OF THE LETTER OF THE WORD IS IN ITS FULLNESS, IN ITS HOLINESS, AND IN ITS POWER.

37. The reason why the Word in the sense of the letter is in its fullness, in its holiness, and in its power, is that the two prior or interior senses, which are called the spiritual and the celestial, are together or simultaneous in the natural sense, which is the sense of the letter, as was said above (n. 28). But how they are simultaneous in that sense shall now be told.

38. There are in heaven and in this world a successive order and a simultaneous order. In successive order one thing succeeds and follows another from highest to lowest; but in simultaneous order one thing is next to another from inmost to outmost. Successive order is like a column with successive parts next to each other from the top to the bottom; but simultaneous order is like a connected structure with successive circumferences from center to surface.

Successive order becomes simultaneous order in the outermost in this way: The highest things of successive order become the inmost ones of simultaneous order, and the lowest things of successive order become the outermost ones of simultaneous order. Comparatively speaking it is as if the column of successive parts were to sink down and become a connected body in a plane.

[2] Thus the simultaneous is formed from the successive in all things both in general and in particular of the natural world, and also of the spiritual world; for everywhere there is a first, a middle, and a last, and the first aims at and goes through the middle to its last. Apply this to the Word. The celestial, the spiritual, and the natural proceed from

147

the Lord in successive order, and in the outmost are in simultaneous order; and it is in this way that the celestial and spiritual senses of the Word are simultaneous in its natural sense. When this is comprehended, it may be seen how the natural sense of the Word, which is the sense of the letter, is the basis, containant, and support of its spiritual and celestial senses; and how in the sense of the letter of the Word divine good and divine truth are in their fullness, in their holiness, and in their power.

39. From all this it is evident that in the sense of the letter the Word is the very Word itself, for within this sense there are spirit and life, the spiritual sense being its spirit, and the celestial sense its life. This is what the Lord says:

The words that I speak unto you are spirit and are life (Jn 6:63).

The Lord spoke His words before the world, in the natural sense. The spiritual sense and the celestial sense without the natural sense which is the sense of the letter, are not the Word; for without it they are like spirit and life without a body; and are (as before said, n. 33) like a palace without a foundation.

40. The truths of the sense of the letter of the Word are in part not naked truths, but appearances of truth, and are as it were likenesses and comparisons taken from things such as exist in nature, and thus accommodated and adapted to the apprehension of the simple and of little children. But being correspondences they are receptacles and abodes of genuine truth; and are like enclosing and containing vessels, as a crystal cup encloses noble wine, and as a silver plate holds palatable food. They are also like garments which clothe, as swathings do an infant, and a pretty dress a maiden. They are also like the memory-knowledges of the natural man which contain within them perceptions and affections of truth of the spiritual man. The naked truths themselves which are enclosed, held, clothed, and contained, are in the spiritual sense of the Word; and the naked goods are in its celestial sense.

[2] But let this be illustrated from the Word. Jesus said:

Woe unto you, Scribes and Pharisees, because ye cleanse the outside of the cup and the platter, but within they are full of extortion and excess. Thou blind Pharisee, cleanse first the inside of the cup and the platter, that the outside of it may be clean also (Mt 23:25, 26).

The Lord here spoke by means of most external things which are containants, and said "cup and platter." "Cup" means wine, and "wine" the truth of the Word; and "platter" means food, and "food" the good of the Word. To "cleanse the inside of the cup and platter," means to purify by means of the Word the interior things which belong to will and thought and thus to love and faith. "That the outside may be clean also," means that in this way, exterior things, which are the actions and the conversation, will have been made pure, for these derive their essence from the interior things.

[3] Again, Jesus said:

There was a certain rich man, who was clothed in crimson and fine linen, and living in mirth and splendor every day; and there was a certain poor man, named Lazarus, who was laid at his porch, full of sores (Lu 16:19, 20).

Here also the Lord spoke by means of natural things that were correspondences, and contained spiritual things. The "rich man" means the Jewish nation, which is called "rich" because it possessed the Word, in which are spiritual riches. The "crimson and fine linen" with which he was clothed, signify the good and truth of the Word; "crimson," its good, and "fine linen" its truth. To "live in mirth and splendor every day," signifies the delight they had in possessing and reading the Word. The "poor man Lazarus," means the Gentiles who had not the Word; and that these were despised and scorned by the Jews, is meant by Lazarus lying at the rich man's porch full of sores.

[4] The reason the Gentiles are meant by "Lazarus" is that the Gentiles were beloved by the Lord, as Lazarus, who was raised from the dead was beloved by the Lord (Jn 11:3, 5, 36), and is called His friend (verse 11), and reclined with the Lord at table (12:2).

From these two passages it is evident that the truths and goods of the sense of the letter of the Word are as vessels and as garments for the naked truth and good that lie hidden in its spiritual and celestial senses.

41. Such being the Word in the sense of the letter, it follows that they who are in divine truths, and in the faith that the Word within, in its bosom, is divine holiness—and much more they who are in the faith that it is from its spiritual and celestial senses that the Word is divine holiness—see divine truths in natural light while reading the Word in enlightenment from the Lord. For the light of heaven (in which is the spiritual sense of the Word) flows into the natural light in which is its sense of the letter, and illumines a man's intellectual called the rational, and causes him to see and recognize divine truths, both where they stand in plain view, and where they lie concealed. With some these divine truths flow in with the light of heaven; sometimes even when they are not aware of it.

42. In its inmost bosom, from its celestial sense, our Word is like a flame that enkindles; and in its middle bosom, from its spiritual sense, it is like a light that enlightens. It follows that in its outmost bosom, from its natural sense which has within it the two more interior senses, the Word is like a ruby and a diamond; like a ruby from its celestial flame, and like a diamond from its spiritual light. And as from its transparency the Word is like this in the sense of the letter, this sense is meant by the foundations of the wall of the New Jerusalem; by the Urim and Thummim in Aaron's ephod; by the garden of Eden in which had been the king of Tyre; by the curtains and veils of the tabernacle; and by the externals of the temple at Jerusalem. But in its very glory the Word was represented by the Lord when He was transfigured.

43. *The truths of the Word's literal sense are meant by the foundations of the wall of the New Jerusalem* (Apoc 21), as follows from the fact that the "New Jerusalem" means the New Church as to doctrine (as has been shown in the *Doctrine of the Lord*, nn. 62, 63); so that its "wall," and the "foundations of the wall," can mean nothing but the external of the Word which is the sense of the letter, for this is the source of doctrine, and through doctrine of the church; and this sense is like a wall with its foundations that encloses and protects a city. Concerning the wall of the New Jerusalem and its foundations we read in the Apocalypse:

The angel measured the wall thereof, a hundred and forty-four cubits, which was the measure of a man, that is, of an angel. And the wall had twelve foundations, adorned with every precious stone. The first foundation was jasper; the second, sapphire; the third, chalcedony; the fourth, emerald; the fifth, sardonyx; the sixth, sardius; the seventh, chrysolite; the eighth, beryl; the ninth, topaz; the tenth, chrysoprase; the eleventh, jacinth; the twelfth, amethyst (21:17-20).

The number "144" signifies all the truths and goods of the church derived from doctrine that is drawn from the sense of the letter of the Word. The like is signified by "12." A "man" signifies intelligence; an "angel" divine truth, the source of intelligence; "measure" the quality of these; the "wall" and its "foundations" the sense of the letter of the Word; and the "precious stones" the truths and goods of the Word in their order, which are the source of doctrine, and through doctrine of the church.

44. *The truths and goods of the sense of the letter of the Word are meant by the Urim and Thummim.* The Urim

and Thummim were on the ephod of Aaron, whose priesthood represented the Lord as to divine good and as to the
work of salvation. The garments of the priesthood or of
holiness represented divine truth from divine good. The
ephod represented divine truth in its outmost, thus the
Word in the sense of the letter, for this, as before said, is
divine truth in its outmost expression. Consequently the
twelve precious stones bearing the names of the twelve
tribes of Israel (which were the Urim and Thummim)
represented divine truths from divine good in their whole
complex.

[2] Concerning these we read in Moses:

They shall make the ephod of [gold,] hyacinthine blue, and bright
crimson, of scarlet doubledyed, and fine linen intertwined. And thou
shalt make a breast-plate of judgment according to the work of the
ephod; and thou shalt set it with settings of stones, four rows of
stones: a ruby, a topaz, and an emerald, the first row; a chrysoprase,
a sapphire, and a diamond, the second row; a cyanus, an agate, and
an amethyst, the third row; a thalassius, a sardius, and a jasper, the
fourth row. These stones shall be according to the names of the sons
of Israel; the engravings of a signet according to his name shall be
for the twelve tribes. And Aaron shall carry upon the breast-plate
of judgment the Urim and Thummim; and let them be upon the
heart of Aaron when he goeth in before Jehovah (Ex 28:6, 15-21,
29, 30).

[3] What was represented by Aaron's garments—his
ephod, robe, vest, mitre, belt—has been unfolded in
Arcana Coelestia on this chapter, where it is shown that
the ephod represented divine truth in its outermost; the
precious stones in it, truths transparent from good; the
twelve precious stones, all outermost truths transparent
from the good of love in their order; the twelve tribes of
Israel, all things of the church; the breast-plate, divine
truth from divine good; the Urim and Thummim, the shining forth in outmost things of divine truth from divine
good (for Urim means a shining fire; and Thummim, in the

angelic language, means a shining forth, and in the Hebrew, entirety). Besides many other things, it is there shown also that answers were given by variegations of light and a simultaneous tacit perception, or by a living voice. From all this it is evident that these precious stones signified truths from good in the literal sense of the Word; nor are answers from heaven given by other means, for in this sense the Divine proceeding is in its fullness.

[4] That precious stones and diadems signify divine truths on their lowest level, such as are the truths of the literal sense of the Word, has been made very evident to me from precious stones and diadems in the spiritual world, among the angels and spirits there whom I have seen wearing them—I have seen them in their casings also—and it has been given me to know that they correspond to truths in externals, and, what is more, that from these truths they exist and come into view. As these truths are signified by diadems and precious stones, John saw diadems upon the head of the dragon (Apoc. 12:3): upon the horns of the beast (13:1); and precious stones upon the harlot that sat on the scarlet beast (17:4).

Diadems and precious stones were seen upon the dragon, the beast, and the harlot, because these signify the people in the Christian world who are in possession of the Word.

45. *The truths of the sense of the letter of the Word are meant by the precious stones in the garden of Eden, in which, in Ezekiel, the king of Tyre is said to have been.* We read in Ezekiel:

King of Tyre, thou sealest up thy sum, full of wisdom, and perfect in beauty. Thou hast been in Eden the garden of God; every precious stone was thy covering, the ruby, the topaz, and the diamond, the beryl, the sardonyx, and the jasper, the sapphire, the chrysoprase, and the emerald, and gold (28:12, 13).

"Tyre," in the Word, signifies the knowledges of truth and good; a "king," the truth of the church; the "garden of

Eden," wisdom and intelligence from the Word; "precious stones," truths transparent from good such as are in the sense of the letter of the Word. As the stones signify these truths, they are called his "covering." That the sense of the letter covers up the interiors of the Word, may be seen in a preceding chapter.

46. *The sense of the letter of the Word is signified by the curtains and veils of the tabernacle.* The tabernacle represented heaven and the church, and therefore the form of it was shown by Jehovah upon Mount Sinai. Consequently all the things in the tabernacle—the lampstand, the golden altar for incense, and the table whereon were the loaves of the Presence—represented and consequently signified holy things of heaven and the church. The Holy of Holies where the ark of the covenant was represented and consequently signified what is inmost of heaven and the church; and the Law itself written on the two tables of stone and enclosed in the ark signified the Lord as to the Word. Now as external things derive their essence from internal things, and both of these from the inmost, which in this case was the Law, it follows that holy things of the Word were represented and signified by all the things of the tabernacle. Therefore the external things of the Tabernacle which were the curtains and veils (and thus its coverings and containants), signified the outmost things of the Word, which are the truths and goods of the literal sense. And because these outmosts of the Word were signified,

All the curtains and veils were made of fine linen intertwined, of hyacinthine blue and bright crimson, and of scarlet double-dyed, with cherubim (Ex 26:1, 31, 36).

What the tabernacle and all the things in it represented and signified generally and specifically, has been unfolded in *Arcana Coelestia* on this chapter of Exodus. It is there shown that the "curtains" and "veils" represented external

things of heaven and the church, and therefore of the
Word; and that "fine linen" signified truth from a spiritual
origin; "hyacinthine blue," truth from a celestial origin;
"bright crimson," celestial good; "scarlet double-dyed," spiritual good; and "cherubim," guards of the interior things
of the Word.

47. *The external things of the temple at Jerusalem represented external things of the Word, which belong to the
sense of its letter.* This is because the temple represented
the same as did the tabernacle, namely, heaven and the
church, and consequently the Word. That the temple at
Jerusalem represented the Lord's Divine Human, He Himself teaches in John:

Destroy this Temple, and in three days I will raise it up; He
spake of the Temple of His Body (2:19, 21).

Where the Lord is meant, there also is meant the Word,
for the Lord is the Word. Now as the interior things of the
temple represented interior things of heaven and the church
(and therefore of the Word), its exterior things represented
and signified exterior things of heaven and the church, and
therefore exterior things of the Word, which belong to the
sense of its letter. Concerning the exterior things of the
temple we read:

That they were built of whole stone, not hewn, and within of
cedar; and that all its walls within were carved with cherubim,
palm-trees, and openings of flowers; and that the floor was overlaid
with gold (1 Kgs. 6:7, 29, 30);

all of which also signify external things of the Word, which
are holy things of the sense of the letter.

48. *The Word in its glory was represented by the Lord
when He was transfigured.* About the Lord as transfigured
before Peter, James, and John, we read:

His face did shine as the sun, and His garments became white as
the light. Moses and Elias appeared talking with Him; A bright cloud

overshadowed the disciples; and a voice was heard out of the cloud, saying, This is My beloved Son, hear ye Him (Mt 17:1-5).

I have been instructed that the Lord then represented the Word; "His face that did shine as the sun," His divine good; "His garments that became as the light," His divine truth; "Moses and Elias," the historical and the prophetical Word; "Moses," the Word that was written through him and the historical Word in general, and "Elias," the prophetical Word; and the "bright cloud that overshadowed the disciples," the Word in the sense of the letter; and therefore a voice was heard from this cloud which said, "This is My beloved Son, hear ye Him." For all utterances and answers from heaven are made exclusively by means of most external things such as are in the literal sense of the Word. For there they are made in fullness, from the Lord.

49. So far we have shown that the Word in the natural sense which is the sense of the letter, is in its holiness and its fullness. Something shall now be said to show that in this sense the Word is also in its power. How great the power of divine truth is, and what its nature is in the heavens and also on earth, is evident from what has been said in *Heaven and Hell* concerning the power of the angels of heaven (nn. 228-233). The power of divine truth is directed especially against falsities and evils, thus against the hells. The fight against these must be waged by means of truths from the sense of the letter of the Word. Moreover it is by means of the truths in a man that the Lord has the power to save him; for man is reformed and regenerated and is at the same time taken out of hell and introduced into heaven, by means of truths from the sense of the letter of the Word. This power the Lord took upon Himself, even as to His Divine Human, after He had fulfilled all things of the Word down to its very letters.

[2] Therefore when by the passion of the cross He was about to fulfill those which remained, He said to the chief priest,

Hereafter ye shall see the Son of man sitting at the right hand of power, and coming in the clouds of heaven (Mt 26:64; Mk 14:62).

The "Son of man," is the Lord as the Word; the "clouds of heaven," are the Word in the sense of the letter; to "sit at the right hand of God," is omnipotence by means of the Word (as also in Mark 16:19). The Lord's power from the most external expressions of truth was represented by the Nazirites in the Jewish Church; and by Samson, of whom it is said that he was a Nazirite from his mother's womb, and that his power lay in his hair. Nazirite and Naziriteship also mean the hair.

[3] That Samson's power lay in his hair, he himself made plain, saying,

There hath not come a razor upon my head, because I have been a Nazirite from my mother's womb; if I be shaven, then my strength will go from me, and I shall become weak, and be like any other man (Judg 16:17).

No one can know why the Naziriteship (by which is meant the hair) was instituted, or whence it came that Samson's strength was from the hair, unless he knows what is signified in the Word by the "head." The "head" signifies the heavenly wisdom which angels and men have from the Lord by means of divine truth; consequently the "hair of the head" signifies heavenly wisdom in outermost things, and also divine truth in its outermost expressions.

[4] As, from correspondence with the heavens, this is the signification of the "hair," it was a statute for the Nazirites that:

They should not shave the hair of their heads, because this is the Naziriteship of God upon their heads (Num 6:1-21).

And for the same reason it was ordained that:

The high priest and his sons should not shave their heads, lest they should die, and wrath should come upon the whole house of Israel (Lev 10:6.)

[5] It was on account of this signification, which is from correspondence, that the hair was so holy; and so the Son of man, who is the Lord as the Word, is described even as to His hairs:

That they were white like wool, as white as snow (Apoc 1:14): In like manner the Ancient of days (Da 7:9).

(On this subject see also above, n. 3:5 [2] & [4].) In short, the reason why the power of divine truth or of the Word is in the sense of the letter, is that there the Word is in its fullness; and it is also because the angels of both the Lord's kingdoms are at the same time and together in that sense with men on earth.

V.

THE DOCTRINE OF THE CHURCH IS TO BE DRAWN FROM THE SENSE OF THE LETTER OF THE WORD, AND IS TO BE CONFIRMED THEREBY.

50. It has been shown in the preceding chapter that the Word in the sense of the letter is in its fullness, in its holiness, and in its power; and as the Lord is the Word (for He is the all of the Word), it follows that He is most of all present in the sense of the letter, and that from it He teaches and enlightens man. But these things shall be set forth in the following order:

i. The Word cannot be understood without doctrine.

ii. Doctrine must be drawn from the sense of the letter of the Word.

iii. But the divine truth which must be of doctrine appears to none but those who are in enlightenment from the Lord.

51. i. *The Word cannot be understood without doctrine.* This is because the Word in the sense of the letter consists exclusively of correspondences, to the end that things spiritual and celestial may be simultaneous or together therein, and that every word may be their containant and support. For this reason, in some places in the sense of the letter the truths are not naked, but clothed, and are then called appearances of truth. Many truths also are accommodated to the capacity of simple folk, who do not lift their thoughts above such things as they see before their eyes. There are also some things that appear like contradictions, although the Word when viewed in its own light contains no contradiction. And again in certain passages in the Prophets, names of persons and places are gathered together from which, in the letter, no sense can be drawn, as in those passages cited above (n. 15). Such being the Word in the sense of the letter, it is evident that it cannot be understood without doctrine.

[2] But to illustrate this by examples. It is said:

That Jehovah repents (Ex 32:12, 14; Jonah 3:9; 4:2);

And also

That Jehovah does not repent (Num 23:19; 1 Sa 15:29).

Without doctrine these passages cannot be reconciled. It is said that

Jehovah visits the iniquity of the fathers upon the sons to the third and fourth generation (Num 14:18);

And it is also said that

The father shall not die for the son, nor the son for the father, but every one for his own sin (Dt 24:16).

According to doctrine these passages do not disagree, but are in agreement.

[3] Jesus says:

Ask, and it shall be given you; seek, and ye shall find; knock, and it shall be opened unto you; for every one that asketh shall receive; and he that seeketh shall find; and to him that knocketh it shall be opened (Mt 7:7, 8; 21:21, 22).

Without doctrine it might be believed that every one will receive what he asks for; but from doctrine it is believed that whatever a man asks not from himself but from the Lord is given; for this also is what the Lord says:

If ye abide in Me, and My words abide in you, ye shall ask what ye will, and it shall be done unto you (Jn 15:7).

[4] The Lord says:

Blessed are the poor, for theirs is the kingdom of God (Lu 6:20).

Without doctrine it may be thought that heaven is for the

poor and not for the rich, but doctrine teaches that the poor in spirit are meant, for the Lord says:

Blessed are the poor in spirit; for theirs is the kingdom of heaven (Mt 5:3).

[5] The Lord says:

Judge not, that ye be not judged; for with what judgment ye judge ye shall be judged (Mt 7:1, 2; Lu 6:37).

Without doctrine this might be cited to confirm the notion that it is not to be said of what is evil that it is evil, thus than an evil person is not to be judged to be evil; yet according to doctrine it is lawful to judge, but justly; for the Lord says:

Judge righteous judgment (Jn 7:24).

[6] Jesus says:

Be not ye called teacher, for One is your Teacher, even the Christ. And call no man your father on the earth; for One is your Father in the heavens. Neither be ye called masters; for One is your Master, the Christ (Mt 23:8-10).

Without doctrine it would seem that it is not lawful to call any person teacher, father, or master; but from doctrine it is known that in the natural sense it is lawful to do this, but not in the spiritual sense.

[7] Jesus said to His disciples:

When the Son of man shall sit upon the throne of His glory, ye also shall sit upon twelve thrones, judging the twelve tribes of Israel (Mt 19:28).

From these words it may be inferred that the Lord's disciples will sit in judgment, when yet they can judge no one. Doctrine therefore must reveal this secret by explaining that the Lord alone, who is omniscient and knows the hearts of all, will sit in judgment, and is able to judge; and that His twelve disciples mean the church as to all the truths and goods it possesses from the Lord through the Word; from which doctrine concludes that these truths will judge every one, according to the Lord's words in John 3:17, 18; 12:47, 48.

[8] He who reads the Word without doctrine does not see the consistency of what is said in the Prophets about the Jewish nation and Jerusalem—that the church with that nation, and its seat in that city, will remain to eternity; as in the following passages:

Jehovah will visit His flock the house of Judah, and will make them as a horse of glory in war; from him shall come forth the corner stone, from him the nail, and from him the bow of war (Zech 10:3, 4, 6, 7).

Behold I come, that I may dwell in the midst of thee. And Jehovah shall make Judah an inheritance, and shall again choose Jerusalem (2:10, 12).

It shall come to pass in that day that the mountains shall drop new wine, and the hills shall flow with milk, and Judah shall be to eternity, and Jerusalem from generation to generation (Joel 3:18-20).

Behold, the days come in which I will sow the house of Israel and the house of Judah with the seed of man, and in which I will make a new covenant with the house of Israel, and with the house of Judah; and this shall be the covenant, I will put My law in their inward parts, and will write it upon their heart; and I will be their God, and they shall be My people (Je 31:27, 31, 33).

In that day ten men shall take hold, out of all the languages of the nations, of the skirt of a man that is a Jew, saying, We will go with you, for we have heard that God is with you (Zech 8:23).

So in other places, as Isa 44:21, 24, 26; 49:22, 23; 65:9; 66:20, 22; Je 3:18; 23:5; 50:19, 20; Na 1:15; Mal 3:4.

In these passages the Lord's advent is treated of, and that this [establishment of the Jews] will then come to pass.

[9] But the contrary is declared in many other places, of which this passage only shall be cited:

I will hide My face from them, I will see what their latter end shall be, for they are a generation of perversions, sons in whom is no faithfulness. I said, I will cast them into outermost corners, I will make the remembrance of them to cease from man, for they are a nation void of counsel, neither is there understanding in them; their vine is of the vine of Sodom, and of the fields of Gomorrah; their grapes are grapes of gall; their clusters are of bitternesses; their wine is the poison of dragons, and the cruel venom of asps. Is not this hidden with Me, sealed up among My treasures? To Me belongeth vengeance and retribution (Dt 32:20-35).

It is of that same nation that these things are said. And things of the same purport are said elsewhere:

As in Isa 3:1, 2, 8; 5:3, 6; Dt 9:5, 6; Mt 12:39; 23:27, 28; Jn 8:44; and in Je and Ezek throughout.

These passages which seem contradictory will however from doctrine be seen to accord, for this teaches that in the Word "Israel" and "Judah" do not mean Israel and Judah, but the church in both senses, in one that it is devastated, in the other that it is to be set up anew by the Lord.

Other things like these exist in the Word, from which it plainly appears that the Word cannot be understood without doctrine.

52. From all this it is evident that they who read the Word without doctrine, or who do not acquire for themselves doctrine from the Word, are in obscurity as to every truth, and that their minds are wavering and uncertain, prone to errors, and pliant to heresies, which they also embrace wherever inclination or authority favors, and their reputation is not endangered. For the Word is to them like a lampstand without a lamp, and in their gloom they seem to see many things, and yet see scarcely anything, for doctrine alone is a lamp. I have seen such persons examined by angels, and found to be able to confirm from the Word whatever they please, and it was also found that they confirm what is of their own love and of the love of those whom they favor. I have seen them stripped of their garments, too, a sign that they were devoid of truths; for in the spiritual world garments are truths.

53. ii. *Doctrine must be drawn from the literal sense of the Word, and be confirmed thereby.* The reason for this is that there and not elsewhere is the Lord present with man, and enlightens him and teaches him the truths of the church. Moreover the Lord never operates anything except in what is full, and the Word is in its fullness in the sense of the letter, as has been shown above. This is why doctrine must be drawn from the sense of the letter.

54. It is by means of doctrine that the Word not only becomes intelligible, but also as it were shines with light. This is because without doctrine it is not understood, and is like a lampstand without a lamp, as has been shown above. By means of doctrine therefore the Word is understood, and is like a lampstand with a lighted lamp. A man then sees more things than he had seen before, and also understands those things which before he had not understood. Dark and contradictory things he either does not see and passes over, or sees and interprets them so that they agree with the doctrine. The experience of the Christian world demonstrates that the Word is seen from doctrine, and is also interpreted according to it. All the Reformed see and interpret the Word from and according to their own doctrine; so do the Papists from and according to theirs; and even the Jews do so from and according to theirs; thus from a false doctrine all see falsities, and from a true doctrine truths. It is evident therefore that true doctrine is like a lamp in the dark, and a guide-post on the way.

However, doctrine is not only to be drawn from the sense of the letter of the Word, but must also be confirmed therby; for if not so confirmed the truth of doctrine appears as if only man's intelligence were in it, and not the Lord's divine wisdom; and so the doctrine would be like a house in the air, and not on the earth, thus lacking a foundation.

55. The doctrine of genuine truth can also be drawn in

full from the sense of the letter of the Word, because in this sense the Word is like a man clothed whose face and hands are bare. All things that concern man's life, and consequently his salvation, are bare; but the rest are clothed. In many places also where they are clothed they shine through their clothing, like a face through a sheer veil of silk. The truths of the Word also appear and shine through their clothing more and more clearly in proportion as they are multiplied by a love for them, and are ranged in order by this love. This also is by means of doctrine.

56. It might be believed that the doctrine of genuine truth could be procured by means of the spiritual sense of the Word which is furnished through a knowledge of correspondences. But doctrine is not procured by means of that sense, but is only lighted up and corroborated. For as said before (n. 26), no one comes into the spiritual sense of the Word by means of correspondences unless he is first in genuine truths from doctrine. If a man is not first in genuine truths he may falsify the Word by means of some correspondences with which he is acquainted, by connecting them together and interpreting them so as to confirm that which cleaves to his mind from some principle previously received. Moreover the spiritual sense of the Word is not given any one except by the Lord alone, and it is guarded by Him as heaven is guarded, for heaven is in it. It is better therefore for man to study the Word in the sense of the letter; from this alone is doctrine derived.

57. iii. *The genuine truth which must be from doctrine appears in the sense of the letter only to those who are in enlightenment from the Lord.* Enlightenment is from the Lord alone, and exists with those who love truths because they are truths and make them of use for life. With others there is no enlightenment in the Word. The reason why enlightenment is from the Lord alone is that the Lord is in all things of the Word. The reason why enlightenment

exists with those who love truths because they are truths
and make them of use for life, is that such are in the Lord
and the Lord in them. For the Lord is His own divine
truth, and when this is loved because it is divine truth
(and it is loved when it is made of use), the Lord is in it
with the individual. This the Lord teaches in John:

> In that day ye shall know that ye are in Me and I in you. He
> that hath My commandments, and doeth them, he loveth Me, and I
> will love him, and will manifest Myself to him; and I will come
> unto him, and make My abode with him (14:20, 21, 23).

And in Matthew:

> Blessed are the pure in heart, for they shall see God (5:8).

These are they who are in enlightenment when they are
reading the Word, and to whom the Word shines and is
translucent.

58. The reason why the Word shines and is translucent
with such, is that there is a spiritual and celestial sense in
every particular of the Word, and these senses are in the
light of heaven, so that through these senses and by their
light the Lord flows into the natural sense, and into the
light of it with a man. This causes the man to acknowledge
the truth from an interior perception, and afterwards to see
it in his own thought, and this as often as he is in the affection of truth for the sake of truth. For perception comes
from affection, and thought from perception, and thus is
produced the acknowledgment which is called faith. But of
these things more will be said in the following chapter
concerning the conjunction of the Lord with man by means
of the Word.

59. With such men the first thing is to acquire for themselves doctrine from the literal sense of the Word, and thus
light a lamp for their further advance. Then after doctrine
has been procured, and a lamp thus lighted, they see the

Word by its means. Those however who do not acquire doctrine for themselves, first make investigation as to whether the doctrine delivered by others and received by the general body accords with the Word, and they agree to what accords, and from what does not accord they disagree. In this way it becomes to them their own doctrine, and through doctrine their faith. But this takes place only with those who not being taken up with worldly affairs are able to exercise discernment. If these persons love truths because they are truths, and make them of use for life, they are in enlightenment from the Lord. All others who are in some life according to truths can learn from them.

60. The contrary takes place with those who read the Word from the doctrine of a false religion, and still more with those who confirm that doctrine from the Word, having in view their own glory or this world's riches. With them the truth of the Word is as it were in the shade of night, and what is false is as in the light of day. They read what is true, but do not see it; and if they see the shadow of it they falsify it. These are they of whom the Lord says that they have eyes, but see not; and ears, but do not understand (Mt 13:13).

For nothing else blinds a man except his [proprium, or what is his] Own and the confirmation of what is false. Man's Own [or proprium] is the love of self and the derivative conceit of self-intelligence; and the confirmation of what is false is thick darkness counterfeiting the light. The light of such men is merely natural, and their sight is like that of one who sees phantoms in shadows.

61. I have been permitted to converse with many after death who had believed that they would shine in heaven like the stars, because, as they said, they had regarded the Word as holy, had often read it through, had collected from it many things by which they had confirmed the

tenets of their faith, and had thereby been celebrated in the world as learned men. On this account they believed they would be Michaels and Raphaels.

[2] Many of them however have been examined as to what was the love from which they had studied the Word, and some of them were found to have done so from the love of self, that they might appear great in the world, and be revered as dignitaries of the church; and others of them had done so from the love of the world, that they might get rich. When examined as to what they knew from the Word, it was found that they knew nothing of genuine truth from it, but only such as is called truth falsified, which in itself is falsity. They were told that this was because their "ends" (or their loves which is the same thing) had been themselves and the world, and not the Lord and heaven. When men read the Word while themselves and the world are the ends in view, their minds cleave to themselves and the world, and this causes them to be constantly thinking from their Own, which is in thick darkness as to all the things of heaven, in which state man cannot be withdrawn by the Lord from his selfhood, and thus be raised into the light of heaven, and consequently cannot receive through heaven any influx from the Lord.

[3] I have even seen such people admitted into heaven, but when they were found to be devoid of truths, they were cast down; yet the conceit remained that they deserved heaven. Very different has it been with those who had studied the Word from the affection of knowing truth because it is truth, and because it is of service to the uses of life, not only to their own uses but also to those of the neighbor. I have seen these raised up into heaven, and thus into the light in which divine truth is there, and at the same time exalted into angelic wisdom and its happiness, which is eternal life.

VI

62. The reason why there is conjunction with the Lord by means of the Word is that it treats solely of Him, and the Lord is consequently its all in all and is called the Word, as has been shown in the *Doctrine of the Lord*. The reason why the conjunction is in the sense of the letter, is that in this sense the Word is in its fullness, its holiness, and its power, as has been shown above in its proper chapter. The conjunction is not apparent to the man, but is in the affection of truth and his perception of it, thus is in the man's love for and faith in divine truth.

63. The reason why there is association with the angels of heaven by means of the sense of the letter, is that the spiritual sense and celestial sense are in it, and the angels are in these senses, the angels of the spiritual kingdom being in the Word's spiritual sense, and those of the celestial kingdom in its celestial sense. These senses are evolved from the Word's natural sense which is the sense of the letter while a true man is in it. The evolution is instantaneous; consequently so is the association.

64. It has been made plain to me by much experience that the spiritual angels are in the spiritual sense of the Word, and the celestial angels in its celestial sense. While reading the Word in its literal sense it has been given me to perceive that communication was effected with the heavens, now with this society of them, now with that, and that what I understood according to the natural sense, the spiritual angels understood according to the spiritual sense, and the celestial angels according to the celestial sense, and this is an instant. As I have perceived this communication many thousands of times, no doubt about it remains with me. Moreover there are spirits beneath the heavens who abuse this communication: they recite some sayings from the sense of the letter, and immediately observe and take note of the society with which communication is effected. This I have frequently seen and heard. From these things it has been given me to know by actual experience that the Word in its literal sense is the divine medium of conjunction with the Lord and with heaven. (On this conjunction by the Word see also what is said in the work on *Heaven and Hell,* nn. 303-310).

65. The way in which the evolution of these senses is effected shall also be told briefly. However, for the understanding of this it will be necessary to recall what has been said above about successive order and simultaneous order, namely, that in successive order what is celestial, what is spiritual, and what is natural follow one after another, from highest things in heaven down to lowest things in the world, and that the same things are in the lowest (which is natural) in simultaneous order, one next another from the inmost things to the outermost ones, and that in like manner there are successive senses of the Word, celestial and spiritual, simultaneously in the natural sense. When these things are comprehended, the way in which the two senses, celestial and spiritual, are evolved from the natural sense while one is reading the Word may in some measure be unfolded before the understanding; for a spiritual angel then calls forth what is spiritual, and a celestial angel what is celestial, nor can they do otherwise, because such things are homogeneous and in accordance with their nature and essence.

66. This may be illustrated in the first place by comparisons drawn from the three kingdoms of nature: animal, vegetable, and mineral. *From the animal kingdom:* When food becomes chyle, the blood vessels extract and call forth from it their blood, the nervous fibres their fluid, and the substances that are the origins of the fibres their animal spirit. *From the vegetable kingdom:* A tree, with its trunk, branches, leaves, and fruit, stands upon its root, and by means of its root it extracts and calls forth from the ground a grosser sap for the trunk, branches, and leaves, a purer for the pulp of the fruit, and the purest for the seeds within the fruit. *From the mineral kingdom:* In some places in the bowels of the earth there are minerals impregnated with gold, silver, and iron, and each of these metals draws its own element from the exhalations stored up in the earth.

67. We may now illustrate by an example how from the natural sense in which the Word is with men, the spiritual angels draw forth their own sense, and the celestial angels theirs. Take as an example five commandments of the Decalogue:

Honor thy father and thy mother. By "father and mother" a man understands his father and mother on earth, and all who stand in their place, and by to "honor" he understands to hold in honor and obey them. A spiritual angel understands the Lord by "father," and the church by "mother," and by to "honor" he understands to love. A celestial angel understands the Lord's divine love by "father," and His divine wisdom by "mother," and by to "honor" to do what is good from Him.

[2] *Thou shalt not steal.* By to "steal" a man on earth understands to steal, defraud, or under any pretext take from his neighbor his goods. A spiritual angel understands to deprive others of their truths of faith and goods of charity by means of falsities and evils. A celestial angel understands to attribute to himself what is the Lord's, and to claim for himself His righteousness and merit.

[3] *Thou shalt not commit adultery.* By "committing

adultery" a man understands to commit adultery and fornication, to do obscene things, speak lascivious words, and
harbor filthy thoughts. A spiritual angel understands to
adulterate the goods of the Word, and falsify its truths. A
celestial angel understands to deny the Lord's divinity and
to profane the Word.

[4] *Thou shalt not kill.* By "killing," a man understands
also bearing hatred, and desiring revenge even to the death.
A spiritual angel understands to act as a devil and destroy
men's souls. A celestial angel understands to bear hatred
against the Lord, and against what is His.

[5] *Thou shalt not bear false witness.* By "bearing false
witness" a man understands also to lie and defame. A
spiritual angel understands to say and persuade that what
is false is true and what is evil good, and the reverse. A
celestial angel understands to blaspheme the Lord and the
Word.

[6] From these examples it may be seen how the spiritual
and celestial of the Word are evolved and drawn out from
the natural sense in which they are hidden. Wonderful to
say, the angels draw out their senses without knowing what
the reader is thinking, and yet the thoughts of the angels
and of the readers make one by means of correspondences,
like end, cause, and effect. Moreover ends actually are in
the celestial kingdom, causes in the spiritual kingdom, and
effects in the natural kingdom. This conjunction by means
of correspondences is such from creation. This then is the
source of man's association with angels by means of the
Word.

68. Another reason why association of man with angels
exists by means of the natural or literal sense of the Word,
is that in every man from creation there are three degrees
of life, celestial, spiritual, and natural, but as long as he is
in this world he is in the natural, and is at the same time in
the spiritual in so far as he is in genuine truths, and in the

celestial in so far as he is in a life according to them; but still he does not come into the spiritual or celestial itself until after death. But more about this elsewhere.

69. From all this it is evident that in the Word alone (through the fact that it is conjunction with the Lord and association with the angels) there is spirit and life, as the Lord teaches:

The words that I speak unto you, they are spirit and they are life (Jn 6:63).

The water that I shall give you shall be in you a fountain of water springing up into eternal life (4:14).

Man doth not live by bread alone, but by every word that proceedeth out of the mouth of God (Mt 4:4).

Labor for the meat that endureth unto eternal life, which the Son of man shall give unto you (Jn 6:27).

VII.

THE WORD IS IN ALL THE HEAVENS, AND IS THE SOURCE OF
ANGELIC WISDOM.

70. It has not been known that the Word is in the heavens, nor could it be made known so long as the church was ignorant that angels and spirits are men like the men in this world, and that they possess in every respect things like those possessed by men [on earth], with the sole difference that they themselves are spiritual, and that all the things they possess are from a spiritual origin; while men in this world are natural, and all the things they possess are from a natural origin. So long as this fact was hidden it could not be known that the Word exists in the heavens also, and is read by angels there, and also by spirits who are beneath the heavens. But that this might not be forever hidden, it has been granted me to be in company with angels and spirits, to converse with them, see what exists with them, and afterwards relate many things that I have heard and seen. This has been done in the work *Heaven and Hell,* published in London in 1758; in which it may be seen that angels and spirits are men, and that they possess in abundance all the things that men possess in this world. That angels and spirits are men, may be seen in that work (nn. 73-77, and 453-456): That they possess things like those possessed by men in this world (nn. 170-190): also that they have Divine worship, and preachings in places of worship (nn. 221-227): that they have writings and also books (nn. 258-264): and that they have the Word (n. 259).

71. As regards the Word in heaven, it is written in a spiritual style, which differs entirely from a natural style. The spiritual style consists solely of letters, each of which

contains a meaning, and there are points above the letters
which exalt the meaning. With the angels of the spiritual
kingdom the letters resemble printed letters in our world;
and with the angels of the celestial kingdom the letters
(each of which also contains a complete meaning) resemble the ancient Hebrew letters, curved in various ways, and
with marks above and within. Such being the style of their
writing, there are no names of persons and places in their
Word such as there are in ours, but instead of the names
there are the things which they signify. Thus instead of
Moses there is the historical Word, instead of Elijah, the
prophetical Word; instead of Abraham, Isaac, and Jacob,
the Lord as to His Divinity and Divine Human; instead of
Aaron, the priestly office; instead of David, the kingly office,
each of the Lord; instead of the names of the twelve sons
of Jacob, or of the tribes of Israel, various things of heaven
and the church; and similar things instead of the names of
the Lord's twelve disciples; instead of Zion and Jerusalem,
the church in respect to the Word and doctrine from the
Word; instead of the land of Canaan, the church itself;
instead of the cities therein on this side and beyond Jordan, various things of the church and of its doctrine; and
so with all the other names. It is the same with the numbers: these do not appear in the Word that is in heaven,
but instead of them the things to which the numbers that
are in our Word correspond. It is evident from these examples that the Word in heaven is a Word that corresponds
to our Word, and thus that the two are a one, for correspondences make a one.

72. It is a wonderful thing that the Word in the heavens
is so written that the simple understand it in simplicity,
and the wise in wisdom, for there are many points and
marks over the letters, which as has been said exalt the
meaning, and to these the simple pay no attention, nor are
they even aware of them; whereas the wise pay attention
to them, each one according to his wisdom, even to the

highest wisdom. In every larger society of heaven, a copy of the Word, written by angels inspired by the Lord, is kept in its sanctuary, lest being elsewhere it should be altered in some point. In respect to the fact that the simple understand it in simplicity and the wise in wisdom, our Word is indeed like that in heaven, but this is effected in a different way.

73. The angels acknowledge that all their wisdom comes through the Word, for they are in light in proportion to their understanding of the Word. The light of heaven is divine wisdom, which to their eyes is light. In the sanctuary where the copy of the Word is kept, there is a flaming and bright light that surpasses every degree of light in heaven that is outside of it. The cause is the same as above mentioned; it is that the Lord is in the Word.

74. The wisdom of the celestial angels surpasses that of the spiritual angels almost as much as this surpasses the wisdom of men, and the reason is that the celestial angels are in the good of love from the Lord, while the spiritual angels are in truths of wisdom from Him, and wherever there is the good of love there resides at the same time wisdom; but where there are truths there resides no more of wisdom than there is good of love together with it. This is the reason why the Word in the celestial kingdom is written differently from that in the spiritual kingdom; for goods of love are expressed in the Word of the celestial kingdom, and the marks denote affections, whereas truths of wisdom are expressed in the Word of the spiritual kingdom, and the marks denote perceptions.

75. From what has been said one may infer the nature of the wisdom that lies hidden in the Word that is in this world. In fact all angelic wisdom, which is unutterable, lies hidden in it, for it is the containant of the same, and after death a man who is being made an angel by the Lord by means of the Word comes into that wisdom.

VIII.

THE CHURCH IS FROM THE WORD, AND IS SUCH AS IS ITS UNDERSTANDING OF THE WORD.

76. That the church is from the Word does not admit of doubt, for the Word is divine truth itself (nn. 1-4); the doctrine of the church is from the Word (nn. 50-61); and through the Word there is conjunction with the Lord (nn. 62-69). But doubt may arise as to whether the understanding of the Word is what makes the church, for there are those who believe that they are of the church because they have the Word, read it or hear it from a preacher, and know something of its literal meaning; yet how this or that in the Word is to be understood they do not know, and some of them little care. It shall therefore be proved that it is not the Word that makes the church, but the understanding of it; and that such as the understanding of the Word is among those who are in the church, such is the church itself. Substantiation of this follows.

77. The Word is the Word according to the understanding of it in a man, that is, as it is understood. If it is not understood, the Word is indeed called the Word, but it is not the Word with the man. The Word is the truth according to the understanding of it, for it may not be the truth, because it may be falsified. The Word is spirit and life according to the understanding of it, for its letter if not understood is dead. And as a man has truth and life according to his understanding of the Word, so has he faith and love according thereto, for truth is of faith, and love is of life. Now as the church exists by means of faith and love, and according to them, it follows that the church is the church through the understanding of the Word and according thereto; a noble church if in genuine truths, an ignoble church if not in genuine truths, and a destroyed church if in falsified truths.

78. Further: it is through the Word that the Lord is present with a man and is conjoined with him, for the Lord is the Word, and as it were speaks with the man in it. The Lord is also divine truth itself, as is the Word. From this it is evident that the Lord is present with a man and is at the same time conjoined with him, according to his understanding of the Word, for according to this the man has truth and the derivative faith, and also love and the derivative life. The Lord is indeed present with a man through the reading of the Word, but He is conjoined with him through the understanding of truth from the Word, and according thereto; and in proportion as the Lord has been conjoined with a man, in the same proportion the church is in him. The church is within man; the church that is outside of him is the church with a number of men who have the church within them. This is meant by the Lord's words to the Pharisees who asked when the kingdom of God would come:

The kingdom of God is within you (Lu 17:21).

Here the "kingdom of God" means the Lord, and from Him, the church.

79. In many places in the Prophets where the church is treated of, the understanding of the Word is also the subject, and it is taught that there is no church except where the Word is rightly understood, and that such as is the understanding of the Word with those in the church, such is the church. In many places also in the Prophets the church with the Israelitish and Jewish nation is described as being totally destroyed and annihilated through their falsification of the meaning or understanding of the Word, for nothing else destroys the church.

[2] The understanding of the Word, both true and false, is described in the Prophets by "Ephraim," especially in Hosea, for in the Word "Ephraim" signifies the understanding of the Word in the church. And as the understanding of the Word makes the church, Ephraim is called,

A dear son, and a child of delights (Je 31:20);
The first-born (verse 9);
The strength of Jehovah's head (Ps 60:7; 108:8);
Mighty (Zech 10:7);
Filled with the bow (9:13);

and the sons of Ephraim are called,

Armed, and shooters with the bow (Ps 78:9).

The "bow" signifies doctrine from the Word fighting against falsities. Therefore also,

Ephraim was passed over to Israel's right hand, and was blessed; and was also accepted instead of Reuben (Ge 48:5, 11-15).

And therefore,

Ephraim, together with his brother Manasseh (under the name of Joseph their father), was exalted above all by Moses when he blessed the sons of Israel (Dt 33:13-17).

[3] The quality of the church when the understanding of the Word has been destroyed, is also described in the Prophets by "Ephraim," especially in Hosea, as is evident from the following passages:

Israel and Ephraim shall stagger; Ephraim shall be in the solitude; Ephraim is oppressed and shattered in judgment. I will be unto Ephraim as a lion; I will tear and go away; I will carry off, and there shall be none to deliver (Hosea 5:5, 9, 11-14).
O Ephraim, what shall I do unto thee? for thy holiness is as a cloud of the dawn, and like the dew that falleth in the morning, it goeth away (6:4).
They shall not dwell in the land of Jehovah; but Ephraim shall return to Egypt, and shall eat in Assyria that which is unclean (9:3).

[4] The "land of Jehovah" is the church; "Egypt" is the memory-knowledge of the natural man; "Assyria" is the derivative reasoning: by these two the Word is falsified in respect to the understanding of it, and therefore it is said that "Ephraim shall return to Egypt, and shall eat in Assyria that which is unclean."

[5] Again:

Ephraim feedeth on wind, and followeth after the east wind; every day he multiplieth lying and wasteness; he maketh a covenant with Assyria, and oil is carried down into Egypt (12:1).

To "feed on wind," to "follow after the east wind," and to "multiply lying and wasteness," is to falsify truths, and thus destroy the church.

[6] The like is signified also by the "whoredom" of Ephraim (for "whoredom" signifies the falsification of the understanding of the Word, that is, of its genuine truth) in the following passages:

I know Ephraim, that he hath altogether committed whoredom, and Israel is defiled (Hosea 5:3).

In the house of Israel I have seen a foul thing; there Ephraim hath committed whoredom, and Israel hath been defiled (6:10).

"Israel" is the church itself, and "Ephraim" is the understanding of the Word, from and according to which is the church, and therefore it is said "Ephraim hath committed whoredom, and Israel hath been defiled."

[7] As the church among the Jews had been utterly destroyed through falsifications of the Word, it is said of Ephraim,

I will give thee up, Ephraim, I will deliver thee over, Israel, as Admah, and I will set thee as Zeboim (Hosea 11:8).

Now as the prophet Hosea, from the first chapter to the last, treats of the falsification of the Word, and of the destruction of the church thereby; and as the falsification of truth is there signified by "whoredom," therefore in order that he might represent this state of the church, that prophet was commanded to take unto himself a harlot for a woman, and of her to beget sons (chap. 1); and, a second time, to take a woman who was an adulteress (chap. 3).

[8] These passages have been cited in order that it may be known and confirmed from the Word that such as is the understanding of the Word in the church, such is the church: excellent and precious if this understanding is from genuine truths of the Word, but ruined and even foul if it is from truths falsified. In confirmation of the truth that Ephraim signifies the understanding of the Word, and in the opposite sense the same falsified, and that the destruction of the church comes from this, other passages in which Ephraim is treated of may be consulted,

As Hosea 4:17, 18; 7:1, 11; 8:9, 11; 9:11-13, 16; 10:11; 11:3; 12:1, 8, 14; 13:1, 12; Isa 17:3; 28:1; Je 4:15; 31:6, 18; 50:19; Ezek 37:16; 48:5; Obad 19; Zech 9:10.

IX.

80. This has not been seen previously, nor could it be seen, because the spiritual sense of the Word has not until now been disclosed, and it cannot be seen except by means of this sense. For in the Word two senses, the spiritual and the celestial, lie hidden within the letter. In the spiritual sense the things in the Word refer especially to the church, and in the celestial sense, especially to the Lord. In the spiritual sense they also refer to divine truth, and in the celestial to divine good. From this comes the marriage in question in the sense of the letter of the Word. But this appears to those only who know from the Word's spiritual and celestial sense the meanings of the words and names, for some of these are predicated of good, and some of truth, and some include both, so that without this knowledge the marriage that exists in each and every particular of the Word could not be seen—which is the reason why this arcanum has not been disclosed before.

81. As there is such a marriage in each and every thing of the Word, there frequently occur in it two expressions that appear like repetitions of the same thing. They however are not repetitions, for one of them has reference to good and the other to truth, and both taken together effect a conjunction of good and truth, and thus form one thing. From this too comes the divinity of the Word and its holiness, for in every divine work good is conjoined with truth and truth with good.

82. It is said that in each and every thing of the Word

there is a marriage of the Lord and the church and a derivative marriage of good and truth, because wherever there is a marriage of the Lord and the church there is also a marriage of good and truth, for the latter is from the former. For when the church or man of the church is in truths, the Lord inflows into his truths with good, and vivifies them. Or what is the same, when through truths the church or man of the church is in intelligence, the Lord inflows into his intelligence through the good of love and of charity, and thus pours life into it.

83. With every man there are two faculties of life, called understanding and will. The understanding is the receptacle of truth and the derivative wisdom, and the will is the receptacle of good and the derivative love. For a man to be a man of the church these two must make a one, and this they do when the man forms his understanding from genuine truths, which to all appearance is done by himself; and when his will is infilled with the good of love, which is done by the Lord. From this the man has a life of truth and a life of good, a life of truth in the understanding from the will, and a life of good in the will through the understanding. This is the marriage of truth and good in a man, and also the marriage of the Lord and the church in him. But concerning this reciprocal conjunction called a marriage, more will be seen in *Divine Providence, Divine Love and Wisdom, and Doctrine of Life.**

84. Readers of the Word who pay attention to the matter can see that there are pairs of expressions in it that appear like repetitions of the same thing, such as "brother [and companion," "poor] and needy," "waste and solitude," "vacuity and emptiness," "foe and enemy," "sin and iniquity," "anger and wrath," "nation and people," "joy and gladness," "mourning and weeping," "righteousness and judgment," etc. These expressions appear synonymous but

* Third work in *The Four Doctrines.*

are not so, for "brother," "poor," "waste," ["vacuity,"] "foe," "sin," "anger," "nation," "joy," "mourning," and "righteousness," are predicated of good, and in the opposite sense of evil; whereas "companion," "needy," "solitude," "emptiness," "enemy," "iniquity," "wrath," "people," "gladness," "weeping," and "judgment," are predicated of truth, and in the opposite sense of falsity. And yet it seems to a reader who is not acquainted with this secret, that "poor and needy," "waste and solitude," "vacuity and emptiness," "foe and enemy," are one and the same thing; and in like manner "sin and iniquity," "anger and wrath," "nation and people," "joy and gladness," "mourning and weeping," "righteousness and judgment;" and yet they are not one thing, but become one thing by conjunction. Many things are also joined together in the Word, such as "fire and flame," "gold and silver," "brass and iron," "wood and stone," "bread and water," "bread and wine," "bright crimson and fine-linen," etc., which is done because "fire," "gold," "brass," "wood," "bread," and "bright crimson," signify good; and "flame," "silver," "iron," "stone," "water," "wine," and "fine-linen," signify truth. In the same way it is said that men are to "love God with all the heart and with all the soul;" and that God will "create in a man a new heart and a new spirit;" for "heart" is predicated of the good of love, and "soul" (and "spirit") of the truth from that good. There are also words that are used alone, or without a mate, because they partake of both good and truth. But these and many other things are not apparent except to the angels, and to those also who while in the natural sense are also in the spiritual sense.

85. That such pairs of expressions which appear like repetitions of the same thing, run through the Word, would be too prolix a matter to show from the Word, for whole sheets could be filled with it; but to remove all doubt about it I will quote passages in which occur the expressions "righteousness (or "justice") and judgment," "nation and people," and "joy and gladness." First, "righteousness and judgment:"

The city was full of judgment, righteousness lodged in her (Isa 1:21).

Zion shall be redeemed in judgment, and they that return of her in righteousness (verse 27).

Jehovah of Hosts shall be exalted in judgment, and God the Holy One shall be sanctified in righteousness (5:16).

He shall sit upon the throne of David, and upon his kingdom, to establish it in judgment and in righteousness (9:7).

Jehovah shall be exalted, for He dwelleth on high; He hath filled Zion with judgment and righteousness (33:5).

Thus saith Jehovah, Keep ye judgment, and do righteousness; for My salvation is near, that My righteousness may be revealed (56:1).

As a nation that did righteousness, and forsook not the judgment of their God; they ask of Me the judgments of righteousness (58:2).

Swear by the living Jehovah in judgment and in righteousness (Je 4:2).

Let him that glorieth glory in this, that Jehovah doeth judgment and righteousness in the earth (9:24).

Do ye judgment and righteousness; Woe unto him that buildeth his house without righteousness, and his chambers without judgment; did not thy father do judgment and righteousness? and then it was well with him (22:3, 13, 15).

I will raise unto David a righteous offshoot, and He shall reign as king, and shall do judgment and justice in the land (23:5; 33:15).

If a man be just, and do judgment and righteousness (Ezek 18:5).

If the wicked turn from his sin, and do judgment and righteousness, it shall not be mentioned against him: he hath done judgment and righteousness; he shall surely live (33:14, 16, 19).

I will betroth thee unto Me to eternity; in righteousness and in judgment; and in mercy and in compassions (Hosea 2:19).

Let judgment flow as water, and righteousness as a mighty torrent (Amos 5:24).

Ye have turned judgment into gall, and the fruit of righteousness into wormwood (6:12).

Jehovah will plead my cause, and execute judgment for me: He will bring me forth into the light, and I shall behold His righteousness (Mic 7:9).

O Jehovah, Thy righteousness is like the mountains of God; Thy judgments are a great abyss (Ps 36:6).

Jehovah will bring forth thy righteousness as the light, and thy judgment as the noonday (37:6).

Jehovah shall judge thy people in righteousness, and thy miserable in judgment (72:2).

Righteousness and judgment are the support of Thy throne (89:14).

When I shall have learned the judgments of Thy righteousness. Seven times a day do I praise Thee, because of the judgments of Thy righteousness (119:7, 164).

God executeth the justice of Jehovah, and His judgment with Israel (Dt 33:21).

The Spirit of Truth shall convict the world of sin, of righteousness, and of judgment (Jn 16:8, 9, 10). (And in other places.)

The reason "judgment" and "righteousness" are mentioned so frequently is that "judgment" is predicated of truths, and "righteousness" of good, and therefore to "do judgment and righteousness" means to act from truth and from good. The reason "judgment" is predicated of truth, and "righteousness" of good, is that the Lord's government in the spiritual kingdom is called "judgment," and in the celestial kingdom "righteousness" (on which subject see the work *Heaven and Hell*, nn. 214, 215). As "judgment" is predicated of truth, in some passages we read

Truth and righteousness (as in Isa 11:5; Ps 85:11; and elsewhere).

86. That repetitions of the same thing occur in the Word on account of the marriage of good and truth, may be seen quite clearly from passages where "nations" and "peoples" are mentioned:

Woe to the sinful nation, to a people laden with iniquity (Isa 1:4).

The peoples that walk in darkness have seen a great light: Thou hast multiplied the nation (9:2, 3).

Asshur, the rod of Mine anger, I will send him against a hypocritical nation, and against the people of My wrath will I give him a charge (10:5, 6).

It shall come to pass in that day, that the root of Jesse, which standeth for an ensign of the peoples, shall the nations seek (11:10).

Jehovah that smiteth the peoples with an incurable stroke, that ruleth the nations with anger (14:6).

In that day shall a present be brought unto Jehovah of hosts of a people scattered and peeled, and a nation meted out and trodden down (18:7).

The mighty people shall honor Thee, the city of the powerful nations shall fear Thee (25:3).

Jehovah will swallow up the covering over all peoples, and the veil over all nations (verse 7).

Come near ye nations, and hearken ye peoples (34:1).

I have called thee for a covenant for the people, for a light of the nations (42:6).

Let all the nations be gathered together, and let the peoples assemble (43:9).

Behold, I will lift up My hand toward the nations, and My standard toward the peoples (49:22).

I have given Him for a witness to the peoples, a prince and a lawgiver to the nations (55:4, 5).

Behold, a people cometh from the land of the north; and a great nation from the sides of the earth (Je 6:22).

I will not make thee hear the calumny of the nations any more, neither shalt thou bear the reproach of the peoples any more (Ezek 36:15).

All peoples and nations shall worship Him (Da 7:14).

Let not the nations make a byword of them, and say among the peoples, Where is their God? (Joel 2:17).

The remnant of My people shall spoil them, and the residue of My nation shall inherit them (Zeph 2:9).

Many peoples and numerous nations shall come to seek Jehovah of hosts in Jerusalem (Zech 8:22).

Mine eyes have seen Thy salvation, which Thou has prepared before the face of all peoples, a light for revelation to the nations (Lu 2:30-32).

Thou hast redeemed us by Thy blood out of every people and nation (Apoc 5:9).

Thou must prophesy again concerning peoples and nations (10:11).

Thou shalt set me for a head of the nations: a people whom I have not known shall serve me (Ps 18:43).

Jehovah bringeth the counsel of the nations to nought, He overturneth the thoughts of the peoples (33:10).

Thou makest us a byword among the nations, a shaking of the head among the peoples (44:14).

Jehovah shall subdue the peoples under us, and the nations under our feet. Jehovah hath reigned over the nations; the willing ones of the peoples are gathered together (47:3, 8, 9).

Let the people confess unto Thee; let the nations be glad and shout for joy; for Thou shalt judge the peoples with equity, and lead the nations upon earth (67:3, 4).

Remember me, O Jehovah, in the good pleasure of Thy people; that I may rejoice in the joy of Thy nations (106:4, 5).

The reason "nations" and "peoples" are mentioned together is that "nations" mean those in good, and in the opposite sense in evil; and "peoples" those in truths, and in the opposite sense in falsities. For this reason those of the Lord's spiritual kingdom are called "peoples," and those of His celestial kingdom "nations;" for in the spiritual kingdom all are in truths and consequently in wisdom, and in the celestial kingdom all are in good and consequently in love.

87. The same rule holds good for other words; for example, where "joy" is mentioned, so is "gladness:"

Behold joy and gladness, slaying the ox (Isa 22:13).

They shall obtain joy and gladness, and sorrow and sighing shall flee away (35:10; 51:11).

Gladness and joy are cut off from the house of our God (Joel 1:16).

There shall be taken away the voice of joy, and the voice of gladness (Je 7:34; 25:10).

The fast of the tenth [month] shall be to the house of Judah for joy and gladness (Zech 8:19).

That we may rejoice all our days, make Thou us glad (Ps 90:14, 15).

Be ye glad in Jerusalem, and rejoice in her (Isa 66:10).

Rejoice and be glad, O daughter of Edom (La 4:21).

The heavens shall be glad, and the earth shall rejoice (Ps 96:11).

Make me to hear joy and gladness (51:8).

Joy and gladness shall be found in Zion, confession and the voice of singing (Isa 51:3).

There shall be gladness, and many shall rejoice at his birth (Lu 1:14).

I will cause to cease the voice of joy and the voice of gladness, the voice of the bridegroom and the voice of the bride (Je 7:34; 16:9; 25:10).

There shall be heard in this place the voice of joy and the voice of gladness, the voice of the bridegroom and the voice of the bride (33:10, 11).

The reason why both "joy" and "gladness" are mentioned is that "joy" is of good and "gladness" of truth, or "joy" is of love and "gladness" of wisdom. For joy is of the heart and gladness of the soul, or joy is of the will and gladness of the understanding. A marriage of the Lord and the church in these expressions also, is evident from its being said,

The voice of joy and the voice of gladness, the voice of the bridegroom and the voice of the bride (Je 7:34; 16:9; 25:10; 33:10, 11).

The Lord is the "bridegroom," and the church is the "bride."

That the Lord is the bridegroom, see (Mt 9:15; Mk 2:19, 20; Lu 5:34, 35;

And that the church is the bride, Apoc 21:2, 9; 22:17.

And therefore John the Baptist said of Jesus:

He that hath the bride is the bridegroom (Jn 3:29).

88. On account of the marriage of the Lord with the church, or what is the same, on account of the marriage of divine good and divine truth in each and every thing of the Word, "Jehovah" and "God," and also "Jehovah" and the "Holy One of Israel," are mentioned in very many places as if they were two although they are one, for by "Jehovah" is meant the Lord as to divine good, and by "God" and the "Holy One of Israel" the Lord as to divine truth. That "Jehovah" and "God," and also "Jehovah" and the "Holy One of Israel," are mentioned in very many places in the Word although One is meant who is the Lord, may be seen in *Doctrine of the Lord* (nn. 34, 38, and 46).

89. As there is the marriage of the Lord and the church in all things of the Word and in every single particular of it, it is evident that all things of the Word and also every particular of it treat of the Lord, as we set out to show in *Doctrine of the Lord* (nn. 1-7). The church (which likewise is treated of) is also the Lord; for the Lord teaches that the man of the church is in Him, and He in the man (Jn 6:56; 14:20, 21; 15:5, 7).

90. As the subject here treated of is the divinity and holiness of the Word, to what has already been said we may add something worthy of mention. A small piece of paper marked with Hebrew letters, but written as the ancients wrote them, was once sent me from heaven. In those times some of the letters that now are partly formed with straight lines were curved, and had little horns that turned upward. The angels who were then with me said that they themselves discerned complete meanings from the very letters, and that they knew them especially from the curvings of the lines and of the points of each letter. And they explained what the letters meant when taken each by itself and what when taken together; and said that the H that was added to the names of Abram and Sarai means what is infinite and eternal. They also explained in my presence from the letters or syllables alone the meaning of the Word in Psalm 32:2, showing that the sum of their meaning is, *That the Lord is merciful even to those who do evil.*

[2] They informed me that the writing in the third heaven consists of curved letters that are bent in various ways, and that each letter possesses a complete meaning; that the vowels there indicate a sound that corresponds to the affection, and that in that heaven they cannot utter the

vowels *i* and *e*, but instead of them *y* and *eu*, but that they do use the vowels *a*, *o*, and *u*, because they give a full sound.° Further: they do not pronounce any consonants as hard, but soft, and it is from this that certain Hebrew letters have a dot in the center as a sign that they are to be pronounced as [hard, and are without this dot when] soft. They said that hardness in pronouncing the letters is in use in the spiritual heaven because there they are in truths, and truth permits what is hard, but good does not, and in good are the angels of the celestial kingdom or third heaven. They also said that these angels possess the Word written with curved letters that have significant points and little horns. This shows what is meant by the words of the Lord:

One jot or one tittle shall in no wise pass from the law till all be fulfilled (Mt 5:18);

It is easier for heaven and earth to pass away than for one tittle of the law to fail (Lu 16:17).

° These letters are to be pronounced as follows:

    i as in mach*i*ne.
    e like the *a* in b*a*by.
    y like the German *ü*, or the French *u*.
    eu as in French, or like the German *ö*.
    a as in f*a*ther.

In Swedish, *o* and *oo* are sounded as follows:—
    o either as *oo* b*oo*th, or as *o* in n*o*te.
    u somewhat like the *ew* in h*ew*.

But the natural scale as set forth by Helmholtz and Donders would assign to *o* the sound of *o* in note, and to *u* the sound of *oo* in booth. [Tr.]

X.

IT IS POSSIBLE FOR HERESIES TO BE DRAWN FROM THE LITERAL
SENSE OF THE WORD, BUT IT IS HURTFUL TO CONFIRM THEM.

91. It has been shown above that the Word cannot be
understood without doctrine, and that doctrine is like a
lamp that enables genuine truths to be seen. The reason is
that the Word has been written entirely by correspondences,
and consequently many things in it are appearances of
truth and not naked truths; and many things also have been
written in adaptation to the apprehension of the natural
and even of the sensuous man, yet so that the simple may
understand it in simplicity, the intelligent in intelligence,
and the wise in wisdom. The result is that the appearances
of truth in the Word, which are truths clothed, may be
seized upon as naked truths, and when they are confirmed
they become falsities. But this is done by those who believe
themselves wise above others, although they are not wise,
for being wise consists in seeing whether a thing is true before it is confirmed, and not in confirming whatever one
pleases. This last is done by those who excel in a genius for
confirming and are in the conceit of self-intelligence, but
the former is done by those who love truths and are affected
by them because they are truths, and who make them uses
of the life, for these persons are enlightened by the Lord,
and see truths by the light of the truths; whereas the others
are enlightened by themselves and see falsities by the
"light" of the falsities.

92. That appearances of truth, which are truths clothed,
may be seized upon from the Word as naked truths, and
that when confirmed they become falsities, is evident from
the many heresies which have existed in Christendom

and still do. The heresies themselves do not condemn men, but an evil life does, as also do the confirmations from the Word, and from reasonings from the natural man, of the falsities that are in the heresy. For every one is born into the religion of his parents, is initiated into it from his infancy, and afterwards holds to it, being unable to withdraw himself from its falsities through being engaged with his business in the world. But to live in evil, and to confirm falsities even to the destruction of genuine truth, is what condemns. For he who remains in his own religion, and believes in God, or if in Christendom, in the Lord, regarding the Word as holy, and from a religious principle living according to the ten commandments, does not swear allegiance to falsities, and therefore as soon as he hears truths, and perceives them in his own way, he can embrace them and so be led away from falsities; but not so the man who has confirmed the falsities of his religion, for confirmed falsity remains and cannot be rooted out. For after confirmation a falsity becomes as if the man had sworn to the truth of it, especially if it agrees with his own self-love, and the derivative conceit of his own wisdom.

93. I have talked with some in the spiritual world who had lived many ages ago, and had confirmed themselves in the falsities of their religion; and I found that they still remained steadfast in the same. I have also spoken there with some who had been of the same religion as they, and had thought as they did, but had not confirmed themselves in its falsities, and I found that after being instructed by angels they had rejected the falsities and had accepted truths, and so they were saved, but not the others. After death every man is instructed by angels, and those who see truths, and from truths falsities, are received. For the power to see truths spiritually is then given every one, and those see them who have not confirmed themselves in falsities, but those who have confirmed themselves do not want to see truths, and if they do see them they turn their backs on them, and then either ridicule or falsify them.

94. Let us illustrate this by an example. In many places in the Word, anger, wrath, and vengeance are attributed to the Lord, and it is also said that He punishes, that He casts into hell, that He tempts, and many other such things. He who believes all this in simplicity, and on that account fears God and takes care not to sin against Him, is not condemned for that simple belief. But the man who confirms himself in these ideas as far as to believe that anger, wrath, revenge, thus things that are evil, exist in the Lord; and that from anger, wrath, and revenge He punishes a man and casts him into hell—such a man is condemned, because he has destroyed the genuine truth that the Lord is love itself, mercy itself, and good itself, and that one who is all these cannot be angry, wrathful, and revengeful. These things are attributed to the Lord because such is the appearance. So with many other things.

95. Many things in the sense of the letter are apparent truths, having genuine truths hidden within them, and it is not hurtful to think and speak in accordance with such truths, but it is hurtful to confirm them to such a degree as to destroy the genuine truth hidden within. This may be illustrated by an example in nature, which is presented because what is natural teaches and convinces more clearly than what is spiritual.

[2] To the eye the sun appears to revolve around the earth daily, and also annually, and therefore in the Word the sun is said to rise and set, thus making morning, noon, evening, and night, and also making the seasons of spring, summer, autumn, and winter, and thus days and years; when yet the sun stands motionless, for it is an ocean of fire, and it is the earth that revolves daily, and is carried around the sun annually. The man who in simplicity and ignorance supposes that the sun is carried around the earth, does not de-

stroy the natural truth that the earth daily rotates on its axis, and is annually carried along the ecliptic. But the man who by the Word and by reasonings from the natural man confirms as real the apparent motion and course of the sun, does invalidate the truth and does destroy it.

[3] That the sun moves is an apparent truth; that it does not move is a genuine truth. Every one may speak in accordance with the apparent truth, and does so speak, but to think in accordance with it from confirmation blunts and darkens the rational understanding. It is the same with respect to the stars in the sidereal heavens. The apparent truth is that they too, like the sun, are carried around the earth once a day, and it is therefore said of the stars also that they rise and set. But the genuine truth is that the stars are fixed, and that their heavens stand motionless. Still, every one may speak in accordance with the appearance.

96. The reason why it is hurtful to confirm the apparent truth of the Word to the point of destroying the genuine truth that lies hidden within, is that each and all things of the sense of the letter of the Word communicate with heaven, and open it, as before shown (nn. 62-69). So when a man applies this sense to confirm worldly loves that are contrary to heavenly ones, the internal of the Word is made false, and the result is that when its external or literal sense, which now has a false internal, communicates with heaven, heaven is closed; for the angels, who are in the internal of the Word, reject that external of it. Thus it is evident that a false internal, or truth falsified, takes away communication with heaven, and closes heaven. This is why it is hurtful to confirm any heretical falsity.

96a. The Word is like a garden, a heavenly paradise, that contains delicacies and delights of every kind, delicacies in its fruits and delights in its flowers; and in the midst of the garden trees of life with fountains of living water near them, while forest trees surround it. The man who from doctrine is in divine truths is at its center where the trees of life are, and is in the actual enjoyment of its delicacies and delights; whereas the man who is in truths not from doctrine, but from the sense of the letter only, is at the outskirts, and sees nothing but the forest vegetation. And one who is in the doctrine of a false religion, and who has confirmed himself in its falsity, is not even in the forest, but is out beyond it in a sandy plain where there is not even grass. That such are their different states after death will be shown in its own place.

97. Moreover the literal sense of the Word is a guard to the genuine truths that lie hidden within. It is a guard in this respect, that it can be turned this way or that, and explained according to the way it is taken, yet without injury or violence to its internal. It does no harm for the sense of the letter to be understood in one way by one person and in a different way by another; but it does harm for the divine truths that lie hidden within to be perverted, because this inflicts violence on the Word. The sense of the letter is a guard against this, and the guard is effective in the case of those who are in falsities from their religion, but do not confirm those falsities, for these persons do the Word no violence.

[2] This guard is signified by cherubs, and in the Word is described by them, as by the cherubs that were stationed at the entrance of the garden of Eden after Adam and his wife had been cast out, of which we read as follows:

When Jehovah God had driven out the man, He made to dwell at the east of the garden of Eden the cherubim, and the flame of a sword which turned every way, to keep the way of the tree of life (Ge 3:24).

The "cherubim" signify a guard; the "way of the tree of life," signifies the access to the Lord which men have by means of the Word; the "flame of a sword that turned every way," means divine truth in the most external things, this being like the Word in the sense of the letter, which can be so turned.

[3] The same is meant by

the cherubs of gold that were placed upon the two ends of the mercy-seat that was upon the ark in the tabernacle (Ex 25:18-21).

As this was signified by cherubs,

the Lord spoke with Moses from between them (25:22; 37:9; Num 7:89).

That the Lord does not speak to man except in what is full, and that the Word in the sense of the letter is divine truth in fullness, may be seen above (nn. 37-49). So therefore did the Lord speak to Moses from between the cherubs. This also was the signification of

the cherubs on the curtains of the tabernacle, and on the veil (Ex 26:1, 31),

for the curtains and veils of the tabernacle represented the outmost things of heaven and the church, and therefore of the Word, as may be seen above (n. 46). Such, too, was the meaning of

the cherubs in the midst of the temple in Jerusalem (1 Kgs 6:23-28); the cherubs carved on the walls and doors of the temple (verses 29, 32, 35); or the cherubs in the new temple (Ezek 41:18-20);

as also may be seen above (n. 47).

[4] As cherubs signified a guard that the Lord, heaven, and divine truth such as is within the Word, be not approached immediately, but mediately through externals, it is said of the king of Tyre,

Thou sealest up the measure, full of wisdom and perfect in beauty; thou has been in Eden the garden of God; every precious stone was thy covering; thou, O cherub, art the outspreading of that which covereth; I have destroyed thee, O covering cherub, in the midst of the stones of fire (Ezek 28:12-14, 16).

"Tyre" signifies the church in respect to the knowledges of truth and good, and therefore its "king" signifies the Word, in which and from which are these knowledges. It is evident that the Word in its literal sense is here signified by that king, and also that a guard is signified by a "cherub," for it is said, "thou sealest up the measure; every precious stone was thy covering;" and "thou, O cherub, art the outspreading of that which covereth;" and also "O covering cherub." That the "precious stones" mentioned in this passage mean truths of the literal sense of the Word, may be seen above (n. 45). As "cherubs" signify the outmost expression of divine truth as a guard, it is said in the Psalms of David:

Jehovah bowed the heavens also and came down; and He rode upon a cherub (18:9, 10).

O Shepherd of Israel, Thou that sittest upon the cherubim, shine forth (80:1).

Jehovah sitteth upon the cherubim (99:1).

To "ride upon cherubs," and to "sit upon them," means upon the literal sense of the Word.

[5] Divine truth in the Word, and the quality of it, are described by the cherubs in the first, ninth, and tenth chapters of Ezekiel; but as no one can know what is signified by the particulars of the description of them, except one to whom the spiritual sense has been opened, it has been disclosed to me what in brief is signified by all the things said about the cherubs in the first chapter of Ezekiel, which are as follows:

The external divine sphere of the Word is described (verse 4);
It is represented as a man (verse 5);
And conjoined with spiritual and celestial things (verse 6);
The natural of the Word, its quality (verse 7);

The spiritual and the celestial of the Word conjoined with its natural, their quality (verses 8, 9);

The divine love of the good and truth celestial, spiritual, and natural therein, and also together (verses 10, 11);

They all look to the one thing (verse 12);

The sphere of the Word from the Lord's divine good and divine truth, from which the Word is alive (verses 13, 14);

The doctrine of good and truth in the Word and from the Word (verses 15-21);

The divine of the Lord above the Word and in it (verses 22, 23);

And from it (verses 24, 25);

The Lord is above the heavens (verse 26);

And divine love and divine wisdom are His (verses 27, 28).

These summaries have been compared with the Word in heaven, and are in conformity with it.

XI.

THE LORD CAME INTO THE WORLD TO FULFILL EVERYTHING IN THE WORD, AND THEREBY TO BECOME DIVINE TRUTH OR THE WORD EVEN IN OUTMOSTS.

98. That the Lord came into the world to fulfill all things of the Word, may be seen in *Doctrine of the Lord* (nn. 8-11). And that He thereby became divine truth or the Word even in outmosts, is meant by these words in John:

The Word became flesh, and dwelt among us, and we beheld His glory, the glory as of the Only-begotten of the Father, full of grace and truth (1:14).

To "become flesh" is to become the Word in outmosts. What the Lord was as the Word in outmosts He showed His disciples when He was transfigured:

Mt 17:2, etc.; Mk 9:2, etc.; Lu 9:28, etc.;

and it is there said that Moses and Elias were seen in glory. By "Moses and Elias" is meant the Word, as may be seen above (n. 48). The Lord, as the Word in outmosts, is also described by John in the Apocalypse, chapter 1: 13-16, where all things in the description of Him signify the most external things of divine truth or of the Word. The Lord had indeed been the Word before, but only in first things, for it is said:

In the beginning was the Word, and the Word was with God, and God was the Word; the same was in the beginning with God (Jn 1:1, 2);

but when the Word became flesh, then the Lord became the Word in last things also. It is from this that He is called,

The First and the Last (Apoc 1:8, 11, 17; 2:8; 21:6; 22:13).

99. The state of the church was completely changed by the Lord's becoming the Word in last things. All the churches that had existed before His advent were representative churches, and could see divine truth in obscurity only; but after the Lord's coming into the world a church was instituted by Him that saw divine truth in the light. The difference is like that between evening and morning, and the state of the church before His advent is also called "the evening," and that of the church after it "the morning." Before His coming into the world the Lord was indeed present with the men of the church, but mediately through heaven, whereas since His coming into the world He is present with them immediately, for in the world He put on the divine natural, in which He is present with men. The glorification of the Lord is the glorification of His Human that He assumed in the world, and the Lord's glorified Human is the divine natural.

100. Few understand how the Lord is the Word, for they think that the Lord may indeed enlighten and teach men by means of the Word without His being on that account called the Word. It should be known however that every man is his own love, and consequently his own good and his own truth. It is solely from this that a man is a man, and there is nothing else in him that is man. It is from the fact that a man is his own good and his own truth that angels and spirits are men, for all the good-and-truth proceeding from the Lord is in form a man. And as the Lord is divine good and divine truth itself, He is *the* Man, from whom every man is a man. That all divine good and divine truth is in form a man, may be seen in the work *Heaven and Hell* (n. 460), and more clearly in treatises to follow, on the subject of *Angelic Wisdom.*

XII.

101. From what is related in the books of Moses it is evident that worship by means of sacrifices was known, and that men prophesied from the mouth of Jehovah, before the Word was given to the Israelitish nation through Moses and the prophets. That such worship by means of sacrifices was known, is evident from these facts:

The sons of Israel were commanded to overturn the altars of the nations, break in pieces their images, and cut down their groves (Ex 34:13; Dt 7:5; 12:3).

In Shittim Israel began to commit whoredom with the daughters of Moab; they called the people to the sacrifices of their gods, and the people did eat, and bowed down to their gods; and Israel joined himself especially to Baal-peor, and on that account the anger of Jehovah was kindled against Israel (Num 25:1-3).

Balaam, who was from Syria, caused altars to be built, and sacrificed oxen and sheep (22:40; 23:1, 2, 14, 29, 30).

[2] That men prophesied from the mouth of Jehovah, is evident from the prophecies of Balaam (Num 23:7-10, 18-24; 24:3-9, 16-24).

He also prophesied concerning the Lord that a Star should arise out of Jacob, and a Scepter out of Israel (verse 17).

And he prophesied from the mouth of Jehovah (22:13, 18; 23:3, 5, 8, 16, 26; 24:1, 13).

From these facts it is evident that there existed among the nations a divine worship similar to that instituted through Moses among the Israelitish nation.

[3] That it existed even before the time of Abram is in some measure apparent from the words in Moses (Dt 32:7,

8), but more evidently from what is said of Melchizedek king of Salem:

He brought forth bread and wine, and blessed Abram, and that Abram gave him tithes of all (Ge 14:18-20);

and that Melchizedek represented the Lord, for he is called

Priest of God Most High (verse 18);

and it is said in David concerning the Lord:

Thou art a priest to eternity, after the manner of Melchizedek (Ps 110:4).

Hence it was that Melchizedek brought forth bread and wine as holy things of the church, even as they are holy things in the sacrament of the Supper; and that Melchizedek could bless Abram, and that Abram gave him tithes of all.

102. I have been told by angels of heaven that there was among the ancients a Word written entirely by correspondences, but that it had been lost, and they said that it is still preserved, and is in use in that heaven where those ancient people dwell who had possessed it in this world. The ancients who still use that Word in heaven came partly from the land of Canaan and the neighboring countries, such as Syria, Mesopotamia, Arabia, Chaldea, Assyria, and Egypt, and also from Sidon, Tyre, and Nineveh. The inhabitants of all these kingdoms were in representative worship, and consequently in the knowledge of correspondences. The wisdom of that time was derived from this knowledge, and by its means they had an interior perception, and a communication with the heavens. Those who had an interior acquaintance with the correspondences of that Word were called wise and intelligent, and later, diviners and magi. But as that Word was full of correspondences which only in a remote way signified celestial and spiritual things, and consequently began to be falsified by many of them, under

the Lord's divine providence it disappeared in course of time, and at length was utterly lost, and another Word, written by correspondences less remote than the other, was given by means of prophets among the sons of Israel. Yet many names of places in the land of Canaan and in the surrounding countries were retained in this Word with significations like those they had in the ancient Word. It was for this reason that Abram was commanded to go into that land, and that his descendants, from Jacob, were brought into it.

103. That there was a Word among the ancients is evident from Moses, who mentions it, and who took some things from it (Num 21:14, 15, 27-30); the historical parts of that Word being called the *Wars of Jehovah*, and its prophetical parts the *Enunciations*. From the historical parts of that Word Moses took the following:

> Wherefore it is said in the book of the Wars of Jehovah: At Vaheb in Suphah, and the rivers of Arnon; and the watercourse of the rivers that inclineth toward the dwelling of Ar, and betaketh itself to the border of Moab (verses 14, 15).

In that Word, as in ours, the "Wars of Jehovah" meant and described the Lord's combats with hell and His victories over it at the time when He should come into the world. The same combats are meant, and are described, in many passages of the historical parts of our Word, such as the wars of Joshua with the nations of the land of Canaan, and those of the judges and kings of Israel.

[2] From the prophetical parts of that Word Moses took the following:

> Wherefore the Enunciators say: Come ye to Heshbon, let the city of Sihon be built and strengthened; for a fire is gone out of Heshbon, a flame from the city of Sihon, it hath devoured Ar of Moab, the possessors of the high places of Arnon. Woe to thee, Moab! thou hast perished, O people of Chemosh: he hath given his sons as fugitives, and his daughters into captivity unto Sihon king of the Amo-

rites. With darts have we destroyed them. Heshbon hath perished even unto Dibon, and we have laid waste even unto Nophah, which reacheth unto Medeba (verses 27-30).

The translators say *They that speak in Proverbs,* but the rendering should be *Enunciators,* or *Prophetic Enunciations,* as is evident from the meaning of the word *m'shalim* in the Hebrew tongue, which is not merely proverbs, but also prophetic enunciations, as in Numbers 23:7, 18; 24:3, 15, where it is said that Balaam uttered "his enunciation" which was prophetic, and which also was about the Lord. His enunciation is called *mashal,* in the singular. Consider also that the things taken from them by Moses are not proverbs, but prophecies.

[3] That ancient Word, like ours, was divine or divinely inspired, as is evident from Jeremiah, where almost the same words occur:

A fire is gone forth out of Heshbon, and a flame from the midst of Sihon, that hath devoured the corner of Moab, and the crown of the head of the sons of clamor. Woe unto thee, O Moab! the people of Chemosh is undone, for thy sons have been carried off into captivity, and thy daughters into captivity (48:45, 46).

Besides these books, a prophetic book of the ancient Word called the *Book of Jashar,* or the *Book of the Upright,* is mentioned by David and by Joshua. By David:

David lamented over Saul and over Jonathan; and wrote, To teach the sons of Judah the bow. Behold it is written in the Book of Jashar (2 Sa 1:17, 18).

And by Joshua:

Joshua said, Sun, be silent in Gibeon, and thou, Moon, in the valley of Ajalon. Is not this written in the Book of Jashar? (Josh 10:12, 13).

Furthermore: I have been told that the first seven chapters of Genesis appear in that ancient Word complete to the slightest expression.

XIII.

104. There can be no conjunction with heaven unless somewhere on earth there is a church where the Word is, and where by it the Lord is known; for the Lord is the God of heaven and earth, and apart from Him there is no salvation. It is sufficient that there be a church where the Word is, even if it consists of comparatively few, for even in that case the Lord is present by its means in the whole world, for by its means heaven is conjoined with the human race. That there is conjunction by means of the Word may be seen above (nn. 62-69).

105. But how the presence and conjunction of the Lord and heaven exist in every country by means of the Word shall now be told. Before the Lord the universal heaven is like one man, and so is the church. And that they actually appear as a man may be seen in the work *Heaven and Hell* (nn. 59-86). In this man, the church where the Word is read and the Lord thereby known, is like the heart and lungs; the celestial kingdom like the heart, and the spiritual kingdom like the lungs.

[2] As all the other members and viscera subsist and live from these two sources of the life of the human body, so also do all those in the whole earth who have some sort of religion, worship one God, and live aright, and who are thereby in that man and correspond to its members and viscera outside the chest which contains the heart and lungs —so do all these subsist and live from the conjunction of the Lord and heaven with the church by means of the Word. For the Word in the church, although existing with

206

comparatively few, is life to all the rest, from the Lord through heaven, just as there is life for the members and viscera of the whole body from the heart and lungs; and there is a similar relationship.

[3] This is why those Christians among whom the Word is read constitute the breast of that man. They are in the center of all; round about them are the Papists; around these again are those Mohammedans who acknowledge the Lord as the greatest Prophet and as the Son of God; beyond these are the Africans; while the nations and people of Asia and the Indies constitute the furthest compass. Concerning this ranking of them something may be seen in the little work on the *Last Judgment* (n. 48). Moreover all who are in that man depend upon the middle region where the Christians are.

106. The greatest light is in this middle region where are the Christians who possess the Word; for light in the heavens is divine truth proceeding from the Lord as the sun there; and as the Word is this divine truth, the light is greatest where dwell those who possess the Word. From this region as from its own center, the light propagates itself to all the perimeters even to the uttermost of them; and in this way comes the enlightening, by means of the Word, of all the nations and peoples that are outside the church. That the light in the heavens is divine truth which proceeds from the Lord, and that this light confers intelligence not only on angels but also on men, may be seen in the work *Heaven and Hell* (nn. 126-140).

107. That this is the case in the universal heaven may be inferred from the similar conditions that prevail in each of the heavenly societies; for every society of heaven is a heaven in a smaller form, and is also like a man. This may be seen in the work *Heaven and Hell* (nn. 41-87). In each society of heaven also, those in the center correspond to the heart and lungs, and they possess the greatest light. This light, and the consequent perception of truth, propagates it-self from that center toward the successive circuits in every direction, thus to all in the society, and it makes their spirit-ual life. It has been shown that when those in the center who constituted the province of the heart and lungs and possessed the greatest light, were taken away, those around them came into shadow, and into a perception of truth so scanty as to be almost none at all; but as soon as the others came back, the light reappeared, and they had perception of truth the same as before.

108. The same thing may be illustrated by the following experience. African spirits from Abyssinia were present with me. On a certain occasion their ears were opened so that they heard the singing of a Psalm of David in some place of worship in this world, which affected them with such delight that they too sang along with that congrega-tion. Presently their ears were closed so that they heard nothing of the singing, but they were then affected with a delight still greater, because spiritual; and they were at the same time filled with intelligence, because that Psalm treated of the Lord and of redemption. The cause of this increase of delight was that there was opened to them a communication with that society in heaven which was in conjunction with those in this world who were singing that Psalm. From this and many other such experiences it has become evident to me that communication with the univer-sal heaven is effected by means of the Word. And for this reason there exists under the Lord's divine providence, a universal commercial intercourse of the kingdoms of Eu-rope—and chiefly of those where the Word is read—with the nations outside the church.

109. In this respect a comparison may be made with heat and light from the sun of this world, which causes vegeta-tion in trees and shrubs even when they are out of its direct rays and under a clouded sky, provided the sun has risen and shown itself in the world. It is the same with the light and heat of heaven from the Lord as the sun, this light being divine truth, the source of all intelligence and wisdom to angels and men. It is therefore said of the Word:

That it was with God, and was God; that it enlightens every man that comes into the world (Jn 1:1, 9); and also that that light appears in the darkness (verse 5).

110. From all this it is evident that the Word which exists in the Church of the Reformed enlightens all nations and peoples by a spiritual communication; and also that it is provided by the Lord that there shall always be a church on earth where the Word is read, and where consequently the Lord is known. It was for this reason that when the Word had been almost completely rejected by the Papists, of the Lord's divine providence the Reformation was brought about, whereby the Word was again received, as also that the Word is accounted holy by a notable nation among the Papists.

111. As without the Word there is no knowledge of the Lord, and therefore no salvation, it pleased the Lord, when the Word had been wholly falsified and adulterated among the Jewish nation and thus as it were brought to nothingness, that He should descend from heaven and come into the world, and fulfill the Word, and thereby repair and restore it, and again give light to the earth's inhabitants, in accordance with His declaration:

The people that sat in darkness have seen a great light; and to those who sat in the region and shadow of death, light is sprung up (Mt 4:16; Isa 9:2).

112. As it had been foretold that darkness would arise at the end of the present church in consequence of the lack of knowledge and acknowledgment of the Lord as being the God of heaven and earth, and also in consequence of the separation of faith from charity, therefore in order that by reason of this a genuine understanding of the Word might not perish, it has pleased the Lord at this present time to reveal the spiritual sense of the Word and make it plain that the Word in this sense, and from this in the natural sense, treats of the Lord and the church, and indeed of these alone, and to uncover many other things besides, by means of which the light of truth from the Word, now almost extinguished, may be restored. That the light of truth would be almost extinguished at the end of the present church is foretold in many places in the Apocalypse, and is also what is meant by the following words of the Lord in Matthew:

Immediately after the affliction of those days shall the sun be darkened, and the moon shall not give her light, and the stars shall fall from heaven, and the powers of the heavens shall be shaken; and then they shall see the Son of man coming in the clouds of heaven with glory and power (24:29, 30).

The "sun" here means the Lord as to love; the "moon," the Lord as to faith; the "stars," the Lord as to the knowledges of good and truth; the "Son of man," the Lord as to the Word; a "cloud," the literal sense of the Word; and "glory,' its spiritual sense and the shining through of this in the sense of the letter.

113. It has been given me to know by much experience that by means of the Word man has communication with heaven. While I read the Word through from the first chapter of Isaiah to the last of Malachi, and the Psalms of David, I was permitted clearly to perceive that each verse communicated with some society of heaven, and thus the whole Word with the universal heaven.

XIV.

WITHOUT THE WORD NO ONE WOULD HAVE KNOWLEDGE OF GOD, OF HEAVEN AND HELL, OF LIFE AFTER DEATH, AND STILL LESS OF THE LORD.

114. This follows as a general conclusion from what has been already said and shown; as that the Word is divine truth itself (nn. 1-4); that it is a medium of conjunction with the angels of heaven (nn. 62-69); that everywhere in it there is a marriage of the Lord and the church, and a consequent marriage of good and truth (nn. 80-89); that the quality of the church is such as is its understanding of the Word (nn. 76-79); that the Word exists in the heavens also, and the angels have their wisdom from it (nn. 70-75); that the nations and peoples outside the church also have spiritual light by means of the Word (nn. 104-113); and much more besides. From all this it can be concluded that without the Word no one would possess spiritual intelligence, which consists in having knowledge of God, of heaven and hell, and of life after death; nor would anyone know anything whatever about the Lord, about faith in Him and love to Him, nor anything about redemption, by means of which nevertheless comes salvation. As the Lord also says to His disciples:

Without Me ye can do nothing (Jn 15:5);

and John:

A man can receive nothing except it be given him from heaven (Jn 3:27).

115. However, as there are those who maintain, and have confirmed themselves in the opinion, that without a Word it is possible for a man to know of the existence of God, and of heaven and hell, and of all the other things taught by the Word, and as they thereby weaken the authority and holiness of the Word, if not with the lips, yet in the heart, therefore it is not practicable to deal with them from the Word, but only from rational light, for they do not believe in the Word, but in themselves. [To all such we would say,] Investigate the matter from rational light, and you will find that in man there are two faculties of life called the understanding and the will, and that the understanding is subject to the will, but not the will to the understanding, for the understanding merely teaches and shows the way. Make further investigation, and you will find that man's will is what is his Own (*proprium*)*, and that this, regarded in itself, is nothing but evil, and that from this springs what is false in the understanding.

[2] Having discovered these facts you will see that from himself a man does not desire to understand anything but what comes from the Own of his will, and also that it is not possible for him to do so unless there is some other source from which he may know it. From the Own of his will a man does not desire to understand anything except what relates to himself and to the world; everything above this is to him in thick darkness. So, when he sees the sun, the moon, the stars, and chances to think about their origin, how is it possible for him to think otherwise than that they exist of themselves? Can he raise his thoughts higher than do many of the learned in the world who acknowledge only nature, in spite of the fact that from the Word they know of the creation of all things by God? What then would these same have thought if they had known nothing from the Word?

[3] Do you believe that the wise men of old, Aristotle, Cicero, Seneca, and others, who wrote about God and the

* See n. 60 above.

immortality of the soul, got this from themselves? They did not, but from others who had it by tradition from those who first knew it from the [ancient] Word. Neither do the writers on natural theology get any such matters from themselves. They merely confirm by rational arguments what they have already become acquainted with from the church in which is the Word; and there may be some among them who confirm without believing it.

116. I have been permitted to see peoples who had been born in [remote] islands, who were rational in respect to civil matters, but had known nothing whatever about God. In the spiritual world such appear like apes, and their life is very similar to that of apes. But having been born men, and consequently being endowed with a capacity to receive spiritual life, they are instructed by angels and are made spiritually alive by means of knowledges about God as a Man. What man is, of himself, is very evident from the character of those who are in hell, among whom are to be found leading and learned men who are unwilling even to hear of God, and therefore cannot utter His name. I have seen such and have talked with them. I have spoken also with some who burned with angry passion when they heard any mention of God. Such being the character of some who have heard about God, who have written about God, and have preached about God (and there are many such from among the Jesuits), consider what a man would be who had never even heard of Him. It is from the will, which is evil, that these are of such a character; for, as before said, the will leads the understanding, and takes away from it the truth that is in it from the Word. If man had been able of himself to know that there is a God and a life after death, why has he not known that after death a man is still a man? Why does he believe that his soul or spirit is like a breath of air, or like the ether, and that it has no eyes with which to see, nor ears with which to hear, nor mouth

with which to speak, until it shall have been conjoined and combined with its carcass and with its skeleton? Assume then the existence of a doctrine of worship that has been hatched solely from rational light, and will not that doctrine be that a man's own self is to be worshiped? For ages this is what has been done, and is done at the present day by some who know from the Word that God alone ought to be worshiped. From what is man's Own, any other kind of worship, even that of the sun and moon, is impossible.

117. Religion has existed from the most ancient times; so everywhere the inhabitants of the world have had knowledge of God, and have known something about a life after death, but this has not originated in themselves or their own discernment, but from the ancient Word (spoken of above, nn. 101-103), and, at a later period, from the Israelitish Word. From these two Words the things of religion have spread into the Indies and their islands, and through Egypt and Ethiopia into the kingdoms of Africa, and from the maritime parts of Asia into Greece, and from thence into Italy. But as the Word could not be written in any other way than by means of representatives, which are such things in this world as correspond to heavenly things, and therefore signify them, the things of religion among many of the nations were turned into idolatry, and in Greece into fables, and the divine attributes and properties into so many gods, over whom they set one supreme, whom they called "Jove" [perhaps—see *True Christian Religion*, n. 275—] from "Jehovah." It is known that they had knowledge of paradise, of the flood, of the sacred fire, and of the four ages, from the first or golden age to the last or iron age, by which are meant the four states of the church (as in Daniel 2:31-35). It is also known that the Mohammedan religion, which came later and destroyed the former religions of many nations, was taken from the Word of both Testaments.

118. Lastly, I will state what those people become like

after death who ascribe all things to their own intelligence, and little or nothing to the Word. They first become as if inebriated, then as if silly, and finally stupid, and they sit in darkness. Of such insanity, therefore, let all beware.

THE DOCTRINE OF LIFE

FOR

THE NEW JERUSALEM

————

I.

ALL RELIGION IS OF THE LIFE, AND THE LIFE OF RELIGION IS TO DO WHAT IS GOOD.

1. Every man who has religion knows and acknowledges that one who leads a good life is saved, and that one who leads an evil life is condemned; for he knows and acknowledges that the man who lives aright thinks aright, not only about God but also about his neighbor. This is not so with the man whose life is evil. The life of man is his love, and what he loves he not only likes to be doing, but also likes to be thinking.

The reason therefore why we say that the life of religion is to do what is good is that doing what is good acts as one with thinking what is good; for if in a man these two things do not act as one, they are not matters of life with him. The demonstration of these points shall now follow.

2. That religion concerns life and that the life of religion is to do what is good is seen by every one who reads the Word, and is acknowledged by him while he is reading it. The Word contains the following declarations:

Whosoever shall break the least of these commandments, and shall teach men so, shall be called the least in the kingdom of the heavens; but whosoever shall do and teach them, the same shall be called great in the kingdom of the heavens. For I say unto you that except your righteousness shall exceed that of the Scribes and Pharisees, ye shall not enter into the kingdom of the heavens (Mt 5:19, 20).

Every tree that bringeth not forth good fruit is hewn down, and cast into the fire. Therefore by their fruits ye shall know them (Mt 7:19, 20).

Not every one that saith unto Me, Lord, Lord, shall enter into the kingdom of the heavens; but he that doeth the will of My Father who is in the heavens (verse 21).

Many will say to Me in that day, Lord, Lord, have we not prophesied by Thy name, and in Thy name done many mighty things? And then will I declare unto them, I never knew you, depart from Me ye that work iniquity (verses 22, 23).

Every one who heareth these words of Mine, and doeth them, shall be likened to a wise man who built his house upon the rock; and every one that heareth these words of Mine, and doeth them not, shall be likened unto a foolish man who built his house upon the sand (verses 24, 26).

Jesus said, Behold, the sower went forth to sow; some seeds fell on the hard way, others fell upon the rocky places, others fell among the thorns, and others fell into good ground; he that was sown upon the good ground, this is he that heareth the Word, and thereto giveth heed, who thence beareth fruit, and bringeth forth, some a hundredfold, some sixty, and some thirty. When Jesus had said these things, He cried, saying, He that hath ears to hear, let him hear (Mt 13:3-9, 23, 43).

For the Son of man shall come in the glory of His Father, and then shall He render unto every one according to his deeds (16:27).

The kingdom of God shall be taken away from you, and shall be given unto a nation bringing forth the fruits thereof (21:43).

When the Son of man shall come in His glory, then shall He sit on the throne of His glory. And He shall say to the sheep on His right hand, Come ye blessed, inherit the kingdom prepared for you from the foundation of the world; for I was hungry, and ye gave Me meat; I was thirsty, and ye gave Me drink; I was a stranger, and ye took Me in; naked, and ye clothed Me; I was sick, and ye visited Me; I was in prison, and ye came unto Me. Then shall the righteous answer, When saw we Thee so? And the king shall answer and say unto them, Verily I say unto you, Inasmuch as ye did it unto one of the least of these My brethren, ye did it unto Me. And the king shall say the like things to the goats on the left, and because they have not done such things, He shall say, Depart from Me, ye cursed, into the eternal fire which is prepared for the devil and his angels (25:31-41).

Bring forth therefore fruits worthy of repentance; even now is the axe laid unto the root of the trees; every tree therefore that bringeth not forth good fruit is hewn down and cast into the fire (Lu 3:8, 9).

Jesus said, Why call ye Me Lord, Lord, and do not the things which I say? Every one that cometh unto Me, and heareth My words, and doeth them, he is like a man building a house, and he laid a foundation upon the rock; but he that heareth, and doeth not, is like a man that built a house upon the earth without a foundation (6:46-49).

Jesus said, My mother and My brethren are these who hear the Word of God, and do it (8:21).

Then shall ye begin to stand, and to knock at the door, saying, Lord, open to us; and He shall answer and say to you, I know you not whence ye are; depart from Me, all ye workers of iniquity (13:25-27).

This is the judgment: that the light is come into the world, and men loved the darkness rather than the light, for their works were evil; for every one that doeth evil hateth the light, lest his works should be reproved. But he that doeth the truth cometh to the light, that his works may be made manifest, that they have been wrought in God (Jn 3:19-21).

And shall come forth; they that have done good, unto the resurrection [of life; and they that have done evil, unto the resurrection] of judgment (5:29).

We know that God heareth not sinners; but if any man be a worshiper of God, and do His will, him He heareth (9:31).

If ye know these things, blessed are ye if ye do them (13:17).

He that hath My commandments, and keepeth them, he it is that loveth Me; and I will love him, and will manifest Myself unto him; and We will come unto him, and make our abode with him. He that loveth Me not keepeth not My words (14:21-24).

Jesus said, I am the true vine, and My Father is the vine-dresser; every branch in Me that beareth not fruit, He taketh away; and every branch that beareth fruit, He cleanseth it, that it may bear more fruit (15:1, 2).

Herein is My Father glorified, that ye bear much fruit, and ye shall be made My disciples (verse 8).

Ye are My friends if ye do the things which I command you; I have chosen you, that ye should bear fruit, and your fruit should abide (verses 14, 16).

The Lord said to John, To the angel of the church in Ephesus write: I know thy works; I have this against thee, that thou hast left thy first charity; repent, and do the first works, or else I will move thy lampstand out of its place (Apoc 2:1, 2, 4, 5).

To the angel of the church in Smyrna write: I know thy works (verses 8, 9).

To the angel of the church in Pergamos write: I know thy works, repent (verses 12, 16).

To the angel of the church in Thyatira write: I know they works and charity, and thy last works are more than the first (verses 18, 19).

To the angel of the church in Sardis write: I know thy works, that thou hast a name that thou livest, but art dead; I have not found thy works perfect before God; repent (3:1-3).

To the angel of the church in Philadelphia write: I know thy works (verses 7, 8).

To the angel of the church of the Laodiceans write: I know thy works; repent (verses 14, 15, 19).

I heard a voice from heaven saying, Write, Blessed are the dead who die in the Lord from henceforth; yea, saith the Spirit, that they may rest from their labors, for their works follow with them (14:13).

Another book was opened, which is the book of life, and the dead were judged out of the things which were written in the books, all according to their works (20:12, 13).

Behold, I come quickly, and My reward is with Me, to give to every one according to his work (22:12).

In like manner in the Old Testament:

Recompense them according to their work, and according to the deed of their hands (Je 25:14).

Jehovah, whose eyes are open upon all the ways of the sons of men, to give every one according to his ways, and according to the fruit of his works (32:19).

I will visit according to his ways, and will reward him his works (Hosea 4:9).

Jehovah, according to our ways, according to our works doth He to us (Zech 1:6).

And in many places it is said that the statutes, commandments, and laws were to be done:

Ye shall observe My statutes, and My judgments, which if a man do, he shall live by them (Lev 18:5).

Ye shall observe all My statutes, and My judgments, that ye may do them (19:37; 20:8; 22:31).

The blessings, if they did the commandments; and the curses if they did them not (26:4-46).

The sons of Israel were commanded to make for themselves a fringe on the borders of their garments, that they might remember all the commandments of Jehovah, to do them (Num 15:38, 39).

So in a thousand other places. That works are what make a man of the church, and that he is saved according to them, is also taught by the Lord in the parables, many of which imply that those who do what is good are accepted, and that those who do what is evil are rejected. As in the parable

Of the husbandmen in the vineyard (Mt 21:33-44);

Of the fig-tree that did not yield fruit (Lu 13:6-9);

Of the talents, and the pounds, with which they were to trade (Mt 25:14-31; Lu 19:13-25);

Of the Samaritan who bound up the wounds of him that was wounded by robbers (10:30-37);

Of the rich man and Lazarus (16:19-31);

Of the ten virgins (Mt 25:1-12).

3. Every one who has religion knows and acknowledges that whoever leads a good life is saved, and that whoever leads an evil one is condemned This is due to the conjunction of heaven with the man who knows from the Word that there is a God, that there is a heaven and a hell, and that there is a life after death. Such is the source of this general perception. Therefore in the doctrine of the *Athanasian Creed* on the Trinity, which has been received throughout the Christian world, the following declaration, at its end has also been received there:

Jesus Christ, who suffered for our salvation, ascended into heaven, and sitteth at the right hand of the Father Almighty, whence He will come to judge the quick and the dead; and then they that have done good will enter into life eternal, and they that have done evil into everlasting fire.

4. In the Christian Churches, however, there are many who teach that faith alone saves, and not any good of life, or good works, and they add that evil of life or evil works do not condemn those who have been justified by faith alone, because such are in God and in grace. However, it is remarkable that although they teach such things, they nevertheless acknowledge (due to a perception from heaven common to all) that those who lead a good life are saved, and that those who live an evil one are not. That they do acknowledge this is evident from the *Exhortation* which not only in England but also in Germany, Sweden, and Denmark is read in the places of worship before the people coming to the Holy Supper. As is well known, it is in these kingdoms that those are found who teach that faith alone saves.

5. The *Exhortation* read in England before the people who approach the Sacrament of the Supper, is as follows:

The way and means to be received as worthy partakers of that Holy Table is, first, to examine your lives and conversations by the rule of God's commandments; and whereinsoever ye shall perceive yourselves to have offended, either by will, word, or deed, there to bewail your own sinfulness, and to confess yourselves to Almighty God, with full purpose of amendment of life; and if ye shall perceive your offenses to be such as are not only against God, but also against your neighbors, then ye shall reconcile yourselves unto them, being ready to make restitution and satisfaction, according to the uttermost of your powers, for all injuries and wrongs done by you to any other, and being likewise ready to forgive others that have offended you, as ye would have forgiveness of your offenses at God's hand; for otherwise the receiving of the Holy Communion doth nothing else but increase your damnation. Therefore if any of you be a blasphemer of God, a hinderer or slanderer of His Word, an adulterer, or be in malice or envy, or in any other grievous crime, repent you of your sins, or else come not to that Holy Table; lest after the taking of that Holy Sacrament the devil enter into you as he entered into Judas, and fill you full of all iniquities, and bring you to destruction both of body and soul.

6. [In this paragraph Swedenborg presents a translation into Latin of the foregoing *Exhortation*.]

7. I have been permitted to ask some of the English clergy who had professed and preached faith alone (this was done in the spiritual world), whether while they were reading in church this *Exhortation*—in which faith is not even mentioned—they believed it to be true; for example, that if people do evil things, and do not repent, the devil will enter into them as he did into Judas, and destroy them both body and soul They said that in the state in which they were when reading the *Exhortation* they had no other knowledge or thought than that this was religion itself; but that while composing and elaborating their discourses or sermons they had a different thought about it, because they were then thinking of faith as being the sole means of salvation, and of the good of life as being a moral accessory for the public good. Nevertheless it was incontestably proved to them that with them too there was that common perception that he who leads a good life is saved, and that he who leads an evil one is damned; and that they are in this perception when they are not engrossed in their own selfhoods.

8. The reason why all religion concerns the life, is that after death every one is his own life, for it stays the same as it had been in this world, and undergoes no change. An evil life cannot be converted into a good one, nor a good life into an evil one, because they are opposites, and conversion into what is opposite is extinction. And, being opposites, a good life is called life, and an evil one death. This is why religion is a matter of life, and why its life is to do what is good. (That after death a man is such as his life in this world had been may be seen in the work on *Heaven and Hell,* nn. 470-484).

II.

FROM HIMSELF NO ONE CAN DO GOOD THAT IS REALLY GOOD.

9. Scarcely any one has known heretofore whether the good done by him is from self or from God, because the church has separated faith from charity, and the good comes from charity. A man gives to the poor; relieves the needy; endows places of worship and hospitals; has regard for the church, his country, and his fellow-citizen; is diligent in his attendance at a place of worship, where he listens and prays devoutly; reads the Word and books of piety; and thinks about salvation; and yet is not aware whether he is doing these things from himself, or from God. He may be doing the very same things from God, or he may be doing them from self. If he does them from God they are good, if from self they are not good. In fact there are goods of this kind done from self which are eminently evil, such as hypocritical goods, the purpose of which is deception and fraud.

10. Goods from God, and goods from self, may be compared to gold. Gold that is gold from the inmost, called pure gold, is good gold. Gold alloyed with silver is also gold, but is good according to the amount of the alloy. Less good still is gold that is alloyed with copper. But a gold made by art, and resembling gold only from its color, is not good at all, for there is no substance of gold in it. There is also what is gilded, such as gilded silver, copper, iron, tin, lead, and also gilded wood and gilded stone, which on the surface may appear like gold; but not being such, they are valued either according to the workmanship, the value of the gilded material, or whatever gold can be scraped off. In goodness these differ from real gold as a garment differs from a man. Moreover rotten wood, dross, or even ordure, may be overlaid with gold; and such is the gold to which pharisaic good may be likened.

11. From science a man knows whether gold is good in substance, is alloyed and falsified, or is merely overlaid; but he does not know from science whether the good he does is good in itself. This only does he know: that good from God is good, and that good from man is not good. Therefore, as it concerns his salvation for him to know whether the good he does is from God, or is not from God, this must be revealed. But first something shall be said about goods.

12. There are civic good, moral good, and spiritual good. Civic good is what a man does from the civic law: by means of and according to this good the man is a citizen in the natural world. Moral good is whatever a man does from the law of reason: by means of and according to this good he is a man. Spiritual good is what a man does from spiritual law: by means of and according to this good he is a citizen in the spiritual world. These goods succeed one another in the following order: spiritual good is the highest, moral good is intermediate, and civic good is last.

13. A man who possesses spiritual good is also a moral man and a civic man; but a man who does not possess spiritual good may appear to be a moral man and a civic man, yet is not so. The reason why a man who possesses spiritual good is also a moral man and a civic man, is that spiritual good has the essence of good within it, and moral and civic good have this essence from spiritual good. The essence of good can be from no other source than from Him who is good itself. Think the matter over from every point of view, and try to find out from what it is that good is good, and you will see that it is so from its inmost being, and that good is what has within it this *esse* of good; consequently that that is good which is from good itself, thus from God; and therefore that good which is not from God, but from man, is not good.

14. From what has been said in *Doctrine of the Sacred Scripture* (nn. 27, 28, 38), it may be seen that what is highest, what is intermediate, and what is last, make a one, like end, cause, and effect; and that because they make a one, the end itself is called the first end, the cause the intermediate end, and the effect the last end. From this it must be evident that in the case of a man who possesses spiritual good, what is moral in him is intermediate spiritual, and what is civic is the outmost spiritual. And for this reason it has been said that a man who possesses spiritual good is also a moral man and a civic man; and that a man who does not possess spiritual good is neither a moral man nor a civic man, although he may appear to be so both to himself and to others.

15. A man who is not spiritual can yet think rationally and speak from that thought, like a spiritual man, because man's understanding can be uplifted into the light of heaven, which is truth, and can see from it; but his will cannot be in the same way uplifted into the heat of heaven, which is love, so as to act from that heat. The reason is that truth and love do not make one in a man unless he is spiritual. It is for this reason also that man can speak; and it is this which makes the difference between a man and an animal. It is by means of this capacity of the understanding to be uplifted into heaven when as yet the will is not so uplifted, that it is possible for a man to be reformed and to become spiritual; but he does not begin to be reformed and become spiritual until his will also is uplifted. It is from this superior endowment of the understanding over the will, that a man, of whatever character he may be, even if evil, is able to think and therefore to speak rationally, as if he were spiritual. In spite of this he is still not rational, because the understanding does not lead the will, but the will leads the understanding. The understanding merely teaches and shows the way, as has been said in *Doctrine of the Sacred*

Scripture (n. 115). So long as the will is not in heaven together with the understanding, the man is not spiritual, and consequently is not rational; for when he is left to his will or love, he throws off the rational things of his understanding of God, heaven, and eternal life, and adopts in their stead such things as are in agreement with his will's love, and these he calls rational. But these matters have been explained in the works on *Angelic Wisdom*, etc.*

16. In the following pages, those who do what is good from themselves will be called natural men, because with them the moral and the civic is in its essence natural; and those who do what is good from the Lord will be called spiritual men, because with them the moral and the civic is in its essence spiritual.

17. That no one can from himself do any good that is really good, is taught by the Lord in John:

A man can receive nothing except it be given him from heaven (3:27).

He that abideth in Me, and I in him, the same beareth much fruit; for without Me ye can do nothing (15:5).

"He that abideth in Me, and I in him, the same beareth much fruit," means that all good is from the Lord; "fruit" means what is good. "Without Me ye can do nothing," means that no man can from himself do anything. Those who believe in the Lord, and from Him do what is good, are called

Sons of light (Jn 12:36; Lu 16:8);
Sons of the bridechamber (Mk 2:19);
Sons of the resurrection (Lu 20:36);
Sons of God (same; Jn 1:12);
Born of God (verse 13);
It is said that they shall see God (Mt 5:8);
That the Lord will make His abode with them (Jn 14:23);
That they have the faith of God (Mk. 11:22);
That their works are done from God (Jn 3:21).

*This refers to *Divine Providence* and Divine *Love and Wisdom.*

These things are all summed up in the folowing words:

As many as received Him, to them gave He power to be sons of God, to them that believe in His name; who were born, not of bloods, nor of the will of the flesh, nor of the will of man, but of God (Jn 1:12, 13).

To "believe in the name of the Son of God," is to believe the Word and to live according to it; "the will of the flesh," is what is proper to man's will, which in itself is evil; "the will of man," is what is proper to his understanding, which in itself is falsity from evil; those "born of" these, are those who will and act, and also think and speak, from what pertains to themselves; those "born of God," are those who do all this from the Lord. In short: what is from man is not good; but what is good is from the Lord.

III.

18. Who does not or may not know that evils stand in the way of the Lord's entrance to a man? For evil is hell, and the Lord is heaven, and hell and heaven are opposites. In proportion therefore as a man is in the one, in the same proportion he cannot be in the other. For the one acts against the other and destroys it.

19. So long as a man is in this world, he is midway between hell and heaven; hell is below him, and heaven is above him, and he is kept in freedom to turn himself to either the one or the other; if he turns to hell he turns away from heaven; if he turns to heaven he turns away from hell. Or what is the same, as long as a man is in this world he stands midway between the Lord and the devil, and is kept in freedom to turn himself to either the one or the other; if he turns to the devil he turns away from the Lord; if he turns to the Lord he turns away from the devil. Or what is again the same, as long as a man is in this world he is midway between evil and good, and is kept in freedom to turn himself to either the one or the other; if he turns to evil he turns away from good; if he turns to good he turns away from evil.

20. We have said that a man is *kept* in freedom to turn himself one way or the other. It is not from himself that every man has this freedom, but he has it from the Lord, and this is why he is said to be kept in it. (On the equilibrium between heaven and hell, and that man is in it and owes his freedom to that fact, see the work *Heaven and Hell* (nn. 589-596; 597-603). That every man is kept in freedom, and that from no one is it taken away, will be seen in its proper place.

21. It is clear from all this that in proportion as a man shuns evils, in the same proportion is he with the Lord and in the Lord; and that in proportion as he is in the Lord, in the same proportion he does goods, not from self but from Him. From this results the general law: In proportion as any one shuns evils, in the same proportion he does goods.

22. Two things however are required: first, the man must shun evils because they are sins, that is, because they are infernal and diabolical, and therefore contrary to the Lord and the divine laws; and secondly, he must do this as from himself, while knowing and believing that it is from the Lord. But these two requirements will be considered in subsequent chapters.

23. From what has been said three things follow:

i. If a man wills and does goods before he shuns evils as sins, the goods are not good.

ii. If a man thinks and speaks pious things while not shunning evils as sins, the pious things are not pious.

iii. If a man knows and is wise in many things, and does not shun evils as sins, he is nevertheless not wise.

24. i. *If a man wills and does goods before he shuns evils as sins, the goods are not good.* This is because, as already said, he is not in the Lord before he does so. For example: if a man gives to the poor, renders aid to the needy, contributes to places of worship and to hospitals, renders good service to the church, his country, and his fellow-citizens, teaches the Gospel and makes converts, does justice in his judgments, acts with sincerity in business, and with uprightness in his works; and yet makes no account of evils as being sins, such as fraud, adultery, hatred, blasphemy, and other like evils, then he can do only such goods as are evil within, because he does them from himself and not from the Lord; and therefore self is in them and not the Lord, and the goods in which is a man's self are all defiled with his evils, and have regard to himself and the world. And yet these very deeds that have just been enumerated are inwardly good if the man shuns evils as sins (such as fraud, adultery, hatred, blasphemy, and other like evils), because in this case he does them from the Lord, and they are said to be "wrought in God" (John 3:19-21).

25. ii. *If a man thinks and speaks pious things while not shunning evils as sins, the pious things are not pious.* This is because he is not in the Lord. If for example he frequents places of worship, listens devoutly to the preaching, reads the Word and books of piety, goes to the sacrament of the Supper, pours forth prayers daily, and even if he thinks much about God and salvation, and yet regards as of no moment the evils which are sins (such as fraud, adultery, hatred, blasphemy, and other like evils), he then cannot do otherwise than think and speak such pious things as inwardly are not pious, because the man himself is in them with his evils. At the time indeed he is not aware of them, yet they are present within deeply hidden out of his sight; for he is like a spring the water of which is foul from its source. His performances of piety are either mere customs of habit, or else are the outcome of self-merit or hyprocrisy. They do indeed rise up toward heaven, but turn back before they get there, and settle down, like smoke in the atmosphere.

26. I have been permitted to see and hear many individuals after death who reckoned up their good works and performances of piety, such as those mentioned above (nn. 24, 25), besides many others. Among them I have also seen some who had lamps and no oil. Inquiry was made as to whether they had shunned evils as sins, and it was found that they had not, and therefore they were told that they were evil. Afterwards also they were seen to go into caverns where evil ones like them had their abode.

27. iii. *If a man knows and is wise about many things, and does not shun evils as sins, he is nevertheless not wise.* This is so for the reason already given: that he is wise from himself and not from the Lord. If for example he has an accurate knowledge of the doctrine of his church and of all things that belong to it, if he knows how to confirm them by the Word and by reasonings, if he knows the doctrines held by all churches for ages, together with the edicts of all the councils, and even if he knows truths, and also sees and understands them; thus if he knows the nature of faith, charity, piety, repentance and the remission of sins, regeneration, baptism, the Holy Supper, the Lord, and redemption and salvation, still he is not wise unless he shuns evils as sins, because his knowledges are devoid of life, being of his understanding only and not at the same time of his will; and such knowledges in time perish, for the reason given above (n. 15). After death also the man himself discards them, because they are not in accordance with his will's love. Nevertheless knowledges are in the highest degree necessary, because they teach how a man is to act; and when he practices them, then they are alive in him, and not till then.

28. All that has been said thus far is taught by the Word in many places, of which only the following shall be presented. The Word teaches that no one can be in good and at the same time in evil, or what is the same, that no one can be (in respect to his soul) in heaven and at the same time in hell. This is taught in the following passages:

No man can serve two masters, for either he will hate the one and love the other, or else he will hold to one and despise the other. Ye cannot serve God and mammon (Mt 6:24).

How can ye, being evil, speak good things? for out of the abundance of the heart the mouth speaketh. The good man out of the good treasure of his heart bringeth forth good things, and the evil man out of its evil treasure bringeth forth evil things (12:34, 35).

A good tree produceth not evil fruit, nor doth an evil tree produce good fruit. Every tree is known by its own fruit; for of thorns men do not gather figs, nor of a bramble bush gather they grapes (Lu 6:43, 44).

29. The Word teaches that no one can do what is good from himself, but that he does it from the Lord:

Jesus said, I am the true vine, and My Father is the vine-dresser. Every branch in Me that beareth not fruit He taketh away; and every branch that beareth fruit He cleanseth it, that it may bear more fruit. Abide in Me, and I in you. As the branch cannot bear fruit of itself, except it abide in the vine, so neither can ye except ye abide in Me. I am the vine, ye are the branches; he that abideth in Me, and I in him, the same beareth much fruit; for without Me ye can do nothing. If a man abide not in Me, he is cast forth as a branch, and is withered; and they gather him, and cast him into the fire, and he is burned (Jn 15:1-6).

30. The Word teaches that in proportion as a man has not been purified from evils, his goods are not good, nor are his pious things pious, and neither is he wise. It also teaches the converse:

Woe unto you, scribes and Pharisees, hypocrites! for ye are like unto whited sepulchres, which outwardly indeed appear beautiful, but inwardly are full of dead men's bones, and of all uncleanness. Even so ye also outwardly indeed appear righteous unto men, but inwardly ye are full of hypocrisy and iniquity. Woe unto you, for ye cleanse the outside of the cup and of the platter, but within they are full of extortion and excess. Thou blind Pharisee, cleanse first the inside of the cup and of the platter, that the outside thereof may become clean also (Mt 23:25-28).

The same appears from these words in *Isaiah:*

Hear the word of Jehovah, ye princes of Sodom: give ear unto the law of our God, ye people of Gomorrah. To what purpose is the multitude of your sacrifices unto Me? bring no more a meat-offering of vanity; incense is an abomination unto Me; new moon and sabbath, I cannot bear iniquity; your new moons and your appointed feasts My soul hateth; therefore when ye spread forth your hands I will hide Mine eyes from you; yea, if ye make many prayers, I will not hear; your hands are full of bloods. Wash you, make you clean;

put away the evil of your doings from before Mine eyes; cease to do evil; though your sins have been as scarlet, they shall be as white as snow; though they have been red, they shall be as wool (1:10-18).

These words in brief amount to this: that unless a man shuns evils, nothing in his worship is good, and in like manner nothing in his works, for it is said, "I cannot bear iniquity, make you clean, put away the evil of your doings, cease to do evil." In Jeremiah:

Return ye every man from his evil way, and make your works good (35:15).

[2] That the same are not wise is declared in Isaiah:

Woe unto them that are wise in their own eyes, and intelligent before their own faces (5:21).

The wisdom of the wise shall perish, and the intelligence of the intelligent; woe unto them that are deeply wise, and their works are done in the dark (29:14, 15).

Woe to them that go down to Egypt for help, and put their stay on horses, and trust in chariots because they are many, and in horsemen because they are strong; but they look not unto the Holy One of Israel, neither seek Jehovah. But He will arise against the house of the evil-doers, and against the help of them that work iniquity. For Egypt is man, and not God; and the horses thereof are flesh, and not spirit (31:1-3).

Thus is described man's self-intelligence. "Egypt" is memory-knowledge; a "horse," the understanding therefrom; a "chariot," the doctrine therefrom; a "horseman," the intelligence therefrom; of all of which it is said, "Woe to them that look not unto the Holy One of Israel, neither seek Jehovah." Their destruction through evils is meant by: "He will arise against the house of the evil-doers, and against the help of them that work iniquity." These things are from man's Own [or his proprium°] and consequently there is no life in them, as is meant by its being said that "Egypt is man and not God," and that "the horses thereof are flesh

° See *Doctrine of the Sacred Scripture,* n. 60, for the definition of "proprium."

and not spirit." "Man," and "flesh," denote what is man's Own; "God," and "spirit," denote life from the Lord; the "horses of Egypt," denote self-intelligence. There are many such things in the Word concerning intelligence from self, and intelligence from the Lord, which can be seen only by means of the spiritual sense.

[3] No one is saved by means of goods from self, because they are not good. This is evident from the following:

Not every one that saith unto Me, Lord, Lord, shall enter into the kingdom of the heavens, but he that doeth the will of My Father: many will say to Me in that day, Lord, Lord, have we not prophesied by Thy name, and by Thy name cast out demons, and in Thy name done many mighty things? but then I will profess unto them, I never knew you, depart from Me, ye that work iniquity (Mt 7:21-23).

Then shall ye begin to stand without, and to knock at the door, saying, Lord, open to us; and ye shall begin to say, We did eat and drink in Thy presence, and Thou has taught in our streets; but He shall say, I tell you I know ye not whence ye are, depart from Me, all ye workers of iniquity (Lu 13: 25-27).

For such persons are like the Pharisee,

Who stood in the temple and prayed, saying that he was not as other men, an extortioner, unjust, an adulterer; that he fasted twice in the week, and gave tithes of all that he possessed (Lu 18:11-14).

Such persons moreover are those who are called "unprofitable servants" (Lu 17:10).

31. The truth is that no man can from himself do what is really good. But so to use this truth as to do away with all the good of charity that is done by a man who shuns evils as sins, is a great wickedness, for it is diametrically contrary to the Word, which commands that a man shall *do*. It is contrary to the commandments of love to God and love toward the neighbor on which the Law and the Prophets hang, and it is to flout and undermine everything relating to religion. For every one knows that religion is to do what is good, and that every one will be judged according to his deeds. Every man is so constituted as to be able (by the Lord's power, if he begs for it) to shun evils as if from himself; and that which he afterwards does is good from the Lord.

IV.

IN PROPORTION AS ANY ONE SHUNS EVILS AS SINS, IN THE SAME PROPORTION HE LOVES TRUTHS.

32. There are two universals that proceed from the Lord: divine good, and divine truth. Divine good is of His divine love, and divine truth is of His divine wisdom. In the Lord these two are a one, and therefore they proceed from Him as a one, but they are not received as a one by angels in the heavens, or by men on earth. There are both angels and men who receive more from divine truth than from divine good; and there are others who receive more from divine good than from divine truth. This is why the heavens are distinguished into two distinct kingdoms, one of which is called the celestial kingdom, and the other the spiritual kingdom. The heavens that receive more from divine good constitute the celestial kingdom, and those which receive more from divine truth constitute the spiritual kingdom. (Concerning these two kingdoms into which the heavens are divided, see the work *Heaven and Hell*, nn. 20–28.) But still the angels of all the heavens are in wisdom and intelligence in proportion to the degree in which the good in them makes one with truth. The good that does not make one with truth is to them not good; and on the other hand the truth that does not make one with good is to them not truth. From this we see that good conjoined with truth constitutes love and wisdom in both angel and man; and as an angel is an angel, and a man a man, from the love and wisdom in him, it is evident that good conjoined with truth causes an angel to be an angel of heaven, and a man a man of the church.

237

33. As good and truth are one in the Lord, and proceed as a one from Him, it follows that good loves truth and truth loves good, and they will to be one. It is the same with their opposites: evil loves falsity, and falsity loves evil, and these will to be one. In the following pages the conjunction of good and truth will be called the heavenly marriage, and that of evil and falsity the infernal marriage.

34. It follows from the foregoing that in proportion as any one shuns evils as sins, in the same proportion he loves truths (for in the same proportion he is in good, as has been shown in the preceding chapter); and also that in proportion as any one does not shun evils as sins, in the same proportion he does not love truths, because in the same proportion he is not in good.

35. It is indeed possible for a man to love truths who does not shun evils as sins; yet he does not love them because they are truths, but because they minister to his reputation, and thereby to his honors or gains, so that if they do not minister to it he loves them not.

36. Good is of the will, truth of the understanding. From the love of good in the will proceeds the love of truth in the understanding; from the love of truth proceeds the perception of truth; from the perception of truth comes thought about truth; and from all of these together comes the acknowledgment of truth which in the true sense is faith. (That this is the progression from the love of good to faith, is shown in the work *Divine Love and Wisdom*.)

37. As good is not good unless it is conjoined with truth, as already said, it follows that previous thereto good does not come into manifest being. But as it continually desires to come into manifest being it longs for and procures truths in order to do so, for truths are the agency of its nourishment and formation. This is the reason why a man loves truths in the same proportion that he is in good, consequently in the same proportion that he shuns evils as sins, for it is in proportion that he does this that any one is in good.

38. In proportion as any one is in good, and from good loves truths, in the same proportion he loves the Lord, because the Lord is good itself and truth itself. The Lord is therefore with man in good and in truth. If the latter is loved from good the Lord is loved, but not otherwise. This the Lord teaches in John:

He that hath My commandments, and doeth them, he it is that loveth Me; He that loveth Me not keepeth not My words (14:21, 24).

If ye keep My commandments, ye shall abide in My love (15:10).

The "commandments" and "words" of the Lord are truths.

39. That good loves truth may be illustrated by comparison with a priest, a soldier, a trader, and an artificer. With a *priest:* If he is in the good of the priesthood, which is to care for the salvation of souls, to teach the way to heaven, and to lead those whom he teaches, then in proportion as he is in this good (thus from his love and its desire) he acquires the truths which he may teach, and by means of which he may lead. But a priest who is not in the good of the priesthood, but is in the delight of his office from the love of self and of the world, which to him is the only good, he too from his love and its desire acquires those truths in abundance in proportion as he is inspired by the delight which is his good. With a *soldier:* If he is in the love of military service, and is sensible of its good, whether it be that of national defense, or that of his own fame, from this good and according to it he acquires its special knowledge, and if he is a commander, its intelligence; these are like truths by which the delight of love which is his good is nourished and formed. With a *trader:* If he has taken up this calling from the love of it, he learns with avidity everything that enters into and makes up that love as its means; these also are like truths, while trading is his good. With a *workman:*

If he applies himself with earnestness to his work, and loves it as the good of his life, he purchases tools, and perfects himself by whatever pertains to a knowledge of it, and by these means he does his work in such a way that it is a good. From these comparisons it is evident that truths are the means through which the good of love comes into manifest being, and becomes something; consequently that good loves truths in order that it may do so. Hence in the Word to "do the truth" means to cause good to come into manifest being. This is meant by

Doing the truth (Jn 3:21);
Doing the Lord's sayings (Lu 6:47);
Keeping His commandments (Jn 14:24);
Doing His words (Mt 7:24);
Doing the Word of God (Lu 8:21); and by
Doing the statutes and judgments (Lev 18:5).

And this also is to "do what is good," and to "bear fruit," for "good" and "fruit" are what come into manifestation.

40. That good loves truth and wills to be conjoined with it, may also be illustrated by comparison with food and water, or with bread and wine. Both are necessary. Food or bread alone effects nothing in the body in the way of nourishment; it does so only together with water or with wine; and therefore the one has an appetite and longing for the other. Moreover in the Word "food" and "bread" mean good, in the spiritual sense; and "water" and "wine" mean truth.

41. From all that has been said it is now evident that he who shuns evils as sins, loves truths and longs for them; and that the more he shuns them, so much the more love and longing does he feel, because so much the more he is in good. The result is that he comes into the heavenly marriage, which is the marriage of good and truth, in which is heaven, and in which must be the church.

V.

42. Faith and life are as distinct from each other as thinking and doing are; and as thinking is of the understanding
and doing is of the will, it follows that faith and life are as
distinct from each other as the understanding and the will.
He who knows the distinction between the two latter knows
that between the two former; and he who knows the conjunction of the two latter knows that of the two former.
For this reason something shall first be set forth about the
understanding and the will.

43. Man possesses two faculties, one of which is called
the will, and the other the understanding. They are distinct
from each other, but are so created that they may be one,
and when they are a one they are called the mind. So the
human mind consists of these two faculties, and the whole
of man's life is in them. Just as all things in the universe
that are in accordance with divine order bear relation to
good and truth, so do all the things in man bear relation to
the will and the understanding; for the good in a man belongs to his will and the truth in him belongs to his understanding, these two faculties being their receptacles and
subjects; the will pertaining to all things good, and the
understanding pertaining to all things true. The goods and
truths in a man are nowhere else, and so therefore neither are the love and faith, because love is of good and
good is of love, and faith is of truth and truth is of
faith.

It is of the utmost importance to know how the will and
the understanding make one mind. They do so in the same

way that good and truth make one, for there is a marriage between the will and the understanding like that between good and truth. The nature of this latter marriage has been in some measure told in the preceding chapter, and to this we should add that just as good is the very being of a thing, and truth is its derivative manifestation, so the will in man is the very being of his life, and the understanding is its derivative manifestation; for the good that is of the will shapes itself forth in the understanding, and presents itself to view so that it may be clearly seen.

44. It has been shown above (nn. 27, 28) that a man may know many things, may think them over, may understand them, and yet may not be wise. And as it is the function of faith to know and to think, and still more to understand, that a thing is true, a man may well believe that he has faith and yet not have it. The reason why he has it not, is that he is in evil of life, and evil of life and truth of faith cannot possibly act as one. The evil of life destroys the truth of faith, because the evil of life is of the will and the truth of faith is of the understanding, and the will leads the understanding and makes it act as one with itself, so that if there is anything in the understanding that is not in accord with the will, and the man is left to himself, and thinks from his own evil and the love of it, he then either rejects the truth that is in the understanding, or else by falsifying it forces it into oneness. Quite different is it with those who are in the good of life: such when left to themselves think from what is good, and love the truth that is in the understanding because it is in agreement. In this way there takes place a conjunction of faith and life like that of truth and good, and both these conjunctions are like that of the understanding and the will.

45. From all this then it follows that in so far as a man shuns evils as sins, just so far has he faith, because just so far is he in good, as shown above. This is confirmed also by its contrary: that he who does not shun evils as sins, has not faith because he is in evil, and evil inwardly hates truth. Outwardly indeed he may act as a friend to truth, and permit it to be in the understanding, may even love to have it there; but when what is outward is put off, as is done after death, he first casts out truth (his friend in this world), then denies that it is truth, and finally feels aversion for it.

46. The faith of an evil man is an intellectual faith, in which there is nothing of good from the will. Thus it is a dead faith, which is like a breathing of the lungs with no life or soul in it from the heart. Moreover the understanding corresponds to the lungs, and the will to the heart. Such faith is also like a good-looking harlot dressed up in crimson and gold, but full of disease and corruption. A harlot also corresponds to the falsification of truth, and therefore in the Word signifies it. Such faith is also like a tree luxuriant in foliage but barren of fruit, which the gardener cuts down. A tree moreover signifies a man, its leaves and blossoms signify the truths of faith, and its fruit the good of love. But very different is that faith in the understanding which has in it good from the will. This faith is living, and is like a breathing of the lungs in which there is life and soul from the heart. It is also like a lovely wife whose chastity endears her to her husband. It is also like a tree that bears fruit.

47. There are many things that appear to be mere matters of faith, such as that there is a God; that the Lord, who is God, is the Redeemer and Savior; that there is a heaven and a hell; that there is a life after death; and many other things of which it is not said that they are to be done, but that they are to be believed. These things of faith also are dead with a man who is in evil, but are living with a man who is in good. The reason is that a man who is in good not only acts aright from the will but also thinks aright from the understanding, and this not only before the world but also before himself when he is alone. It is not so with a man who is in evil.

48. We have said that these things appear to be mere matters of faith. However, the thought of the understanding derives its coming into manifest being from the love of the will, which is the inmost being of the thought in the understanding, as has been said above (n. 43). For whatever anyone wills from love, he wills to do, he wills to think, he wills to understand, and he wills to speak; or, what is the same, whatever anyone loves from the will, he loves to do, he loves to think, he loves to understand, and he loves to speak. To this may be added that when a man shuns evil as sin, he is in the Lord, as shown above, and the Lord then does everything. Therefore to those who asked Him what they should do that they might work the works of God, He said:

This is the work of God, that ye believe in Him whom He hath sent (Jn 6:28, 29).

To "believe in the Lord" is not only to think that He is, but also to do His words, as He teaches elsewhere.

49. Those who are in evils have no faith, no matter how much they may suppose themselves to have it. This has been shown in the spiritual world in the case of persons of this character. They were brought into a heavenly society, which caused the spiritual sphere of faith existing with the angels to enter into the interiors of their faith, and the result was that the angels perceived that those persons possessed only what is a natural or external of faith, and not what is the spiritual or internal of it, and therefore they themselves confessed that they really had no faith whatsoever; although in the world they had persuaded themselves that to believe or to have faith consisted in thinking a thing to be true, no matter what the ground for so thinking. Very different was perceived to be the faith of those who had not been in evil.

50. From all this it may be seen what spiritual faith is; and also what faith not spiritual. Spiritual faith exists with those who do not commit sins, for those who do not commit sins do things that are good, not from themselves but from the Lord (see above, nn. 18-21), and through faith become spiritual. Faith with these is the truth. This the Lord teaches in John:

This is the judgment, that the light is come into the world, and men loved the darkness rather than the light, because their works were evil. For every one that doeth evil hateth the light, and cometh not to the light, lest his works should be reproved. But he that doeth the truth cometh to the light, that his works may be made manifest, that they have been wrought in God (3:19-21).

51. All the foregoing is confirmed by the following passages in the Word:

A good man out of the good treasure of his heart bringeth forth that which is good; and an evil man out of the evil treasure of his heart bringeth forth that which is evil, for out of the abundance of the heart the mouth speaketh (Lu 6:45; Mt 12:34).

The "heart" in the Word means man's will, and as man thinks and speaks from this, it is said: "Out of the abundance of the heart the mouth speaketh."

Not that which goeth into the mouth defileth the man; but that which goeth out of the heart, this defileth the man (Mt 15:11, 18).

The "heart" here too means the will. Jesus said of the woman who anointed His feet with ointment:

Her sins are forgiven; for she loved much; thy faith has saved thee (Lu 7:47, 50);

from which it is evident that when sins have been remitted or forgiven, thus when they exist no longer, faith saves. Those are called "sons of God" and "born of God" who are not in the proprium* of their will, and consequently are not in the proprium of their understanding; that is to say, who are not in evil and from this in falsity. These are they who believe in the Lord, as He Himself teaches in Jn 1:12, 13, which passage may be seen explained above in n. 17, at the end.

52. From the foregoing there follows this conclusion: That no man has in him a grain more of truth than he has of good; thus that he has not a grain more of faith than he has of life. In the understanding indeed there may exist the thought that such or such a thing is true, but not the acknowledgment which is faith, unless there is consent thereto in the will. Thus do faith and life keep step as they advance. From all this it is now evident that in proportion as any one shuns evils as sins, in the same proportion he has faith and is spiritual.

---

* See No. 60, *Doctrine of the Sacred Scripture.*

VI.

53. What nation in the wide world is not aware that it is evil to steal, to commit adultery, to kill, and to bear false witness? If men were not aware of this, and if they did not by laws guard against the commission of these evils, it would be all over with them; for without such laws the community, the commonwealth, and the nation would perish. Who can imagine that the Israelitish nation was so much more senseless than others as not to know that these were evils? One might therefore wonder why these laws, known as they are the world over, were promulgated from Mount Sinai by Jehovah Himself with such a miracle. But consider: they were promulgated so miraculously in order that men may know that these laws are not only civic and moral laws, but are also spiritual laws; and that to act contrary to them is not only to do evil to a fellow-citizen and to the community, but is also to sin against God. For this reason those laws, through promulgation from Mount Sinai by Jehovah, were made laws of religion; for it is evident that whatever Jehovah God commands, He commands in order that it may be of religion, and that it is to be done for His sake, and for the sake of man that he may be saved.

54. As these laws were the first-fruits of the Word, and therefore the first-fruits of the church that was to be again set up by the Lord with the Israelitish nation, and as they were in a brief summary a complex of all those things of religion by means of which there is conjunction of the Lord with man and of man with the Lord, they were so holy that nothing is more so.

55. That they were most holy is evident from the fact that Jehovah Himself (that is, the Lord) came down upon Mount Sinai in fire, and with angels, and promulgated them from it by a living voice, and that the people had prepared themselves for three days to see and to hear; that the mountain was fenced about lest any one should go near it and die; that neither were the priests nor the elders to draw near, but Moses only; that those laws were written by the finger of God on two tables of stone; that when Moses brought the tables down from the mountain the second time, his face shone; that the tables were afterwards laid away in the ark, and the ark in the inmost of the tabernacle, and upon it was placed the mercy-seat, and upon this cherubs of gold; that this was the most holy thing of their church, being called the holy of holies; that outside the veil that hung before it there were placed objects that represented holy things of heaven and the church, namely, the lampstand with its seven golden lamps, the golden altar of incense, and the table overlaid with gold on which were the loaves of the Presence*, and surrounded with curtains of fine linen, bright crimson, and scarlet. The holiness of this whole tabernacle had no other source than the Law that was in the ark.

[2] On account of this holiness of the tabernacle from the Law in the ark, the whole people of Israel, by command, encamped around it in the order of their tribes, and marched in order after it, and there was then a cloud over it by day, and a fire by night. On account of the holiness of that Law, and the presence of the Lord in it, the Lord spoke with Moses above the mercy-seat between the cherubs, and the ark was called "Jehovah there." Aaron also was not allowed to enter within the veil except with sacrifices and incense. Because that Law was the very holi-

---

* In the King James version: "the shew (show)-bread."

ness of the church, the ark was brought by David into Zion; and later it was kept in the midst of the temple at Jerusalem, and constituted its shrine.

[3] On account of the Lord's presence in that Law and around it, miracles were wrought by the ark in which was that Law: the waters of Jordan were cleft asunder, and so long as the ark was resting in the midst of it, the people passed over on dry ground; when the ark was carried round the walls of Jericho they fell; Dagon the god of the Philistines fell down before it, and afterwards lay on the threshold of the temple without his head; and on its account the Bethshemites were smitten to the number of many thousands; not to mention other miracles. These were all performed solely by the Lord's presence in His Ten Words, which are the commandments of the Decalogue.

56. Such great power and such holiness existed in that Law for the further reason that it was a complex of all things of religion; for it consisted of two tables of which the one contains all things that are on the part of God, and the other in a complex all things that are on the part of man. The commandments of this Law are therefore called the "Ten Words," and are so called because "ten" signifies all. But how this Law is a complex of all things of religion will be seen in the following chapter.

57. As by means of this Law there is a conjunction of the Lord with man and of man with the Lord, it is called the "Covenant," and the "Testimony," the "Covenant" because it conjoins, and the "Testimony" because it bears witness, for a "covenant" signifies conjunction, and a "testimony" the attestation of it. For this reason there were two tables, one for the Lord and the other for man. The conjunction is effected by the Lord, but only when the man does the things that have been written in his table. For the Lord is constantly present and working, and wills to enter in, but man must open to the Lord in the freedom which he has from Him; for the Lord says:

> Behold, I stand at the door, and knock; if any man hear My voice, and open the door, I will come in to him, and will sup with him, and he with Me (Apoc 3:20).

58. In the second table, which is for man, it is not said that man must do this or that good, but that he must not do this or that evil, as for example, "Thou shalt not kill, Thou shalt not commit adultery, Thou shalt not steal, Thou shalt not bear false witness, Thou shalt not covet." The reason is that man cannot do any good whatever from himself, but when he no longer does evils, then he does good, not from himself but from the Lord. That by the power of the Lord a man is able to shun evils as of himself if he begs for that power, will be seen in the following pages.

59. What has been said above (n. 55) respecting the promulgation, holiness, and power of that Law, will be found in the following places in the Word:

> That Jehovah came down on Mount Sinai in fire, and that the mountain smoked and quaked, and that there were thunderings, lightnings, a thick cloud, and the voice of a trumpet (Ex 19:16, 18; Dt 4:11; 5:22-26).
>
> That before the descent of Jehovah the people prepared and sanctified themselves for three days (Ex 19:10, 11, 15).
>
> That bounds were set round the mountain, lest any one should come near its base, and should die; and that not even were the priests to come near, but Moses only (verses 12, 13, 20-23; 24:1, 2).
>
> That the Law was promulgated from Mount Sinai (20:2-17; Dt 5:6-21).
>
> That that Law was written by the finger of God on two tables of stone (Ex 31:18; 32:15, 16; Dt 9:10).
>
> That when Moses brought those tables down from the mountain the second time, his face shone (Ex 34:29-35).
>
> That the tables were kept in the ark (25:16; 40:20; Dt 10:5; 1 Kgs 8:39).

That upon the ark was placed the mercy-seat, and upon this the golden cherubs (Ex 25:17-21).

That the ark, together with the mercy-seat and the cherubs, constituted the inmost of the tabernacle, and that the golden lampstand, the golden altar of incense, and the table overlaid with gold on which were the loaves of the Presence, constituted the exterior of the tabernacle; and the ten curtains of fine linen, bright crimson, and scarlet, its outermost (chaps. 25-6; all; 40:17-28).

That the place where the ark was, was called the holy of holies (26:33).

That the whole people of Israel encamped around the habitation in order according to their tribes, and marched in order after it (Num 2:1-end).

That there was then over the habitation a cloud by day and a fire by night (Ex 40:38; Num 9:15-end; 14:14; Dt 1:33).

That the Lord spoke with Moses from over the ark between the cherubs (Ex 25:22; Num 7:89).

That the ark, from the Law within it, was called Jehovah-There, for when the ark set forward, Moses said, Rise up, Jehovah; and when it rested he said, Return Jehovah (Num 10:35, 36), and see further 2 Sa 6:2; Ps 132:7, 8.

That on account of the holiness of that Law Aaron was not allowed to enter within the veil except with sacrifices and with incense (Lev 16:2-14, etc.).

That the ark was brought into Zion by David with sacrifices and with shouting (2 Sa 6:1-19). That on that occasion, Uzzah, who touched it, died (verses 6 and 7).

That the ark was placed in the midst of the temple in Jerusalem, where it constituted the shrine (1 Kgs 6:19, etc.; 8:3-9).

That by the Lord's presence and power in the Law that was in the ark, the waters of Jordan were cleft asunder, and so long as the ark rested in the midst of it, the people passed over on dry ground (Josh 3:1-17; 4:5-20).

That when the ark was carried around them, the walls of Jericho fell (6:1-20).

That Dagon the god of the Philistines fell to the earth before the ark, and afterwards lay upon the threshold of the temple headless (1 Sa 5:1-4).

That on account of the ark the Bethshemites were smitten, to the number of many thousands (6:19).

60. That the tables of stone on which the Law was written were called "the tables of the covenant," and that from them the ark was called "the ark of the covenant," and the Law itself "the covenant," see: Numbers 10:33; Deuteronomy 4:13, 23; 5:2, 3; 9:9; Johsua 3:11; 1 Kings 8:19, 21; Apocalypse 11:19; and in many other places. The reason why the Law was called the "covenant," is that "covenant" signifies conjunction; and it is therefore said of the Lord that:

He shall be for a covenant to the people (Isa 42:6; 49:8;

and He is called:

The messenger of the covenant (Mal 3:1);

and His blood:

The blood of the covenant (Mt 20:28; Zech 9:11; Ex 24:4-10).

And therefore the Word is called the "Old Covenant," and the "New Covenant." Moreover covenants are made for the sake of love, friendship, association, and thus for the sake of conjunction.

61. That the commandments of this Law were called the "Ten Words," see Ex 34:28; Dt 4:13; 10:4. They are so called because "ten" signifies all, and "words" signifies truths, for there were more than ten words. As "ten" signifies all,

The curtains of the tabernacle were ten (Ex 26:1).

And for the same reason the Lord said

That a certain man who was to receive a kingdom, called ten of his servants, and gave them ten pounds to trade with (Lu 19:13).

And for the same reason also the Lord

Likened the kingdom of the heavens to ten virgins (Mt 25:1).

For the same reason also,

The dragon is described as having ten horns, and upon his horns ten diadems (Apoc 12:3).

In like manner the beast that came up out of the sea (13:1).
And another beast also (17:3, 7).
Likeise the beast in Daniel (7:7, 20, 24).
The like is signified by ten in Leviticus (26:26), and in Zechariah (8:23), and in other places.

This is the origin of tithes, for "tithes" (or "tenths") signify something from all.

VII.

62. It is well known that the Law of Sinai was written on two tables, and that the first table contains the things of God, and the other the things of man. That the first table contains all things that belong to God, and the second all that belong to man, does not appear in the letter, yet they are there, all, and it is for this reason that they are called the Ten Words, by which are signified all truths in the complex (as may be seen just above, n. 61). But in what way all things are in them cannot be set forth in a few words, but may be apprehended from what has been presented in the *Doctrine of the Sacred Scripture* (n. 67), which see. This is why it is said "murders, adulteries, thefts, and false witness *of every kind.*"

63. A religious tenet has prevailed to the effect that no one is able to fulfill the law; the law being not to kill, not to commit adultery, not to steal, and not to bear false witness. Every civic man and moral man is able to fulfill these commandments of the law by a civic and moral life; but this tenet denies that he can do so by a spiritual life; from which it follows that his not doing these evils is only for the sake of avoiding penalties and losses in this world, and not for the sake of avoiding penalties and losses after he has left it. It is for this reason that a man with whom this tenet has prevailed, thinks these evils allowable in the sight of God, but not so in that of the world.

[2] In consequence of such thought from this tenet, a man lusts after all these evils, and refrains from doing them

254

merely for the world's sake; and therefore after death such a man, although he had not committed murders, adulteries, thefts, and false witness, nevertheless desires to commit them, and does commit them when the external possessed by him in this world is taken away from him. Every desire he has had remains with him after death. It is owing to this that such persons act as one with hell, and cannot but have their lot among those who are there.

[3] Very different is the lot of those who are unwilling to kill, to commit adultery, to steal, and to bear false witness for the reason that to do these things is contrary to God. These persons, after some battling with these evils, do not will them, thus do not desire to commit them: they say in their hearts that they are sins, and in themselves infernal and devilish. After death, when the external which they had possessed for this world is taken away from them, they act as one with heaven, and as they are in the Lord they come into heaven.

64. It is a common principle of every religion that a man ought to examine himself, repent, and desist from sins, and that if he fails to do so he is in a state of damnation. (That this is a common principle of every religion may be seen above, nn. 4-8.) Teaching the Decalogue is also a common thing throughout the whole Christian world, and by it little children are commonly initiated into the Christian religion, for it is in the hands of all young children. Their parents and teachers tell them that to commit these evils is to sin against God, and in fact while speaking to the children they know nothing different. We may well wonder that these same persons, and the children too when they become adults, think that they are not under this Law, and that they are not able to do the things that belong to it. Can there be any other cause for their learning to think in this way, than that they love evils and consequently the false notions that favor them? These therefore are the

people who do not make the commandments of the Decalogue a matter of religion. And that these same persons
live without religion will be seen in *the Doctrine of Faith*.

65. All the nations in the wide world who have religion
possess precepts like those in the Decalogue, and all who
from religion live them are saved, and all who do not live
them from religion are damned. When those who live
them from religion are instructed after death by the angels,
they receive truths, and acknowledge the Lord; the reason
of which is that they shun evils as sins, and are consequently in good, and good loves truth, and from the desire
of this love, receives it (as has been shown above, nn.
32-41). This is meant by the words of the Lord to the
Jews:

> The kingdom of God shall be taken away from you, and shall be
> given to a nation bringing forth the fruits thereof (Mt 21:43).

And also by these:

> When therefore the Lord of the vineyard shall come, He will de-
> stroy those evil men, and will let out his vineyard to other husband-
> men, who shall render him the fruits in their season (verses 40, 41).

And by these:

> I say unto you that many shall come from the east and the west,
> and from the north and the south, and shall sit down in the kingdom
> of God, but the sons of the kingdom shall be cast forth into the outer
> darkness (8:11, 12; Lu 13:29).

66. We read in Mark:

> A certain rich man came to Jesus, and asked Him what he should
> do to inherit eternal life, and Jesus said to him, Thou knowest the
> commandments: Thou shalt not commit adultery, Thou shalt not kill,
> Thou shalt not steal, Thou shalt not be a false witness, Thou shalt
> not defraud, Honor thy father and mother. And he answering said,
> All these things have I kept from my youth. And Jesus looked upon
> him and loved him, yet said unto him, One thing thou lackest; go,
> sell whatsoever thout hast, and give to the poor; so shalt thou have

treasure in the heavens; and come, take up the cross and follow Me (10:17-22).

It is said that Jesus "loved him." This was because the man said that he had kept those commandments from his youth. But because he lacked three things, which were that he had not removed his heart from riches, had not fought against his sinful desires, and had not yet acknowledged the Lord to be God, the Lord said that he should "sell all that he had," by which is meant that he should remove his heart from riches; that he should "take up the cross," by which is meant that he should fight against his lusts; and that he should "follow Him," by which is meant that he should acknowledge the Lord to be God. The Lord spoke these things as He spoke all things: by correspondences. (See *Doctrine of the Sacred Scripture*, n. 17.) For no one is able to shun evils as sins unless he acknowledges the Lord and goes to Him, and unless he fights against evils and so removes his lusts. But more about these matters in the chapter on combats against evils.

VIII.

67. "Murders of every kind" include enmity, hatred, and revenge of every kind, which breathe murder, for murder lies hidden in them, like fire in wood underneath the ashes. Infernal fire is nothing else, and this is the origin of the expressions to "kindle with hatred," and to "burn with revenge." All these are "murders" in the natural sense. But in the spiritual sense "murders" mean all methods of killing and destroying the souls of men, which methods are varied and many. And in the highest sense "murder" means to hate the Lord. These three kinds of "murder" form a one, and cleave together, for he who wills the murder of a man's body in this world, after death wills the murder of his soul, and wills the murder of the Lord, for he burns with anger against Him, and desires to blot out His name.

68. These kinds of murder lie inwardly hidden in man from his birth, but from early childhood he learns to veil them over with the civic and moral behavior that he is bound to show toward men in the world, and in proportion as he loves honors or gains he guards against their appearance. This forms his external, while his internal is these kinds of murder. Such is man in himself. Now as when he dies he lays aside that external together with his body, and retains the internal, it is evident what a devil he would be unless he were reformed.

69. As the kinds of murder mentioned above lie inwardly hidden in man from his birth, as has been said, and at the same time thefts of every kind, and false witness of every kind, together with inclinations to them (of which we shall speak further on), it is evident that unless the Lord provided means of reformation, a man must perish everlastingly. The means of reformation provided by the Lord are as follows: That man is born into total ignorance; that when newly born he is kept in a state of external innocence; a little after in a state of external charity; and later in a state of external friendship; but in proportion as he comes into the exercise of thought from his own understanding, he is kept in a certain freedom of acting according to reason. This is the state that has been described above (n. 19), and the description shall be here repeated for the sake of what is to follow:

So long as a man is in this world he is midway between hell and heaven; hell is below him, and heaven is above him; and he is kept in freedom to turn himself to either the one or the other; if he turns to hell he turns away from heaven; if he turns to heaven he turns away from hell. Or what is the same, so long as a man is in this world he stands midway between the Lord and the devil, and is kept in freedom to turn himself to either one or the other; if he turns to the devil he turns away from the Lord; if he turns to the Lord he turns away from the devil. Or what is again the same, so long as a man is in this world he is midway between evil and good, and is kept in freedom to turn himself to either the one or the other; if he turns to evil he turns away from good; if he turns to good he turns away from evil. (See also what follows this, nn. 20-22).

70. Now as evil and good are two opposite things, precisely as are hell and heaven, or as are the devil and the Lord, it follows that if a man shuns evil as sin, he comes into the good that is opposite to the evil. The good opposite to the evil that is meant by "murder," is the good of love toward the neighbor.

71. As this good and that evil are opposites, it follows that the latter is removed by means of the former. Two opposites cannot be together, even as heaven and hell cannot; if they were together there would be lukewarmness, of which it is said in the Apocalypse:

I know that thou art neither cold nor hot; I would thou wert cold or hot; but because thou art lukewarm, and neither cold nor hot, I will spew thee out of My mouth (3:15, 16).

72. When a man is no longer in the evil of murder, but in the good of love toward the neighbor, whatever he does is a good of this love, and therefore it is a good work. A *priest* who is in this good does a good work whenever he teaches and leads, because he acts from the love of saving souls. A *magistrate* who is in this good does a good work whenever he delivers a decision or a judgment, because he acts from the love of taking care of his country, of the community, and of his fellow-citizen. The same with a *trader:* if he is in this good everything of his trading is a good work; there is in him the love of the neighbor; and his country, the community, his fellow-citizen, and also the members of his household are the neighbor whose welfare he has care for in providing for his own. A *workman* also who is in this good, works faithfully from it, for others as for himself, fearing his neighbor's loss as he would his own. The reason why the doings of these men are good works, is that in proportion as any one shuns evil, in the same proportion he does good, according to the general law stated above (n. 21), and he who shuns evil as sin, does good not from himself but from the Lord (nn. 18-31).

The contrary is the case with him who does not regard as sins the various kinds of murder, which are enmities, hatred, revenge, and many more. Whether he be priest, magistrate, trader, or workman, whatever he does is not a good work, because every work of his partakes of the evil that is within him; for his internal is what gives it birth. The external may be good, but only as regards others, not as regards himself.

73. The Lord teaches the good of love in many places in the Word. He teaches it in Matthew by what He says about reconciliation with the neighbor:

If thou art offering thy gift upon the altar, and there rememberest that thy brother hath aught against thee, leave there thy gift before the altar, and go thy way; first be reconciled to thy brother, and then come and offer thy gift. Be well-minded to thine adversary quickly, while thou art in the way with him; lest the adversary deliver thee to the judge, and the judge deliver thee to the officer, and thou be cast into prison. Verily I say unto thee, thou shalt not come out thence, till thou hast paid the last farthing (5:23-26).

To be "reconciled to one's brother," is to shun enmity, hatred, and revenge; that it is to shun them as sins is evident. The Lord also teaches in Matthew:

All things whatsoever ye would that men should do to you, do ye even so to them; for this is the Law and the Prophets (7:12);

thus that we should not do evil. He teaches the same in many other places. The Lord also teaches that to be angry with one's brother or the neighbor rashly, and to hold him as an enemy, is also to commit murder (Mt 5:21, 22).

IX.

74. To "commit adultery," as mentioned in the sixth commandment of the Decalogue means, in the natural sense, not only to commit whoredom, but also to do obscene things, to speak lascivious things, and to think about filthy things. But in the spiritual sense to "commit adultery" means to adulterate the goods of the Word, and to falsify its truths. In the highest sense to "commit adultery" means to deny the divinity of the Lord, and to profane the Word. These are the "adulteries of every kind." The natural man is able to know from rational light that to "commit adultery" includes in its meaning the doing of things obscene, the speaking of things lascivious, and the thinking of things that are filthy; but he does not know that to commit adultery means also to adulterate the goods of the Word and to falsify its truths, and still less that it means to deny the divinity of the Lord and to profane the Word. Consequently neither does he know that adultery is so great an evil that it may be called diabolism itself, for he who is in natural adultery is also in spiritual adultery, and the converse. That this is so will be shown in a separate little work entitled *Marriage*. But those who from their faith and their life do not regard adulteries as sins, are in adulteries of every kind at once.

75. In proportion as any one shuns adultery, in the same proportion he loves marriage; or what is the same, in proportion as any one shuns the lasciviousness of adultery, in the same proportion he loves the chastity of marriage. This is because the lasciviousness of adultery and the chastity of marriage are two opposite things, and therefore in propor-

tion as any one is not in the one, he is in the other. It is precisely as has been said above at n. 70.

76. No one can know the nature of the chastity of marriage except the man who shuns as a sin the lasciviousness of adultery. For a man may know that in which he is, but cannot know that in which he is not. If from description or from thinking about it a man knows something in which he is not, he nevertheless knows about it merely as of something in the dark; and there remains some doubt, because no one sees anything in the light and free from doubt until he is actually in it. This last therefore is to know, whereas the other is both to know and not to know. The truth is that the uncleanness of adultery and the chastity of marriage stand toward each other exactly as do hell and heaven, and that the abomination of adultery makes hell in a man, and the chastity of marriage makes heaven. But the chastity of marriage exists solely with the man who shuns as sin the abomination of adultery. (See below, n. 111).

77. From all this we can conclude and see, with no uncertainty, whether a man is a Christian or not, and even whether he has any religion or not. If from his faith and from his life a man does not regard adulteries as sins, then he is not a Christian, and neither has he any religion. On the other hand, if a man shuns adulteries as sins, and especially if on that account he feels aversion for them, and still more especially if he abhors them, then he has religion, and if he is in the Christian Church he is a Christian. (But more about these matters in the little work entitled *Marriage*, and in the meantime see what has been said on this subject in *Heaven and Hell*, nn. 366-386.)

78. To "commit adultery" means also to do obscene things, to speak lascivious things, and to think about filthy things, as is evident from the Lord's words in Matthew:

Ye have heard that it was said to them of old time, Thou shalt not commit adultery; but I say unto you that whosoever looketh on a woman to lust after her hath committed adultery with her already in his heart (5:27, 28).

79. To "commit adultery" in the spiritual sense means to adulterate the good of the Word and to falsify its truth, as is evident from the following passages:

Babylon hath made all the nations drink of the wine of her fornication (Apoc 14:8).

The angel said, I will show thee the judgment of the great harlot that sitteth upon many waters, with whom the kings of the earth have committed fornication (17:1, 2).

Babylon hath made all the nations drink of the wine of the wrath of her fornication, and the kings of the earth have committed fornication with her (18:9).

God hath judged the great harlot who did corrupt the earth with her fornication (19:2).

"Whoredom" is predicated of Babylon, because "Babylon" means those who arrogate to themselves the Lord's divine sovereign power, and profane the Word by adulterating and falsifying it; and for this reason Babylon is called:

The mother of the whoredoms and of the abominations of the earth (Apoc 17:5).

[2] The same is signified by "whoredom" in the Prophets, as in Jeremiah:

In the prophets of Jerusalem I have seen a horrible obstinacy in committing adultery and walking in lying (23:14).

And in Ezekiel:

Two women, the daughters of one mother, committed whoredom in Egypt; they committed whoredom in their youth; the one committed whoredom when she was Mine, and doted on her lovers the Assyrians her neighbors; she bestowed her whoredoms upon them, yet she forsook not her whoredoms in Egypt; the other corrupted her love more than she, and her whoredoms were more than the whoredoms of her sister; she added to her whoredoms, she loved the Chaldeans, the sons of Babel came to her to the bed of loves, and defiled her with their whoredom (23:2-17).

These things are said of the Israelitish and the Jewish Church, here called the "daughters of one mother." Their "whoredoms" mean adulterations and falsifications of the Word, and as in the Word "Egypt" signifies memory-knowledge, "Assyria" reasoning, "Chaldea" the profanation of truth, and "Babel" the profanation of good, it is said that they "committed whoredom" with them.

[3] The same is said of "Jerusalem," by which is signified the church as to doctrine:

Thou didst trust in thy beauty, and didst commit whoredom because of thy renown, so that thou pouredst out thy whoredoms on every one that passed by; thou hast committed whoredom with the sons of Egypt thy neighbors, great of flesh, and hast multiplied thy whoredom; thou hast committed whoredom with the sons of Asshur; and when thou wast not satisfied with those with whom thou didst commit whoredom, thou hast multiplied thy whoredoms unto the land of traffic, to Chaldea. An adulterous woman that receiveth strangers instead of her husband! All give hire to their harlots, but thou hast given hire to all thy lovers that they may come unto thee on every side in thy whoredoms. Wherefore, O harlot, hear the word of Jehovah (Ezek 6:15, 26, 28, 29, 32, 33, 35).

That "Jerusalem" means the church may be seen in *Doctrine of the Lord* (nn. 62, 63).

(The like is signified by "whoredoms" in Isa 23:17, 18; 57:3; Je 3:2, 6, 8, 9; 5:1, 7; 13:27; 29:23; Mic 1:7; Na 3:4; Hosea 4:10, 11; Lev 20:5; Num 14:33; 15:39; and elsewhere.)

For the same reason the Lord called the Jewish nation

An adulterous generation (Mt 12:39; 16:4; Mk 8:38).

X.

IN PROPORTION AS ANY ONE SHUNS THEFTS OF EVERY KIND AS SINS, IN THE SAME PROPORTION HE LOVES HONESTY.

80. To "steal," in the natural sense, means not only to commit theft and robbery, but also to defraud, and under some pretext take from another his goods. In the spiritual sense, however, to "steal" means to deprive another of his truths of faith and his goods of charity. In the highest sense to "steal" means to take from the Lord that what is His, and attribute it to one's self, and thus to claim righteousness and merit for one's self. These are the "thefts of every kind." They also make a one, as do adulteries of every kind, and murders of every kind, of which we have already treated. The reason why they make a one is that they are one within the other.

81. The evil of theft enters more deeply into a man than any other evil, because it is conjoined with cunning and deceit; and cunning and deceit insinuate themselves even into the spiritual mind of man in which is his thought with understanding. That man possesses a spiritual mind and a natural mind will be seen below.

82. In proportion as any one shuns theft as a sin, in the same proportion he loves honesty. This is because theft is also fraud, and fraud and honesty are two opposite things, so that in proportion as any one is not in theft in the same proportion he is in honesty.

83. Honesty is to be understood as including integrity, justice, fidelity, and rectitude. No man can be in these from himself so as to love them from and for their own sakes. But that man is in them who shuns as sins, fraud, cunning, and deceit, and is therefore in them not from himself but from the Lord (as shown above, nn. 18-31).

Such is the case with a priest, a magistrate, a judge, a trader, and with every one in his own office and his own work.

84. This is taught by the Word in many passages, among which are the following:

He that walketh in righteousness, and speaketh uprightnesses; he that despiseth oppressions for gain, that shaketh his hands from holding bribes, that stoppeth his ears from the hearing of bloodshed, and shutteth his eyes from seeing evil; he shall dwell on high (Isa 33:15, 16).

Jehovah, who shall abide in Thy tent? who shall dwell in the mountain of Thy holiness? He that walketh uprightly, and doeth righteousness; he that slandereth not with his tongue, nor doeth evil to his companion (Ps 15:1-3, etc.).

Mine eyes shall be upon the faithful of the land, that they may dwell with Me; he that walketh in the way of the upright, he shall minister unto Me. He that worketh deceit shall not dwell in the midst of My house; he that speaketh lies shall not stand before Mine eyes. In the dawning will I cut off all the wicked of the land, to cut off from the city all the workers of iniquity (101:6-8).

Unless a man is interiorly honest, just, faithful, and upright, he is dishonest, unjust, unfaithful, and debased. This is taught by the Lord in these words:

Except your righteousness shall exceed that of the scribes and Pharisees, ye shall not enter into the kingdom of the heavens (Mt 5:10).

The "righteousness that exceeds that of the scribes and Pharisees" means the interior righteousness in which is the man who is in the Lord. That he is in the Lord is taught by the Lord Himself in John:

The glory which Thou hast given Me I have given unto them, that they may be one even as we are One, I in them, and Thou in Me, that they may be perfected into one; that the love wherewith Thou hast loved Me may be in them, and I in them (17:22, 23, 26).

From this it is evident that they are "perfect" when the Lord is in them. These are they who are called

The pure in heart, who shall see God; [and], Those who are perfect as is their Father in the heavens (Mt 5:8, 48).

85. It has been said above (n. 81), that the evil of theft enters more deeply into a man than any other evil because it is conjoined with cunning and deceit, and that cunning and deceit insinuate themselves even into the spiritual mind of man in which is his thought with understanding. Something shall therefore now be said about the mind of man. (That the mind of man is his understanding and will together, see above, n. 43.)

86. Man possesses a natural mind and a spiritual mind. The natural mind is below, and the spiritual mind above. The natural mind is the mind of man's world, and the spiritual mind is the mind of his heaven. The natural mind may be called the animal mind, and the spiritual mind the human mind. Man is distinguished from the animal by possessing a spiritual mind. By means of this mind he can be in heaven while still in the world; and it is by means of this mind also that man lives after death.

[2] In his understanding a man is able to be in the spiritual mind, and consequently in heaven, but unless he shuns evils as sins he cannot be in the spiritual mind and consequently in heaven with his will. And if he is not there with his will, he is not in heaven, in spite of the fact that he is there in understanding, for the will drags the understanding down, and causes it to be just as natural and animal as it is itself.

[3] Man may be compared to a garden—his understanding to light, and his will to heat. In winter time a garden is in light but not in accompanying heat, but in summer time it is in light accompanied by heat. Just so a man who is in the light of the understanding alone is like a garden in winter time, whereas one who is in the light of the understanding and at the same time in the heat of the will is like a garden in summer time. Moreover the understanding

is wise from spiritual light, and the will loves from spiritual heat, for spiritual light is divine wisdom, and spiritual heat is divine love.

[4] So long as a man does not shun evils as sins, the lusts of evils block up the interiors of his natural mind on the part of his will, being like a thick veil there, and like a black cloud beneath the spiritual mind, and they prevent its being opened. But the very moment a man shuns evils as sins, the Lord inflows from heaven, takes away the veil, dispels the cloud, opens the spiritual mind, and so introduces the man into heaven.

[5] So long as the lusts of evils block up the interiors of the natural mind (in the way we have indicated), so long is the man in hell; the moment however that these inclinations have been dispersed by the Lord, the man is in heaven. Furthermore: so long as the lusts of evils block up the interiors of the natural mind, so long is the man natural; but the moment they have been dispersed by the Lord, he is spiritual. Furthermore: so long as the allurements of evils block up the interiors of the natural mind, so long is the man animal, differing only in his ability to think and speak, even of such things as he does not see with his eyes, which ability he derives from his capacity of uplifting his understanding into the light of heaven. The moment however that these allurements have been dispersed by the Lord, the man is a man, because he then thinks what is true in the understanding from what is good in the will. Furthermore: so long as the lusts of evils block up the interiors of the natural mind, the man is like a garden in winter time, but the moment these lusts have been dispersed by the Lord, he is like a garden in summer.

[6] The conjunction in a man of the will and the understanding is meant in the Word by "heart and soul," and by "heart and spirit." For example: that we must love God

With all the heart, and with all the soul (Mt 22:37).

And that God will give

A new heart, and a new spirit (Ezek 11:19; 36:26, 27).

The "heart" means the will and its love, and the "soul" and the "spirit," the understanding and its wisdom.

XI.

IN PROPORTION AS ANY ONE SHUNS FALSE WITNESS OF EVERY KIND AS SIN, IN THE SAME PROPORTION HE LOVES THE TRUTH.

87. To "bear false witness," in the natural sense, means not only to play the false witness, but also to lie, and to defame. In the spiritual sense, to "bear false witness" means to declare some false thing to be true or some evil thing good, and to persuade others that it is so; and the converse. And in the highest sense, to "bear false witness" means to blaspheme the Lord and the Word. These are the three senses of "bearing false witness." That these make one in the man who bears false witness, utters a lie, or defames, is clear from what has been shown respecting the three senses of everything in the Word, in *Doctrine of the Sacred Scripture* (nn. 5-7, etc. and 57).

88. As lying and the truth are two opposite things, it follows that in proportion as any one shuns falsehood as sin, in the same proportion he loves the truth.

89. In proportion as any one loves the truth, in the same proportion he desires to know it, and in the same proportion is affected at heart when he finds it. No one else comes into wisdom. And in proportion as any one loves to *do* the truth, in the same proportion he is aware of the pleasantness of the light in which the truth is. It is the same with all the other things spoken of above; with honesty and justice in the case of one who shuns thefts of every kind; with chastity and purity in the case of one who shuns adulteries of every kind; and with love and charity in the case of one who shuns murders of every kind; and so forth. On the other hand, one who is in the opposites to these heavenly things knows nothing about them, although every-

271

thing that is truly something is present in them.

90. It is the truth that is meant by the "seed in the field," of which the Lord said:

A sower went forth to sow, and as he sowed some fell upon the pathway, and it was trodden down, and the fowls of heaven devoured it; and some fell upon stony places, and as soon as it was sprung up, because it had no root it withered away; and some fell among thorns, and the thorns sprung up with it and choked it; and other seed fell into the good ground, and sprung up, and bare fruit manifold (Lu 8:5-8; Mt 13:3-8; Mk 4:3-8).

Here the "sower" is the Lord, and the "seed" is His Word, thus the truth; the "seed upon the pathway" exists with those who do not care for the truth; the "seed upon stony places" exists with those who do care for the truth, but not for its own sake, thus not interiorly; the "seed in the midst of thorns" exists with those who are in the lusts of evil; but the "seed in good ground" exists with those who love the truths that are in the Word from the Lord, and do them from Him, thus who bear fruit. That these things are meant is evident from the explanation of the parable by the Lord (Mt 13:19-23, 37; Mk 4:14-20; Lu 8:11-15). From all this it is evident that the truth of the Word cannot take root in those who do not care for the truth, nor in those who love the truth outwardly and not inwardly, nor in those who are in evil allurements, but in those in whom the lusts of evil have been dispersed by the Lord. In these the "seed"—that is, the truth—takes root in their spiritual mind (concerning which above, n. 86 at the end).

91. It is a general opinion at the present day that to be saved consists in believing this thing or that which the church teaches, and that it does not consist in keeping the commandments (which are, Do not kill, Do not commit adultery, Do not steal, Do not bear false witness) in both the narrow and the broad sense. For it is maintained that works are not regarded by God, but that faith is, when

nevertheless the truth is that in proportion as any one is in these evils, in that same proportion he has no faith.. (See above nn. 42-52.) Take counsel of reason and observe whether, as long as he has desires for these evils, any murderer, adulterer, thief, or false witness is able to have faith; and also, further, whether the enticement of these evils can be shaken off in any other way than by refusing to will to commit them for the reason that they are sins, that is, because they are infernal and devilish. So whoever imagines that being saved consists in believing this thing or that which is taught by the church, while himself remaining thus evil in feeling and in character, must needs be a "foolish man," in accordance with the words of the Lord in Matthew 7:26. Such a church is thus described in Jeremiah:

Stand in the gate of Jehovah's house, and proclaim there this word: Thus saith Jehovah of hosts the God of Israel, Amend your ways and your doings; trust ye not in lying words, saying, The temple of Jehovah, the temple of Jehovah, the temple of Jehovah, are these. Will ye steal, murder, and commit adultery, and swear falsely, and come and stand before Me in this house, which is called by My name, and say, We are delivered, while ye do all these abominations? Is this house become a den of robbers? Behold I, even I, have seen it, saith Jehovah (7:2-4, 9-11).

XII.

NO ONE CAN SHUN EVILS AS SINS SO AS TO BE INWARDLY AVERSE
TO THEM EXCEPT BY MEANS OF COMBATS AGAINST THEM.

92. Everybody knows from the Word and from doctrine drawn from it that the proprium° of man is evil from his birth, and that this is the reason why from inborn inclination he loves evils and is drawn into them. This is why he desires to have revenge, and to commit fraud, defamation, and adultery. And unless he takes thought that such things are sins, and on that account resists them, he does them whenever an opportunity offers, provided that his reputation and thereby his honors and gains do not suffer. Consider also that unless he has religion the man does these things with delight.

93. As this proprium of man constitutes the first root of his life, it is evident what kind of a tree a man would be unless this root were plucked up, and a new root planted in its place. He would be a rotted tree, of which it is said that it must be cut down and cast into the fire (Mt 3:10; 7:19.) This root is not removed and a new one set in its place unless the man regards the evils that constitute the root as injurious to his soul, and on this account desires to rid himself of them. But as these evils belong to his proprium, and are therefore delightful to him, he cannot do this except with a struggle against his will, and therefore without a fight.

94. Everyone goes through this struggle who believes in the existence of hell and of heaven: that heaven is eternal happiness, and hell eternal unhappiness; and that those who do evils enter hell, and those who do goods enter

---

° For a definition of this term, see No. 60, *Doctrine of the Sacred Scripture.*

heaven. And one who thus fights acts from within, and against the desire itself which constitutes the root of the evil, for one who fights against anything does not will it, and to desire is to will. This shows that the root of evil is not removed except by means of combat.

95. In proportion therefore as any one fights against and thus removes evil, in the same proportion good takes its place, and from this good the man in the same proportion looks evil in the face, and sees that it is infernal and horrible, and on that account he not only shuns it, but feels averse to it, and at last abhors it

96. A man who fights against evils cannot but do so as if from himself, for one who does not fight as if from himself does not do so at all, but stands like an automaton that sees nothing and does nothing; and from evil he is continually thinking in favor of evil, and not against it. But it is important to know that it is the Lord alone who fights in a man against his evils, and that it only appears to the man that he himself does the fighting; and also that the Lord wills that it should so appear to him, because without this appearance no combat takes place and therefore no reformation.

97. This combat is not severe except in the case of those who have given free rein to their lusts, and have indulged them of set purpose; and also in the case of those who have stubbornly cast off the holy things of the Word and of the church. With others it is not severe; let them even once in a week, or twice in a month, resist the evils they are inclined to, and they will perceive a change.

98. The Christian Church is called the church militant, and it cannot be called militant except as against the devil, and thus against the evils that are from hell. Hell is the devil; and the temptation that the man of the church undergoes is this warfare.

99. Struggles against evils, which are temptations, are

treated of in many places in the Word. They are meant by these words of the Lord:

> I say unto you, Except a grain of wheat fall into the earth and die, it abideth by itself alone; but if it die, it beareth much fruit (Jn 12:24).

And also by these:

> If any man would come after Me, let him deny himself, and take up his cross, and follow Me. For whosoever would save his life shall lose it; and whosoever shall lose his life for My sake and the gospel's, the same shall save it (Mk 8:34, 35).

The "cross" means temptation (as also in Mt 10:38; 16:24; Mk 10:21; Lu 14:27). By his "life" is meant the life of man's proprium (as also in Mt 10:39; 16:25; Lu 9:24; and especially in Jn 12:25), which is also the "life of the flesh that profiteth nothing" (Jn 6:63).

In regard to struggles against evils, and victories over them, the Lord speaks in the Apocalypse to all the churches:

> To the church in Ephesus: To him that overcometh, to him will I give to eat of the tree of life, which is in the midst of the paradise of God (2:7).
> To the church in Smyrna: He that overcometh shall not be hurt of the second death (verse 11).
> To the church in Pergamos: To him that overcometh, to him will I give to eat of the hidden manna, and I will give him a white stone, and upon the stone a new name written, which no one knoweth but he that receiveth it (verse 17).
> To the church in Thyatira: He that overcometh, and that keepeth My words unto the end, to him will I give power over the nations; and the morning star (verses 26, 28).
> To the church in Sardis: [He that overcometh shall be clothed in white garments, and I will not blot his name out of the book of life, and I will confess his name before My Father, and before His angels (3:5).
> To the church in Philadelphia:] He that overcometh I will make a pillar in the temple of My God, and I will write upon him the name of My God, and the name of the city of My God, the New Jerusalem,

which cometh down out of heaven from My God, and My new name (verse 12).

To the church in Laodicea: He that overcometh I will give to him to sit down with Me in My throne (verse 21).
(15:14).

100. These struggles, which are temptations, may be seen specially treated of in *The New Jerusalem and its Heavenly Doctrine,* published in London in the year 1758 (from n. 187 to n. 201): Whence and what they are (nn. 196, 197): How and where they take place (n. 198): What good they effect (n. 199): That the Lord fights for man (n. 200): Concerning the Lord's combats or temptations (n. 201).

XIII.

A MAN OUGHT TO SHUN EVILS AS SINS AND FIGHT AGAINST THEM AS IF FROM HIMSELF.

101. It is in accordance with divine order that man should act in freedom according to reason, because so to act is to act from himself. And yet these two faculties, freedom and reason, are not ascribable to man, but are the Lord's in him; and in so far as he is a man they must not be taken away from him, because without them he cannot be reformed; for without them he cannot perform repentance, he cannot fight against evils, and afterwards bring forth fruits worthy of repentance. Now as it is from the Lord that man possesses freedom and reason, and as mans acts from them, it follows that he does not act from himself, but *as if* from himself.

102. The Lord loves man and wills to dwell with him, yet He cannot love him and dwell with him unless He is received and loved in return. From this alone comes conjunction. For this reason the Lord has given man freedom and reason, freedom to think and will as if from himself, and reason in accordance with which he may do so. To love and to be conjoined with one in whom there is nothing reciprocal is not possible, nor is it possible to enter in and abide with one in whom there is no reception. As there are in man, from the Lord, reception and reciprocation, the Lord says:

Abide in Me, and I in you (Jn 15:4).

He that abideth in Me, and I in him, the same bringeth forth much fruit (verse 5).

At that day ye shall know that ye are in Me, and I in you (Jn 14:20).

The Lord also teaches that He is in the truths and in the goods that a man receives, and that are in him:

> If ye abide in Me, and My words abide in you. If ye keep My commandments, ye shall abide in My love (Jn 15:7, 10).
>
> He that hath My commandments, and doeth them, he it is that loveth Me; and I will love him, and will make My abode with him (14:21, 23).

Therefore, the Lord dwells in a man in what is His own, and the man dwells in those things which are from the Lord, and thus dwells in the Lord.

103. As there is in man, from the Lord, this ability to reciprocate and return, and consequently this *mutuality,* the Lord says that a man must do the work of repentance, which no one can do except as if from himself:

> Jesus said: Except ye repent ye shall all perish (Lu 13:3, 5).
>
> Jesus said: The kingdom of God is at hand; repent ye, and believe the gospel (Mk 1:14, 15).
>
> Jesus said: I am come to call sinners to repentance (Lu 5:32).
>
> Jesus said to the churches: Repent (Apoc 2:5, 16, 21, 22; 3:3).

It is also said:

> They repented not of their works (Apoc 16:11).

104. As there is in man, from the Lord, this ability to reciprocate and return, and consequently this mutuality, the Lord says that a man must keep the commandments, and also that he must bring forth fruit:

> Why call ye Me Lord, Lord, and do not the things which I say? (Lu 6:46-49).
>
> If ye know these things, blessed are ye if ye do them (Jn 13:17).
>
> Ye are My friends, if ye do the things which I command you (15:14).
>
> Whosoever shall do and teach them shall be called great in the kingdom of the heavens (Mt 5:19).
>
> Every one therefore who heareth these words of Mine, and doeth them, I will liken to a wise man (7:24).
>
> Bring forth therefore fruits worthy of repentance (3:8).

Make the tree good, and its fruit good (12:33).

The kingdom shall be given to a nation bringing forth the fruits thereof (21:43).

Every tree that bringeth not forth good fruit is hewn down, and cast into the fire (7:19).

And so in many other places: from all this it is evident that a man must act as if from himself but really from the Lord's power, which he must petition for. For this is to act *as if* from himself.

105. As there is in man, from the Lord, this ability to reciprocate and return, and consequently this mutuality, a man must render an account of his works, and will be requited according to them. For the Lord says:

The Son of man shall come, and shall render to every man according to his deeds (Mt 16:27).

They shall come forth: they that have done good, unto the resurrection of life, and they that have done evils unto the resurrection of judgment (Jn 5:29).

Their works do follow with them (Apoc 14:13).

They were judged every man according to his works (20:13).

Behold, I come, and My reward is with Me, to give every man according to his work (22:12).

If there were in man no reciprocal action, there would be no imputation.

106. As in man there are reception and reciprocality, the church teaches that a man must examine himself, confess his sins before God, desist from them, and lead a new life. It may be seen above (nn. 3-8) that every church in the Christian world teaches this.

107. Unless there were reception by man, and at the same time an awareness as it were by him, nothing could have been said about faith, for faith is not from man. Without this reception and reciprocality, man would be like chaff in the wind, and would stand as if lifeless, with mouth open, and hands hanging down, awaiting influx, devoid of thought and action in regard to the things that concern his salvation. It is indeed true that he is by no means the agent in regard to these things, but yet he is a reagent as if from himself.

XIV.

108. There are moral men who keep the commandments
of the second table of the Decalogue, not committing fraud,
blasphemy, revenge, or adultery; and those among them
who confirm themselves in the belief that such things are
evils because they are injurious to the public weal, and
therefore contrary to the laws of humane conduct, practise
charity, honesty, justice, chastity. But if they do these
goods and shun those evils merely because they are evils,
and not at the same time because they are sins, they are
still merely natural men, and with the merely natural the
root of evil remains imbedded and is not dislodged; for
which reason the goods they do are not goods, because
they are from themselves.

109. Before men, a natural moral man may appear exactly like a spiritual moral man, but not before the angels.
Before the angels in heaven, if he is in goods he appears
like an image of wood, if in truths like an image of marble,
lifeless, and very different from a spiritual moral man. For
a natural moral man is an outwardly moral man, but a
spiritual moral man is an inwardly moral man, and what is
outward without what is inward is lifeless. It does indeed
live, but not the life that is truly life.

110. The allurements of evil that constitute the interiors
of man from his birth can be removed by the Lord alone.
For the Lord inflows from what is spiritual into what is
natural; but man, of himself, from what is natural into
what is spiritual; and this influx is contrary to order, and

does not operate into the lusts and remove them, but shuts them in closer and closer in proportion as it confirms itself. And as the hereditary evil thus lurks there, shut in, after death when the man becomes a spirit it bursts the cover that had hidden it here, and breaks out like the discharge from an ulcer that has been healed only outwardly.

111. There are various and many causes that make a man moral in the outward form, but unless he is moral in the inward form also, he is nevertheless not moral. For example: if a man abstains from adulteries and whoredom from the fear of the civil law and its penalties; from the fear of losing his good name and esteem; from the fear of the consequent diseases; from the fear of his wife's tongue in his home, and the consequent inquietude of his life; from the fear of the husband's vengeance, or that of some relative; from poverty, or avarice; from disability caused either by disease, abuse, age, or impotence; nay, if he abstains from such things on account of any natural or moral law, and not at the same time on account of the spiritual law, he nevertheless is inwardly an adulterer and whoremonger, for none the less does he believe that such things are not sins. As toward God, therefore, in his spirit he makes them not unlawful, and so in spirit he commits them, although not in the body in the sight of the world; and therefore after death, when he becomes a spirit, he speaks openly in favor of them. From all this it is evident that an ungodly man is able to shun evils as injurious, but only a Christian can shun them as sins.

112. It is the same with thefts and frauds of every kind, with murders and revengeful acts of every kind, and with false witness and lies of every kind. No one can of himself be cleansed and made pure from such things, for within every lust there are infinite things which the man sees only as one simple thing, whereas the Lord sees the smallest details of the whole series. In a word, a man cannot regenerate himself, that is, form in himself a new heart and a new spirit, but the Lord alone can do this, who Himself is the reformer and the regenerator. Therefore if a man wills to make himself new by his own sagacity and intelligence, it is merely like painting an ugly face, or smearing a cleansing cream over a part that is infected with inward corruption.

113. Therefore the Lord says in Matthew:

Thou blind Pharisee, cleanse first the inside of the cup and the platter, that the outside may be clean also (23:26).

And in Isaiah:

Wash you, make you clean, put away the evil of your works from before Mine eyes, cease to do evil; and then though your sins be as scarlet, they shall be as white as snow, though they have been red like crimson, they shall be as wool (1:16, 18).

114. To what has already been said shall be added the following:

1. Christian charity, with every one, consists in faithfully performing what pertains to his calling, for by this, if he shuns evils as sins, he is doing goods every day, and is himself his own use in the general body. In this way also the common good is cared for, and the good of each person in particular.

2. All the other things that [the Christian] does are not the special works of charity, but are either its signs, its benefactions, or its obligations.

THE DOCTRINE OF FAITH

FOR

THE NEW JERUSALEM

I.

1. At the present day the term Faith is taken to mean the mere thought that something is so because the church so teaches, and because it is not evident to the understanding. For we are told to believe and not to doubt, and if we say that we do not comprehend, we are told that this is just the reason for believing. So the faith of the present day is a faith in the unknown, and may be called blind faith; and as it is something that somebody has said, *in somebody else,* it is a faith of hearsay. It will be seen presently that this is not spiritual faith.

2. Real faith is nothing else than an acknowledgment that something is so because it is true; for one who is in real faith thinks and says, "This is true, and therefore I believe it." For faith is of truth, and truth is of faith. If such a person does not see the truth of a thing, he says, "I do not know whether this is true, and therefore as yet I do not believe it. How can I believe what I do not intellectually comprehend? Perhaps it is false."

3. But a common remark is that no one can comprehend spiritual or theological matters because they are supernatural. Spiritual truths however can be comprehended just as well as natural ones; and even if they are not clearly comprehended, still as soon as they are heard it is possible to perceive whether they are true or not. This is especially the case with those whose affection is stirred by truths. I have been permitted to know this by much experience.

I have been permitted to speak with the uneducated, with the dull-minded, and with the utterly senseless, as also with persons who had been in falsities, and those who had been in evils, all born within the church, and who had heard something about the Lord and about faith and charity; and I have had the privilege of telling them certain secrets of wisdom, and they comprehended everything and acknowledged it. At the time however they were in that light of the understanding which every human being possesses; and felt withal the pride of being thought intelligent. All this happened during my association with spirits. Many others who were with me were hereby convinced that spiritual things can be comprehended just as well as natural, that is, when they are heard or read.

However, comprehension by the man himself when thinking from himself is by no means so easy. The reason spiritual things can be comprehended is that a man's understanding may be lifted into the light of heaven, in which light none but spiritual things appear, and these are the truths of faith. For the light of heaven is spiritual light.

4. This then is the reason why those who are in the spiritual affection of truth possess an internal acknowledgment of truth. As the angels are in this affection, they discard the dogma that the understanding must be kept in obedience to faith, and say, "What is this? believing when you do not see whether the thing is true?" And if somebody says that still it is to be believed, they reply, "Do you consider yourself the Deity that I am bound to believe you? Or do you think me mad enough to believe a statement in which I do not see the truth? Help me to see it." Thereupon the dogmatizer betakes himself elsewhere. The wisdom of the angels consists solely in this: that they see and comprehend everything they think about.

5. A spiritual idea (about which few know anything) flows into those who are in the affection of truth, and inwardly tells them that what they hear or read is true, or is not true. In this idea are those who read the Word in enlightenment from the Lord. To be in enlightenment is nothing else than to be in the perception, and in the consequent internal acknowledgment, that this or that is true. These are they who are called "the taught of Jehovah" (Isa 54:13; Jn 6:45); and of whom it is said in Jeremiah:

Behold, the days come that I will make a new covenant: this shall be the covenant: I will put My law in their inward parts, and upon their heart will I write it, and they shall teach no more every man his companion, or every man his brother, saying, Know Jehovah; for they shall all know Me (Je 31:31, 33, 34).

6. From all this it is evident that faith and truth are one. For this reason the ancients (who from their affection for truths thought more about them than the men of our time) instead of saying "faith," were accustomed to say "truth." For the same reason also truth and faith are one word in the Hebrew language, namely *Amuna* or *Amen*.

7. The reason the term "faith" is used by the Lord in the Gospels and the Apocalypse is that the Jews did not believe it to be true that He was the Messiah foretold by the prophets; and where truth is not believed, there "faith" is spoken of. But still it is one thing to have faith and believe in the Lord, and another to have faith and believe in some one else. The difference will be explained below.

8. Faith separated from truth came in and took possession of the church along with the dominion of the papacy, because the chief safeguard of that religion was ignorance of truth. For this reason also they forbade the reading of the Word, for otherwise they could not have been worshiped as deities, nor could their saints have been invoked.

nor idolatry instituted to such an extent that dead bodies, bones, and sepulchres were regarded as holy, and made use of for purposes of gain. From this it is evident what enormous falsities a blind faith can bring into being.

9. Blind faith survived later with many of the Reformed, because they had separated faith from charity, for they who separate these two must needs be in ignorance of truth; and they will give the name of faith to the mere thought that something is so, quite apart from any internal acknowledgment. With these also, ignorance is the safeguard of dogma, for so long as ignorance prevails, together with the persuasion that theological matters transcend comprehension, they can speak without being contradicted, and it can be believed that their tenets are true, and that they themselves understand them.

10. The Lord said to Thomas:

Because thou hast seen Me, thou hast believed: blessed are they that do not see, and yet believe (Jn 20:29).

This does not mean a faith separated from the internal acknowledgment of truth; but that they are blessed who do not, like Thomas, see the Lord with their eyes, and yet believe in His existence, for this is seen in the light of truth from the Word.

11. As the internal acknowledgment of truth is faith, and as faith and truth are the same thing (as was said above, nn. 2, 4-6), it follows that an external acknowledgment without an internal one is not faith, and also that a persuasion of what is false is not faith. An external acknowledgment without an internal one is a faith in what is unknown, and a faith in what is unknown is mere memory-knowledge, which if confirmed becomes persuasion. They who are in such knowledge and persuasion think a thing true because somebody has said so, or they think it is true from their having confirmed it; and yet what is false can be confirmed just as well as what is true, and sometimes better. To think a thing true from having confirmed it is to think that something another says is true, and then to confirm it without previous examination.

12. If any one should think within himself, or say to some one else, "Who is able to have the internal acknowledgment of truth which is faith? not I;" let me tell him how he may have it: Shun evils as sins, and come to the Lord, and you will have as much of it as you desire. (That he who shuns evils as sins is in the Lord, see *Doctrine of Life for the New Jerusalem* nn. 18-31; that such a one loves truth, and sees it, nn. 32-41; and that he has faith nn. 42-52).

II.

13. We have already said what faith is, and will now say what charity is. In its origin or beginning, charity is the affection of good; and as good loves truth, the affection of good produces the affection of truth, and through it the acknowledgment of truth which is faith. Through this succession, the affection of good comes forth into manifest being, and becomes charity. This is the progressive advance of charity from its origin which is the affection of good, through faith which is the acknowledgment of truth, to its final end in view, which is charity. The final end is the doing. And this shows how love, here the affection of good, produces faith—which is the same thing as the acknowledgment of truth—and through this produces charity—which is the same thing as the working of love through faith.

14. More clearly: Good is nothing but Use, so that in its very origin charity is the affection of use; and as use loves the means, the affection of use produces the affection of the means, and from this the knowledge of them, and through this progression the affection of use comes forth into manifest being, and becomes charity.

15. The progression of these things is precisely like that of all the things of the will through the understanding into bodily acts. The will brings forth nothing from itself apart from the understanding, nor does the understanding bring forth anything from itself apart from the will. In order that anything may come forth into manifest being, the two must act in conjunction. Or, what is the same: Affection, which belongs to the will, brings forth nothing from itself except by means of thought, which pertains to the understanding (the converse also being true), for in order that anything may come forth into manifest being the two must act in conjunction. For consider: If you take away from thought all affection belonging to some love, can you exercise thought? Or if from the affection you take away all thought, are you then able to be affected by anything? Or, what is much the same, if you take away affection from thought, can you say anything? Or if you take away thought or understanding from affection, can you do anything? It is the same with charity and faith.

16. All this may be illustrated by comparison with a tree. The prime source of a tree is a seed, and in this there is an endeavor to bring forth fruit. This endeavor, roused to activity by heat, brings forth first a root, and then from that a stem or stalk with branches and leaves, and at last the fruit; and in this way the endeavor to bear fruit comes forth into manifest being. From this it is evident that the endeavor to bring forth fruit is constant through the whole progression until it attains manifest being, for if it ceased the capacity to vegetate would die at once. This is the application: The tree is man; in him the endeavor to bring forth the means is from his will in his understanding; the stem or stalk with branches and leaves, in him are the instrumental means, and are called the truths of faith; the fruits which in the tree are the final effects of the endeavor to bear fruit, in man are uses; and in these his will comes forth into manifest being. From this it may be seen that the will to bring forth uses by means of the understanding is constant through the whole progression, until it comes into manifest being. (On the will and the understanding, and their conjunction, see *Doctrine of Life for the New Jerusalem*, n. 43.)

17. From what has now been said it is evident that charity, in so far as it is the affection for good, or for use,

brings forth faith as a means through which it may come into manifest being; and therefore that charity and faith, in performing uses, act in unison; and also that faith does not bring forth good or use from itself, but from charity, for faith is charity in its mediate stage. It is therefore a fallacy that faith brings forth good as a tree does its fruit. The tree is not faith. The tree is the man himself.

18. It should be known that charity and faith make one as do the will and the understanding, for charity pertains to the will, and faith to the understanding. And in the same way that charity and faith make one, so do affection and thought, because affection pertains to the will, and thought to the understanding. Also that charity and faith make one as do good and truth, because good comes of affection which belongs to the will, and truth comes of thought which belongs to the understanding. In a word, charity and faith make one as do essence and form. This shows that faith without charity is like a form without an essence, which is nothing at all; and that charity without faith is like an essence without a form, which likewise is nothing at all.

19. Charity and faith in a man are related to each other precisely as are the motion of the heart called systole and diastole, and that of the lungs called breathing. Moreover there is a full correspondence of these two with man's will and understanding, and therefore with charity and faith. For this reason the will and its affection are meant in the Word by the "heart," and the understanding and its thought by the "breath" and the "spirit," on which account to "give up the breath," or "yield up the spirit," means to cease to respire, or to expire.

This shows that there cannot be faith without charity, nor charity without faith; faith without charity being like breathing with the lungs in the absence of a heart, which is impossible in any living being, except by some artificial apparatus; and charity without faith being like a heart without lungs, which can result in no conscious life; and therefore charity performs uses by means of faith, just as the heart does its work by means of the lungs. So complete is the likeness between the heart and charity, and between the lungs and faith, that in the spiritual world every one is known as to the quality of his faith by his mere breathing, and as to that of his charity by the way his heart beats. For angels and spirits live by a heart-beat and breathing just as men do, and it is for this reason that they, equally with men in this world, feel, think, act, and speak.

20. As charity is love toward the neighbor, we will define the neighbor. In the natural sense, the neighbor is man both collectively and individually. Collectively, man is the church, our country, and society; individually, he is our fellow-citizen, who in the Word is called "brother" and "companion." But in the spiritual sense the neighbor is good, and as use is good, the neighbor in this sense is use. That use is the spiritual neighbor must be acknowledged by every one. For who loves a human being merely as a person? We love him for what he has in him, which gives him his character, thus from his quality; for this is the man. And this quality that we love is use, and is called good, so that this is the neighbor. And as, in its bosom, the Word is spiritual, therefore in its spiritual sense this is to "love the neighbor."

21. But it is one thing to love the neighbor on account of the good or use he is to us, and another to love him from the good or use we may be to him. Even an evil man can do the first, but only a good man the second, for a good man loves good from good, that is, he loves use from affection for use. The difference between the two is described by the Lord in Matthew 5:42-47. Many say, "I love such a man because he loves me and does me good;" but to love any

one for this only is not to love him inwardly, unless he who so loves is himself in good, and from it loves the good of the other. In this case the man is in charity, but in the other he is in a friendship which is not charity. A man who loves the neighbor from charity conjoins himself with his good, and not with his person except in so far and for so long as he is in good. Such a man is spiritual, and loves his neighbor spiritually, whereas one who loves another from mere friendship, conjoins himself with his person, and at the same time with his evil, and after death he cannot without difficulty be separated from the personality that is in evil, but the former can. Charity effects this by means of faith, which faith is the truth; and the man who is in charity by means of the truth examines thoroughly and sees what ought to be loved, and in loving and conferring benefits he regards the quality of the other's use.

22. Love to the Lord is love properly so called, and love toward the neighbor is charity. With man no love to the Lord is possible except in charity; it is in charity that the Lord conjoins Himself with a man. As, in its essence, faith is charity, it follows that no one can have faith in the Lord unless he is in charity. There is conjunction from charity through faith; through charity conjunction of the Lord with man, and through faith conjunction of man with the Lord. (That the conjunction is reciprocal, see *Doctrine of Life for the New Jerusalem,* nn. 102-107.)

23. In brief: In proportion as any one shuns evils as sins, and looks to the Lord, in the same proportion he is in charity, and therefore in the same proportion he is in faith. (That in proportion as any one shuns evils as sins and looks to the Lord, in the same proportion he is in charity, may be seen in *Doctrine of Life for the New Jerusalem,* nn. 67-73, and also nn. 74-91; and that in the same proportion he has faith, nn. 42-52. What charity properly understood is, n. 114).

24. From all said thus far it is evident that saving faith, which is the internal acknowledgment of truth, is impossible to all except those who are in charity.

III.

KNOWLEDGES OF TRUTH AND OF GOOD ARE NOT MATTERS OF
REAL BELIEF UNTIL A MAN IS IN CHARITY, BUT ARE THE STORE-
HOUSE OF MATERIAL OUT OF WHICH THE FAITH OF CHARITY
CAN BE FORMED.

25. From his earliest childhood man has an affection
for knowing, which leads him to learn many things that
will be of use to him, and many that will be of no use.
While he is growing into manhood he learns by application
to some business such things as belong to that business,
and this business then becomes his use, and he feels an
affection for it. In this way commences the affection or love
of use, and this brings forth the affection of the means
which teach him the handling of the business which is his
use. With everybody in the world there is this progression,
because everybody has some business to which he advances
from the use that is his end, by the means, to the actual
use which is the effect. But inasmuch as this use together
with the means that belong to it is for the sake of life in
this world, the affection that is felt for it is natural affection
only.

26. However, as every man regards uses not only for
the sake of life in this world, but also should regard uses
for the sake of his life in heaven (for into this life he will
come after his life here, and will live in it to eternity),
therefore from childhood every one acquires knowledges
of truth and good from the Word, or from the doctrine of
the church, or from preaching, which knowledges are to be
learned and retained for the sake of that life; and these he
stores up in his natural memory in greater or less abundance according to such affection for knowing as may be

inborn with him, and has in various ways been incited to an increase.

27. But all these knowledges, whatever their number and nature, are merely the storehouse of material from which the faith of charity can be formed; and this faith cannot be formed except in proportion as the man shuns evils as sins. If he shuns evils as sins, then these knowledges become those of a faith that has spiritual life within it. But if he does not shun evils as sins, then these knowledges are nothing but knowledges, and do not become those of a faith that has any spiritual life within it.

28. This storehouse of material is in the highest degree necessary, because faith cannot be formed without it, for the knowledges of truth and good enter into faith and make it; so that if there are no knowledges, faith cannot come forth into being, for an entirely void and empty faith is impossible. If the knowledges are scanty, the faith is consequently very small and meager; if they are abundant, the faith becomes proportionately rich and full.

29. However one should know that it is knowledges of genuine truth and good that constitute faith, and by no means knowledges of what is false, for faith is truth (as before said, nn. 5-11), and as falsity is the opposite of truth, it destroys faith. Charity cannot come forth into being where there are only falsities, for (as before said, n. 18) charity and faith make one just as good and truth make one. From all this it follows that an absence of knowledges of genuine truth and good involves an absence of faith, that a few knowledges make some faith, and that many knowledges make a faith which is clear and bright in proportion to their abundance. Such as is the quality of a man's faith from charity, such is the quality of his intelligence.

30. There are many who possess no internal acknowledgment of truth, and yet have the faith of charity. These are they who have had regard to the Lord in their life, and from religion have avoided evils, but have been prevented from thinking about truths by worldly cares and by their businesses, as well as by a lack of truth on the part of their teachers. But inwardly, that is, in their spirit, they are nevertheless in the acknowledgment of truth, because they are in affection for it; and therefore after death, when they become spirits and are instructed by angels, they acknowledge truths and receive them with joy. Very different is the case with those who have had no regard to the Lord in their life, and have not from religion avoided evils. Inwardly, that is, in their spirit, they are in no affection for truth, and consequently are in no acknowledgment of it; and therefore after death, when they become spirits and are instructed by angels, they are unwilling to acknowledge truths, and consequently do not receive them. For evil of life inwardly hates truths, whereas good of life inwardly loves them.

31. Knowledges of good and truth that precede faith appear to some to be matters of faith (or real belief), but still are not so. Their thinking and saying that they believe is no proof that they do; and neither are such knowledges things of faith, for they are matters of mere thought that the case is so, and not of any internal recognition that they are truths; and the faith or belief that they are truths, while it is not known that they are so, is a kind of persuasion quite remote from inward recognition. But as soon as charity is being implanted, these knowledges become things of faith, but no further than there is charity in the faith. In the first state, before charity is felt, faith appears to them as though it were in the first place, and charity in the second; but in the second state, when charity is felt, faith betakes itself to the second place, and charity to the first. The first state is called reformation, and the second regeneration. In this latter state a man grows in wisdom every day, and every day good multiplies truths and causes them to bear fruit.

The man is then like a tree that bears fruit, and deposits seeds in the fruit, from which come new trees, and at last a garden. He then becomes truly a man, and after death an angel, in whom charity constitutes the life, and faith the form, beautiful in accordance with the quality of the faith, which is then no longer called faith, but intelligence. From all this it is evident that the whole sum and substance of faith is from charity, and nothing of it from itself; and also that charity brings forth faith, and not faith charity. The knowledges of truth that go before are like the supply in a granary, which does not feed a man unless he is hungry and takes out the grain.

32. We will also say how faith is formed from charity. Every man has a natural mind and a spiritual mind: a natural mind for the world, and a spiritual mind for heaven. As to his understanding, man is in both minds, but not as to his will, until he shuns and is averse to evils as sins. When he does this his spiritual mind is opened as to the will also; and when it has been opened there is an influx from it into the natural mind of spiritual heat from heaven (which heat in its essence is charity), and life is thereby given to the knowledges of truth and good in the natural mind, and out of them it forms faith. The case here is just as it is with a tree, which does not receive any vegetative life until heat inflows from the sun, and conjoins itself with the light, as takes place in spring. There is also a full parallelism between the quickening of man with life and the growing of a tree, in this respect, that the latter is effected by the heat of this world, and the former by the heat of heaven. It is for this reason also that man is so often likened by the Lord to a tree.

33. From these few words it may be considered settled that the knowledges of truth and good are not really things of faith until the man is in charity, but that they are the storehouse of material out of which the faith of charity can

be formed. With a regenerate person the knowledges of truth become truths, and so do the knowledges of good, for the knowledge of good is in the understanding, and the affection of good in the will, and what is in the understanding is called truth, and what is in the will is called good.

IV.

THE CHRISTIAN FAITH IN ITS UNIVERSAL IDEA.[*]

34. The Christian *Faith* in its universal idea is this: The Lord from eternity who is Jehovah, came into the world to subdue the hells, and to glorify His Human; and without this no mortal could have been saved; and they are saved who believe in Him.

35. It is said "in the *universal* idea" because this is what is universal of the *Faith*, or what must be in every detail of it both in general and in particular. It is a universal of the *Faith* that God is One in Person and in Essence, in whom is the Trinity, and that the Lord is that God. It is a universal of the *Faith* that no mortal could have been saved unless the Lord had come into the world. It is a universal of the *Faith* that He came into the world in order to remove hell from man, and He removed it by combats against it and by victories over it; thus He subdued it, and reduced it into order and under obedience to Himself. It is also a universal of the *Faith* that He came into the world in order to glorify the Human which He took upon Him in the world, that is, in order to unite it to the all-originating Divine; thus hell was disposed into order by Him, and He holds it under His subjection to eternity. And inasmuch as neither of these mighty works could have been accomplished except by means of temptations even to the uttermost of them, which was the passion of the cross, He therefore underwent this uttermost temptation. These are the universals of the Christian *Faith* concerning the Lord.

36. The universal of the Christian *Faith* on the part of

[*] The Latin word *idea* is evidently used here in its original Greek sense of *form*. See *True Christian Religion* (n. 2), where Swedenborg in exactly the same connection uses the word *forma* instead of *idea*. [TR.]

man is that he believe in the Lord, for through believing in Him there is effected conjunction with Him, by which comes salvation. To believe in Him is to have confidence that He will save, and as no one can have this confidence except one who lives aright, therefore this also is meant by believing in Him.

37. These two universals of the Christian *Faith* have already been treated of specifically; the first, which regards the Lord, in *Doctrine of the Lord;* and the second, which regards man, in *Doctrine of Life.* It is therefore unnecessary to discuss them further here.

V.

38. The *Faith* of the present day in its universal idea is this: God the Father sent His Son to make satisfaction for mankind, and for the sake of this merit of the Son He is moved to compassion, and saves those who believe this (or, according to others, saves those who believe this, and at the same time do good works).

39. But in order that the character of this *Faith* may be seen more clearly, I will adduce in their order the various things which it maintains.

The *Faith* of the present day maintains that:

i. God the Father and God the Son are two; and both are from eternity.

ii. God the Son came into the world by the will of the Father to make satisfaction for mankind, who otherwise would have perished in eternal death by the divine justice, which they also call avenging justice.

iii. The Son made satisfaction by fulfilling the law, and by the passion of the cross.

iv. The Father was moved to compassion by these deeds of the Son.

v. The Son's merit is imputed to those who believe this.

vi. This imputation takes place in an instant; and therefore it may take place, if not before, in life's last moments.

vii. There is some measure of temptation, and deliverance thereupon through this belief.

viii. Those possessing this experience, in especial have trust and confidence.

ix. In especial they have justification, the Father's full grace for the sake of the Son, the remission of all their sins, and thereby salvation.

x. The more learned maintain that in such there is an endeavor toward good, which works in secret, and does not manifestly move the will. Others maintain a manifest working. Both classes hold that it is by the Holy Spirit.

xi. Of those who confirm themselves in the belief that no one can from himself do good that is really good and that is not tainted with self-merit, and that they are not under the yoke of the law, very many omit to do what is good, giving no thought to the evil and the good of life, saying to themselves that a good work does not save, and neither does an evil one condemn, because faith alone effects everything.

xii. All maintain that the understanding must be kept in subjection to faith, calling that a matter of faith which is not understood.

40. We forbear to examine and weigh these points separately in regard to their being truths, their real character being very evident from what has already been said, especially from what has been shown from the Word, and at the same time rationally confirmed, in the *Doctrine of the Lord,* and in the *Doctrine of Life.*

41. Still, in order that it may be seen what is the character of faith separated from charity, and what that of faith not separated from it, I will impart something which I heard from an angel of heaven. He said that he had spoken with many of the Reformed, and had heard what was the character of their faith, and he related his conversation with one who was in faith separated from charity, and with another who was in faith not separated, and what he had heard from them. He said that he questioned them, and they made answer. As what was said may throw light upon the subject, I will here present the two conversations.

42. The angel said that with the one who was in faith separated from charity he spoke as follows:

"Friend, who are you?" "I am a Reformed Christian." "What is your doctrine and the religion you have from it?" "It is faith." "What is your faith?" "My faith is that 'God the Father sent the Son to make satisfaction for mankind, and that they are saved who believe this.'" "What more do you know about salvation?" "Salvation is through that faith alone." "What do you know about redemption?" "It was effected by the passion of the cross, and the Son's merit is imputed through that faith." "What do you know about regeneration?" "It is effected through that faith." "What do you know about repentance and the remission of sins?" "They are effected through that faith." "Say what you know about love and charity." "They are that faith." "Say what you know about good works." "They are that faith." "Say what you think about all the things commanded in the Word." "They are in that faith." "There is nothing then that you are to do?" "What is there for me to do? I cannot from myself do good that is really good." "Can you have faith from yourself?" "I cannot." "How then is it possible for you to have faith?" "That I do not inquire into. I am to have faith."

Finally the angel said, "Surely you know something more than this about salvation." He replied, "What more is there for me to know, seeing that salvation is obtained through that faith alone?"

Then the angel said, "You answer like a fifer who sounds only one note: I hear of nothing but faith. If that is all you know, you know nothing. Go, and look at your associates."

So he left, and came upon his [companions] in a desert, where there was no grass. He asked the reason for this, and was told that it was because there was nothing of the church in them.

43. With the one who was in faith not separated from charity, the angel spoke as follows:

"Friend, who are you?" "I am a Reformed Christian." "What is your doctrine and the religion you have from it?" "Faith and charity." "These are two things?" "They cannot be separated." "What is faith?" "To believe what the Word teaches." "What is charity?" "To do what the Word teaches." "Have you only believed these things, or have you also done them?" "I have also done them."

The angel of heaven then looked at him, and said, "My friend, come with me, and dwell with us."

VI.

44. In order that it may be seen what the character of faith is when separated from charity, I will present it in its nakedness, in which it is as follows:

God the Father, being angry with mankind, cast them away from Him, and out of justice resolved to take vengeance by their eternal condemnation; and He said to the Son, "Go down, fulfill the law, and take upon Thyself the condemnation destined for them, and then perchance I shall be moved to compassion." Wherefore He came down, and fulfilled the law, and suffered Himself to be hanged on the cross, and cruelly put to death. When this was done, He returned to the Father, and said, "I have taken upon Myself the condemnation of mankind, therefore now be merciful;" thus interceding for them. But He received for answer, "Toward them I cannot; but as I saw Thee upon the cross, and beheld then Thy blood, I have been moved to compassion. Nevertheless I will not pardon them, but I will impute unto them Thy merit, but to no others than those who acknowledge this. This shall be the faith by which they can be saved."

45. Such is that faith in its nakedness. Who that possesses any enlightened reason does not see in it absurdities that are contrary to the Divine essence itself? As for instance that God, who is love itself, and mercy itself, could out of anger and its consequent revengefulness condemn men and accurse them to hell. Or again, that He wills to be moved to mercy by His Son's taking upon Him their condemnation, and by the sight of His suffering upon the cross, and of His blood. Who that possesses any enlightened reason does not see that the Deity could not say to another coequal Deity, "I do not pardon them, but I impute to them Thy merit?" Or, "Now let them live as they please; only let them believe this and they shall be saved." Besides many other absurdities.

46. The reason why these absurdities have not been seen is that they have induced a blind faith, and have thereby shut men's eyes, and stopped up their ears. Do this, that is, contrive that they do not exercise thought from any understanding, and then say whatever you please to persons in whom some idea of eternal life has been implanted, and they will believe it; even if you should say that God is capable of being angry and of breathing vengeance; that God is capable of inflicting eternal condemnation on any one; that God wills to be moved to mercy through the blood of His Son; that He will impute and attribute this to man as merit and as man's; and that He will save him by his merely thinking so. Or again, that one God could bargain about such things with another God of the one essence, and impose them upon Him; and other things of the same kind. But open your eyes and unstop your ears, that is, think about these things from understanding, and you will see their incongruity with the real truth.

47. Shut men's eyes and stop up their ears, and contrive that they do not think from any understanding, and can you not then lead them to believe that God has given all His authority to a man, to be as God upon earth? Can you not lead them to believe that the dead are to be addressed in prayer? that men are to bare the head and bend the knee before images of the dead? and that their lifeless bodies, their bones, and their graves, are holy and are to be venerated? But if you open your eyes and unstop your ears, that is, think about these things from some understanding, will you not behold absurdities that human reason must abhor?

48. When these things and others like them are received by a man whose understanding has been closed by his religion, may not the temple in which he performs his worship be compared to a den or cavern under-ground, where he does not know what the objects are which he glimpses? And may not his religion be compared to dwelling in a house that has no windows? and the voice of his worship to sound, and not to speech? With such a man an angel of heaven can hold no conversation, because the one does not understand the language of the other.

VII.

IN THE WORD THEY WHO ARE IN FAITH SEPARATED FROM
CHARITY ARE REPRESENTED BY THE PHILISTINES.

49. In the Word all the names of nations and peoples,
and also those of persons and places, signify things of the
church. The church itself is signified by "Israel" and "Judah," because it was instituted among them; and various
religious persuasions are meant by the nations and peoples
around them, those accordant with the church by the good
nations, and those discordant with it by the evil nations.
There are two evil religious concepts into which every
church in course of time degenerates, one that adulterates
its goods, and the other that falsifies its truths. The one
which adulterates the goods of the church springs from the
love of rule; and the one which falsifies the truths of the
church springs from the conceit of self-intelligence. The
religious concept that springs from the love of rule is
meant in the Word by "Babylon," and that which springs
from the conceit of self-intelligence is meant in the Word
by "Philistia." Who at the present day belong to Babylon
is known, but not who belong to Philistia. To Philistia belong those who are in faith and not in charity.

50. That they belong to Philistia who are in faith and
not in charity, is evident from various things said in the
Word about the Philistines, when understood in the spiritual sense, as well from their strife with the servants of
Abraham and of Isaac (recorded in Genesis 21 and 26),
as from their wars with the sons of Israel (recorded in the
book of Judges, and in the books of Samuel and of Kings);
for in the spiritual sense all the wars described in the Word
involve and signify spiritual wars. And as this religion,

309

namely, faith separated from charity, is continually desiring to get into the church, the Philistines remained in the land of Canaan, and often harried the sons of Israel.

51. As the Philistines represented those who are in faith separated from charity, they were called "the uncircumcised," by whom are meant those who are devoid of spiritual love, and consequently are in natural love only: spiritual love is charity. The reason such were called the uncircumcised is that by the circumcised are meant those who are in spiritual love. (That the Philistines are called the "uncircumcised," see 1 Samuel 17:26, 36; 2 Samuel 1:20; and elsewhere.)

52. Those who are in faith separated from charity were represented by the Philistines, as is clear not only from their wars with the sons of Israel, but also from many other things recorded about them in the Word, such as that about Dagon their idol, and about the hemorrhoids and mice with which they were smitten and infested for placing the Ark in the temple of their idol, and from other things occurring at the same time, as recorded in 1 Samuel 5 and 6; and likewise from what is said about Goliath, who was a Philistine, and was slain by David, as related in 1 Samuel 17. For Dagon from the navel upward was like a man, and below was like a fish, and thus represented their religion, in that from faith it seemed to be spiritual, but was merely natural from having no charity. The "hemorrhoids" with which they were smitten, meant their filthy loves. The "mice" by which they were infested, signified the devastation of the church through falsifications of truth. And "Goliath" whom David slew, represented their conceit of self-intelligence.

53. Those who are in faith separated from charity were represented by the Philistines, as is evident also from the prophetic parts of the Word where they are treated of, as from the following:

Against the Philistines: Behold, waters rise up out of the north, and shall become an overflowing stream, and shall overflow the land and the fullness thereof, the city and them that dwell therein, so that men shall cry, and that every inhabitant of the land shall howl. Jehovah shall lay waste the Philistines (Je 47:1, 2, 4).

The "waters that rise up out of the north," are falsities from hell; their "becoming an overflowing stream, and overflowing the land and the fullness thereof," signifies the laying waste of everything pertaining to the church through these falsities; the "city and them that dwell therein," means the laying waste of everything of its doctrine; that "men shall cry, and that every inhabitant of the land shall howl," signifies a lack of all truth and good in the church; "Jehovah shall lay waste the Philistines," means the destruction of such. In Isaiah:

Rejoice not thou, all Philistia, because the rod that smote thee is broken; for out of the serpent's root shall come forth a basilisk, whose fruit shall be a flying fire-serpent (14:29).

"Rejoice not thou, all Philistia," signifies let not those who are in faith separated from charity rejoice that they still remain; "for out of the serpent's root shall go forth a basilisk," means the destruction of all truth in them by the conceit of self-intelligence; "whose fruit shall be a flying fire-serpent," signifies reasonings from falsities of evil against the truths and goods of the church.

54. Circumcision represented purification from evils belonging to merely love natural—which is evident from these passages:

Circumcise your heart, and take away the foreskins of your heart, lest Mine anger go forth because of the evil of your doings (Je 4:4).

Circumcise therefore the foreskin of your heart, and be no more stiff-necked (Dt 10:16).

To "circumcise the heart" or "the foreskin of the heart," is to purify one's self from evils. On the contrary therefore, one who is "uncircumcised" or "foreskinned" means one not purified from the evils of love merely natural, thus one who is not in charity. And as one who is unclean in heart is meant by "one uncircumcised," it is said:

No [son of a stranger] uncircumcised in heart, and uncircumcised in flesh, shall enter into My sanctuary (Ezek 44:9).

No uncircumcised person shall eat the passover (Ex 12:48).

And that such a one is condemned (Ezek 28:10; 31:18; 32:19).

VIII.

THOSE WHO ARE IN FAITH SEPARATED FROM CHARITY ARE MEANT BY THE DRAGON IN THE APOCALYPSE.

55. It has been said above that in course of time every church falls away into two general religious persuasions that are evil, one springing from the love of rule, and the other from the conceit of self-intelligence, and that in the Word the former is meant and described by "Babylon," and the latter by "Philistia." Now as the Apocalypse treats of the state of the Christian Church, especially such as it is at its end, it therefore treats both generally and specifically of these two evil persuasions. The concept meant by "Babylon" is described in chapters 17, 18, 19, and is there the "harlot sitting upon the scarlet beast;" and that meant by "Philistia" is described in chapters 12, 13, and is there the "dragon," also the "beast that came up out of the sea," and the "beast that came up out of the earth." That this religious persuasion is meant by the dragon and his two beasts could not heretofore be known, because the spiritual sense of the Word was not opened, and therefore the Apocalypse has not been understood, and especially because the concept of faith separated from charity has so prevailed in the Christian world that no one was able to see it, for every such persuasion blinds the eyes.

56. That the concept of faith separated from charity is meant and described in the Apocalypse by the dragon and his two beasts has not only been told me from heaven, but has also been shown me in the world of spirits, which lies beneath heaven. Those in this separated faith, when assembled together, I have seen appearing like a great dragon with a tail outstretched toward the sky; and others of the same description I have seen individually appearing like dragons. For there are appearances of this nature in the world of spirits on account of the correspondence of spiritual things with natural. For this reason the angels of heaven call such persons dragonists. There is however more than one kind of them; some constitute the head of the dragon, some its body, and some its tail. They who constitute its tail are they who have falsified all the truths of the Word, and it is therefore said of the dragon in the Apocalypse that with its tail it drew down the third part of the stars of heaven. The "stars of heaven" signify knowledges of truth, and a "third part" means all.

57. Inasmuch as the dragon in the Apocalypse means those who are in faith separated from charity, and as hitherto this has not been known, being indeed actually hidden through a lack of knowledge of the spiritual sense of the Word, a general exposition shall here be given of what is said in the twelfth chapter about the dragon.

58. In Apocalypse 12 it is said:

A great sign was seen in heaven, a woman encompassed with the sun, and the moon under her feet, and upon her head a crown of twelve stars; and she being with child, cried, travailing in birth, and in pain to be delivered. And another sign was seen in heaven; and behold a great red dragon, having seven heads and ten horns, and upon his heads seven diadems. And his tail drew the third part of the stars of heaven, and did cast them into the earth. And the dragon stood before the woman who was ready to be delivered, that when she was delivered, he might devour her child. And she brought forth a man child, who was to pasture all the nations with a rod of iron; and her child was caught up unto God, and unto his throne. And the woman fled into the wilderness, where she hath a place prepared of God, that they may nourish her there a thousand two hundred and sixty days. And there was war in heaven; Michael and his angels fought with the dragon, and the dragon fought and his angels; and they prevailed not, neither was their place found any more in heaven. And when the dragon saw that he was cast into the earth, he persecuted the woman who brought forth the man child. And unto the woman were given two wings of the great

eagle, that she might fly into the wilderness into her place, where
she would be nourished for a time, and times, and half a time, from
the face of the serpent. And the serpent cast out of his mouth water
as a flood after the woman, that he might cause her to be carried
away by the flood. And the earth helped the woman, and the earth
opened her mouth, and swallowed up the flood that the dragon
cast out of his mouth. And the dragon was wroth with the woman,
and went away to make war with the remnant of her seed, who
keep the commandments of God, and hold the testimony of Jesus
Christ (verses 1-8, 13-17).

59. The exposition of these words is as follows: "A great
sign was seen in heaven," signifies a revelation by the Lord
concerning the church to come, and about the reception of
its doctrine, and those by whom it will be assailed. The
"woman encompassed with the sun, and the moon under
her feet," means a church that is in love and in faith from the
Lord; "and upon her head a crown of twelve stars," signifies
wisdom and intelligence from divine truths in the men of
that church; "and she being with child," signifies its nascent
doctrine; "cried, travailing in birth, and in pain to be delivered," signifies resistance by those who are in faith separated from charity. "And another sign was seen in heaven,"
means further revelation; "and behold, a great red dragon,"
signifies faith separated from charity; he is said to be "red"
from love that is merely natural; "having seven heads," signifies a false understanding of the Word; "and ten horns,"
means power in consequence of its reception by many; "and
upon his heads seven diadems," signifies falsified truths of
the Word; "and his tail drew the third part of the stars of
heaven, and did cast them into the earth," means the destruction of all knowledges of truth. "And the dragon stood
before the woman that was ready to be delivered, that when
she was delivered, he might devour her child," signifies their
hatred, and their intention to destroy the doctrine of the
church at its birth. "And she brought forth a man child,"
signifies the doctrine; "who was to pasture all the nations

with a rod of iron," signifies that this doctrine will convince by the power of natural truth from spiritual truth; "and her child was caught up unto God and unto His throne," means the protection of the doctrine by the Lord, from heaven. "And the woman fled into the wilderness," signifies the church among a few; "where she hath a place prepared of God," signifies its state while provision is being made for its existing with many; "that they may nourish her there a thousand two hundred and sixty days," signifies until it grows to its appointed state. "And there was war in heaven; Michael and his angels fought with the dragon; and the dragon fought and his angels," means dissent and battling by those who are in faith separated from charity against those who are in the doctrine of the church pertaining to the Lord and the life of charity; "and they prevailed not," means that they were overcome; "neither was their place found any more in heaven," signifies that they were cast down thence.

"And when the dragon saw that he was cast into the earth, he persecuted the woman who brought forth the man child," signifies the infestation of the church by those in faith separated from charity, on account of its doctrine. "And unto the woman were given two wings of the great eagle, that she might fly into the wilderness into her place," means cautious care and foresight while the church is as yet among few; "where she would be nourished for a time, and times, and half a time, from the face of the serpent," signifies while the church is growing to its appointed state. "And the serpent cast out of his mouth water as a flood after the woman, that he might cause her to be carried away by the flood," means their abundant reasonings from falsities whereby to destroy the church. "And the earth helped the woman, and the earth opened her mouth, and swallowed up the flood that the dragon cast out of his mouth," means that their reasonings, being from falsities, fell of themselves to the ground. "And the dragon was wroth with the woman, and went away to make war with the remnant of her seed," signifies their persistent hatred; "who keep the commandments of God, and hold the testimony of Jesus Christ," signifies against those who live the life of charity, and believe in the Lord.

60. The next chapter (Apoc 13), treats of the dragon's two beasts, the first seen coming up out of the sea, in verses 1-10, and the other one out of the earth, in verses 11-18. That these are the dragon's beasts is evident from verses 2, 4, and 11. The first beast means confirmations from the natural man of faith separated from charity. The other beast signifies faith separated from charity as supported by confirmations of it from the Word, which also are falsifications of truth. As the exposition of these passages contains the arguments of those who are in such faith, and would be too tedious if set forth in detail, I refrain, merely giving the exposition of the concluding words:

He that hath understanding, let him count the number of beast; for it is the number of a man; and his number is six hundred and sixty-six (verse 18).

"He that hath understanding, let him count the number of the beast," means permission given to those who are in enlightenment to examine the nature of the confirmations of that faith devised from the Word; "for it is the number of a man," signifies that the nature of these confirmations is one of self-intelligence; "and his number is six hundred and sixty-six," means all the truth of the Word in a falsified condition.

IX.

61. That the "he-goat" in Daniel 8 and the "goats" in
Matthew 25 mean those in faith separated from charity, is
evident from the fact that they stand contrasted with the
"ram" and the "sheep," by which are meant those who are in
charity. For in the Word the Lord is called the "shepherd,"
the church the "fold," and the men of the church taken collectively the "flock," and individually, "sheep." And as the
"sheep" are those in charity, the "goats" are those who are
not in charity.

62. That those in faith separated from charity are meant
by the "goats" shall now be shown.

i. From experience in the spiritual world.

ii. From the last judgment, and the character of those upon whom
it was executed.

iii. From the description in Daniel of the combat between the
ram and the he-goat.

iv. Lastly, from the neglect of charity by those of whom mention
is made in Matthew.

63. i. *Those who are in faith separated from charity are
meant in the Word by "goats," as is shown from experience
in the spiritual world.* In the spiritual world appear all the
things that are in the natural world. There appear houses
and palaces. There appear paradises and gardens, and in
them trees of every kind. There appear fields and meadow-
land, plains and grassy swards, flocks and herds, all precisely like those on our earth, there being no difference
except that the latter are from a natural origin, while the
former are from a spiritual origin. Therefore angels, being

318

spiritual, behold the things which are of spiritual origin, just as men do those of natural origin.

[2] All the things that appear in the spiritual world are correspondences, for they correspond to the affections of the angels and spirits. For this reason they who are in the love of what is good and true, and consequently in wisdom and intelligence, dwell in magnificent palaces that are surrounded by paradises full of correspondent trees, around which again are fields and plains with flocks lying there, and these are appearances. With those however who are in evil affections there are correspondences of an opposite character; such are either in hells confined in workhouses that are windowless, and yet have light in them like that of a will-o'-the-wisp, or else they are in deserts and dwell in hovels surrounded by an unbroken barrenness where there are serpents, dragons, screech-owls, and many other creatures that correspond to their evils.

[3] Between heaven and hell there is an intermediate place called the world of spirits, into which every human being comes immediately after death, and where one person associates with others just as among men on earth. Here too all things that appear are correspondences. Gardens, groves, forests of trees and shrubs, and flowery and grassy plains, appear with animals of various kinds, both tame and wild, all in correspondence with the affections of those who dwell there.

[4] There I have often seen sheep and goats, and combats between them like that described in Daniel 8. I have seen goats with horns bent forward and bent backward, and I have seen them attack the sheep with fury. I have seen goats with two great horns with which they violently struck the sheep. And when I looked to see what these things meant, I saw some who were disputing about charity and faith; and from this it was evident that faith separated from charity was what appeared as a goat, and that charity from which

is faith was what appeared as a sheep. Moreover as I have seen such things often I have come to know with certainty that those who are in faith separated from charity are meant in the Word by "goats."

64. ii. *Those in faith separated from charity are meant in the Word by "goats," as is shown from the last judgment and the character of those upon whom it was executed.* The last judgment was executed upon no others than those who in externals had been moral, but in internals had not been spiritual, or but little spiritual. As to those who had been evil in both externals and internals, they had been cast into hell long before the last judgment, while those who had been spiritual in externals and at the same time in internals had also long before that event been uplifted into heaven; and the last judgment was not executed upon those in heaven, nor upon those in hell, but upon those who were midway between the two, where they had made for themselves imaginary heavens. That the last judgment was executed upon these exclusively, may be seen in the short work on the *Last Judgment* (nn. 59 and 70); and still further in the *Continuation of the Last Judgment* (nn. 16-19), where it treats of the judgment upon the Reformed, of whom those who had been in faith separated from charity in their life as well as in their doctrine, were cast into hell, while those who had been in that same faith as to their doctrine only, and in their life had been in charity, were uplifted into heaven; from which it was evident that none but these were meant by the "goats" and the "sheep" in Matthew 25, where the Lord is speaking of the last judgment.

65. iii. *Those in faith separated from charity are meant in the Word by "goats," as is shown from the description in Daniel of the combat between the ram and the he-goat.* In the book of Daniel all things treat, in the spiritual sense, of the things of heaven and the church, as do all things in the whole Sacred Scripture (as is shown in *Doctrine of the*

Sacred Scripture, nn. 5-26). So therefore does what is said in Daniel about the combat of the ram and the he-goat, which in substance is as follows:

In vision I saw a ram that had two high horns, and the higher one came up last, and I saw that with the horn he pushed westward, and northward, and southward, and magnified himself. Afterwards I saw a he-goat coming from the west over the faces of the whole earth, that had a horn between his eyes; and he ran at the ram with the fury of his strength, and broke his two horns, cast him to the earth, and trampled upon him. But the great horn of the he-goat was broken, and instead of it there came up four horns, and out of one of them came forth a little horn, that grew exceedingly toward the south, and toward the sunrise, and toward the beauteous land, and even to the army of the heavens, and he cast down some of the army, and of the stars, to the earth, and trampled upon them. Yea, he exalted himself even to the prince of the army, and from him the continual sacrifice was taken away, and the dwelling-place of his sanctuary was cast down, because he cast down the truth to the earth. And I heard a holy one saying, How long shall be this vision, the continual sacrifice, and the wasting transgression, that the holy place and the army shall be given to be trampled upon? And he said, Until evening morning; then shall the holy place be made righteous (8:2-14).

66. It is very evident that this vision foretells future states of the church, for it is said that the continual sacrifice was taken away from the prince of the army, that the dwelling-place of his sanctuary was cast down, and that the he-goat cast down the truth to the earth. Besides all that, a holy one said, "How long shall this vision be, the continual sacrifice, and the wasting transgression, that the holy place and the army shall be given to be trampled upon?" and the answer was, "Until evening morning; then shall the holy place be made righteous;" for "evening" means the end of the church when there will be a new church [which is "morning."] The "kings of Media and Persia," spoken of in the same chapter, mean the same as the "ram;" and the "king of Greece" means the same as the "he-goat." For the names of the kings, nations, and peoples, and also those of persons and places, mentioned in the Word, signify the things of heaven and of the church.

67. The explanation of the foregoing prophetic utterances is as follows:—The "ram that had two high horns, the higher of which came up last," signifies those who are in faith from charity; his "pushing with it westward, northward, and southward," means the dispersing of what is evil and false; his "magnifying himself," means growth; the "he-goat coming from the west over the faces of the whole earth," signifies those who are in faith separated from charity, and the invasion of the church by them, the "west" being the evil of the natural man; his having "a horn between his eyes," means self-intelligence; that he "ran at the ram with the fury of his strength," signifies impetuously attacking charity and the faith of charity; that he "broke the ram's two horns, cast him down to the earth, and trampled upon him," signifies scattering to the winds both charity and faith, for whoever does this to charity does it to faith also, because these make one; that the "great horn of the he-goat was broken," means the non-appearing of self-intelligence; that "instead of it there came up four horns," signifies applications of the sense of the letter of the Word by way of confirmation; and that "out of one of them there came forth a little horn," means an argument that no one is able of himself to fulfill the law, and do what is good; that "this horn grew toward the south, toward the sunrise, and toward the beauteous land," means a rising up thereby against all things of the church; "and unto the army of the heavens, and he cast down some of the army, and of the stars, and trampled upon them," signifies the destruction in this manner of all the knowledges of good and truth pertaining to charity and faith; that he "exalted himself to the prince of the army, and from him was taken away the continual sacrifice, and the dwelling-place of his sanctuary," means that in this way this principle ravaged all things that pertain to the worship of the Lord and to His church; that he "cast down the truth to the earth," means that it falsified the truths of the Word; "evening morning, when the holy place shall be made righteous," signifies the end of that church, and the beginning of a new one.

68. iv. *Those in faith separated from charity are meant by "goats." This is shown from the neglect of charity by those of whom mention is made in* Matthew. That the "goats" and "sheep" in chapter 25:31-46 mean the very same persons as those meant by the "he-goat" and "ram" in Daniel 8: is evident from the fact that works of charity are attributed to the sheep, and it is said that they had done them; and that the same works of charity are attributed to the goats, and it is said that they had done them not, and that the latter are condemned on that account. For works are neglected by those who are in faith separated from charity, in consequence of their denying that there is anything of salvation or of the church therein; and when charity, which consists in works, is set aside in this way, faith also falls to the ground, because faith is from charity; and when there are no charity and faith there is condemnation. If *all* the evil had been meant there by the goats, the works of charity they had not done would not have been enumerated, but instead the evils they had done. The same persons are meant by the "he-goats" also in Zechariah:

Mine anger was kindled against the shepherds, and I will visit upon the he-goats (10:3).

And in Ezekiel:

Behold, I judge between cattle and cattle, between the rams and the he-goats. Is it a small thing to you that ye have eaten up the good pasture, but ye must also tread down with your feet the residue of the pastures? ye have pushed all the feeble sheep with your horns, till ye have scattered them abroad; therefore will I save My flock, that it may no more be for a prey (34:17, 18, 21, 22, etc.).

X.

FAITH SEPARATED FROM CHARITY DESTROYS THE CHURCH AND
ALL THAT BELONGS TO IT.

69. Faith separated from charity is no faith, because
charity is the life of faith: its soul, and its essence. And
where there is no faith because no charity, there is no
church. And therefore the Lord says:

When the Son of man cometh, shall He find faith on the earth?
(Lu 18:8).

70. At times I have heard the goats and the sheep holding a discussion as to whether those who have confirmed
themselves in faith separated from charity possess any
truth; and as they said that they possessed a great deal,
the matter in dispute was submitted to an examination.
They were then questioned as to whether they knew what
love is, what charity is, and what good is; and as these
were the things that they had set aside, the only reply they
could make was that they did not know. They were questioned as to what sin is, as to what repentance is, and what
the remission of sins; and as they replied that those who
have been justified through faith have their sins remitted
so that they no longer appear, it was declared to them,
"This is not the truth." They were questioned as to what
regeneration is, and they replied either that it is baptism,
or that it is the remission of sins through faith. It was
declared to them that "this is not the truth." They were
questioned as to what the spiritual man is, and they replied that it is one who has been justified through the confession of their faith. But it was declared to them that "this

is not the truth." They were questioned concerning redemption, concerning the union of the Father and the Lord, and concerning the unity of God, and they gave answers that were not truths. Not to mention other points on which they were questioned. After these queries and the replies, the matter in dispute came to judgment, and the judgment was that those who have confirmed themselves in faith separated from charity do not possess any truth.

71. That such is the case cannot be believed by them while they are in the natural world, because those who are in falsities see no otherwise than that falsities are truths, and that it is not a matter of much consequence to know more than what belongs to their faith. And as their faith is divorced from the understanding (for it is a blind faith) they make no inquiry into this matter, which is one that can be investigated solely from the Word by the means of an enlightenment of the understanding. The truths therefore that are in the Word they turn into falsities by thinking of faith when they see mention made of "love," "repentance," the "remission of sins," and many other things that must belong to action.

72. But it is most true that it is those who have confirmed themselves by both doctrine and life in faith alone who are of this character, and by no means those who, although they have heard and have believed that faith alone saves, have nevertheless shunned evils as sins.

THE THEOLOGICAL WRITINGS
OF EMANUEL SWEDENBORG

These books may be ordered through your nearest bookstore or direct from—

SWEDENBORG FOUNDATION, INC.
139 East 23rd Street
New York, N.Y. 10010

Complete catalog and current price list sent free on request.

APOCALYPSE EXPLAINED, 6 volumes.

Presents the spiritual (symbolic) sense of the *Book of Revelation* up to chapter 19, verse 10, and many other parts of the *Scriptures,* especially the *Psalms,* the *Prophets,* and the *Gospels.* Extensive and practical doctrinal discussions are introduced.

APOCALYPSE REVEALED, 2 volumes.

A study which primarily concentrates on the exposition of the spiritual (symbolic) sense of the *Book of Revelation.* It is the work, therefore, to which the reader would turn first for the profound meaning in this dramatic book of the New Testament.

ARCANA COELESTIA (Heavenly Secrets), 12 volumes.

An exposition of the spiritual (symbolic) sense within the allegory and history of the books of *Genesis* and *Exodus* with numerous references to other parts of the *Bible.*

CONJUGIAL LOVE.

An ethical discussion of the relation of the sexes and a view of the enduring world of the spirit, of the nature and origin of love truly conjugal (marital), and of its indissoluble nature, of sexual irregularities and the avoidance of them. Also discusses the marriage of the Lord and the Church and its spiritual significance.

DIVINE LOVE AND WISDOM.

This book is an interpretation of the universe as a spiritual-natural or psycho-physical world. It treats of the activity of God's love and wisdom in the creation of this world and of the human being, who is similarly constituted.

DIVINE PROVIDENCE.

A profound philosophical work, revealing the law-abiding ways and merciful means by which God, in His immanence, cares for the individual and for mankind.

HEAVEN AND HELL.

Based on Swedenborg's experiences in the spiritual realm, this is the most comprehensive and concrete description of life hereafter ever given to mankind—the orderly arrangement of heaven into societies, universal speech, the beautiful life there, our entry into the next world, and many other matters enhancing all our conceptions of life both here and hereafter.

MARITAL LOVE, translated by Wm. F. Wunsch.
Another translation of *Conjugial Love* containing teachings regarding the home and marriage. It also deals with the conjugial and scortatory loves, in the framework of morals and ethics.

MISCELLANEOUS THEOLOGICAL WORKS.
Bound together in this volume are the following treatises: *The New Jerusalem and Its Heavenly Doctrine; A Brief Exposition of the Doctrine of the New Church; The Nature of the Intercourse Between the Soul and the Body; On the White Horse Mentioned in the Apocalypse; On the Earths in the Universe; The Last Judgment* (on a first Christian era); and *A Continuation Concerning the Last Judgment.*

POSTHUMOUS THEOLOGICAL WORKS, 2 volumes.
A number of the shorter posthumous works including extracts from Swedenborg's correspondence.

SPIRITUAL DIARY, 5 volumes.
A storehouse of spiritual facts, phenomena and principles which Swedenborg wrote at the time of his experiences in the spiritual realm.

THE SPIRITUAL LIFE, THE WORD OF GOD.
Extracts from Swedenborg's *The Apocalypse Explained*, make devotional reading on the spiritual or regenerating life, the significance of the Ten Commandments, our possible profanation of good and truth, and the power of God's Word.

TRUE CHRISTIAN RELIGION, 2 volumes.
Swedenborg's crowning work giving a complete exposition of doctrines for the New Christian Era. It is a powerful and massive presentation dealing with a broad spectrum of modern Christian concerns and draws upon more than nine hundred passages from all parts of the *Bible.*

OTHER TITLES:

THE CEREBRUM, by Emanuel Swedenborg.
The pursuit of the soul through anatomy with emphasis on the anatomy of the brain.

DICTIONARY OF BIBLE IMAGERY—compiler Alice Spiers Sechrist.
Reveals symbolic meaning of thousands of words of the *Bible.*

DIGEST OF TRUE CHRISTIAN RELIGION, by Arthur Wilde.
A summary of Swedenborg's work of this title.

DREAMS, HALLUCINATIONS, VISIONS, by Ernst Benz.
Explains the psychic and religious significance of these three types of phenomena.

THE ESSENTIAL SWEDENBORG, by Sig Synnestvedt.
Presents the basic elements of Swedenborg's thought.

GIST OF SWEDENBORG, by Smyth & Wunsch.
Topically arranged quotations from Swedenborg's works.

THE HUMAN MIND, by Hugo Lj. Odhner.
A collection of essays on the different degrees of the mind.

INSIGHTS INTO THE BEYOND, by Paul Zacharias.
An introductory guide to Swedenborg's most popular book *Heaven and Hell.*

INTRODUCTION TO SWEDENBORG'S RELIGIOUS THOUGHT, by John Howard Spalding.
A clear, comprehensive, and forcefully reasoned presentation of Swedenborg's teachings.

THE LANGUAGE OF PARABLE, by William L. Worcester.
This work takes commonly used expressions and traces them back to the letter of the Word presenting their spiritual sense.

MARRIAGE (IDEALS AND REALIZATIONS), by William F. Wunsch.
A compilation from several of Swedenborg's works on this subject.

MY RELIGION, by Helen Keller.
A beautifully written and inspiring account of the teachings of Swedenborg regarding the Divine which Miss Keller stated ". . . was a constant source of strength."
Also a recording for the blind and shut-in—set of 2 ten inch records, 8⅓ RPM, dramatized by Lillian Gish. Also available in cassette tapes.

OUTLINES OF SWEDENBORG'S TEACHINGS, by William F. Wunsch.
A study guide dealing with a way of life of particular significance to those in quest of religious insights, emphasizing the Spiritual Life, the Word, and the Lord.

THE PRESENCE OF OTHER WORLDS, by Wilson Van Dusen.
A fascinating account of Swedenborgs inner journey of the mind with spiritual and psychological findings.

THE SERMON ON THE MOUNT, by Richard H. Teed.
An exposition of the acknowledged statement of the ideal religious life.

SEX, EROS, MARITAL LOVE, by Gerhard Gollwitzer.
Scholarly study of the spiritual significance of the subject.

SWEDENBORG, LIFE AND TEACHING, by George Trobridge.
The most widely read biography of the "Aristotle of the North."

TREMULATION, by Emanuel Swedenborg.
The beginning of the theory of motion.